# Petty Capitalists
# and Globalization

SUNY series in Anthropological Studies
of Contemporary Issues

*Jack R. Rollwagen, editor*

# Petty Capitalists and Globalization

*Flexibility, Entrepreneurship, and Economic Development*

*Edited by*
*Alan Smart and Josephine Smart*

STATE UNIVERSITY OF NEW YORK PRESS

Published by
State University of New York Press, Albany

© 2005 State University of New York

For information, address State University of New York Press,
90 State Street, Suite 700, Albany, NY 12207

Production by Diane Ganeles
Marketing by Michael Campochiaro

**Library of Congress Cataloging-in-Publication Data**

Petty capitalists and globalization: flexibility, entrepreneurship, and
economic development / edited by Alan Smart and Josephine Smart.
      p. cm. — (SUNY series in anthropological studies of contemporary
            issues)
   Includes bibliography references and index.
   ISBN 0–7914–6399–0 (hardcover : alk. paper)
1. Small business. 2. International trade. 3. Globalization—Economic
aspects. I. Smart, Alan. II. Smart, Josephine. III. Series.

HD2341.P474 2005
338.6′—dc22                                                    2004008051

HD
2341
.P474
2005

# Contents

# Illustrations

## Figures

## Tables

# 1

## Introduction

*Alan Smart*
*and*
*Josephine Smart*

**1**

This volume contends that while the enterprises operated by petty capitalists may be small, there is nothing petty about their significance for the operation of economies and for our understanding of contemporary societies, families, and localities. Petty capitalists regularly operate in the ambiguous boundaries between capital and labor, cooperation and exploitation, family and economy, tradition and modernity, friends and competitors. By examining how these relationships vary over time, space, and culture, the study of petty capitalists offers insights into an era where assembly lines are deconstructed and scattered across the globe, and where rapid and flexible response to desires can make the difference between economic success and failure.

An ever-increasing proportion of interactions cross national boundaries. At the same time, changing technologies and regulatory contexts have made it more compelling for even the smallest firms to either compete on a transnational terrain, or at least to be wary of competitive threats from beyond their nation's border. Globalization has usually been seen in terms of the activities of large private corporations and the governments of the World Trade Organization (WTO), Group of 7 (G-7) or Organization of Economic Cooperation & Development (OECD-23) who are changing conditions to facilitate freer flow of trade and investment. Hypermobile capital is widely thought to have improved its negotiating position vis-à-vis workers and localities, potentially producing a race to the bottom in terms of working conditions and welfare provisions. Conversely, small business is usually assumed to be local business, while business activities that operate regionally, nationally, or transnationally are seen to be the province of increasingly larger enterprises.

Yet, the greater ease with which goods, money, and ideas move around the world also makes it possible for very small firms and individuals to operate in global markets. Small entrepreneurs can operate in a global economy in ways that would not have been feasible a few decades ago. For example, a study of Canadian companies doing business in Japan found that companies established before 1970 waited an average of over 20 years before exporting to Japan. By the 1980s, the average lag between starting business and exporting to Japan had dropped to 1.9 years and to 1.1 years in the 1990s. The report concluded that relaxed trade barriers, as well as cheaper travel costs and ease of e-mail and fax machines, have helped smaller business globalize more quickly than in the past (Walton 1999:B10).

As Hill Gates (1996; this volume) reminds us, however, small enterprises have operated across borders for at least a millennium, sometimes in the forms of what Weber called pariah capitalism. Brokerage across borders provides risky opportunities that appeal particularly to those with little capital but higher risk tolerance (A. Smart 1999). At the same time, international migration and study abroad creates kin and friendship ties that can facilitate taking advantage of opportunities created by local difference (Smart and Smart 1998; M. P. Smith 2001). In this volume, a variety of scholars explore the impact of contemporary circumstances on petty capitalists. They consider how operating in transnational markets influences the dynamics of these enterprises. An analysis of petty capitalists, we suggest, provides a different perspective on the contemporary era, and on how people respond to its challenges and opportunities. Our argument is not that petty capitalists, or even the larger category of small and medium enterprises, are the most important driving forces of the contemporary global economy, although many studies suggest their increasing significance in a variety of settings (Blim 1990; Buechler and Buechler 1992a). Rather, we are suggesting that when conditions make production across national borders more feasible and attractive, petty capitalists may be among the pioneers in taking advantage of this situation. Doing so may involve mobilizing ethnic links (a major focus of a recent flurry of work on transnationalism, see Glick Schiller, Basch, and Szanton Blane 1992; Faist 2000), particularly when the "rules of the game" are poorly elaborated or are rigged against members of particular ethnic groups. The "rules of the game," in the form of international standards or trading regulations may also work against the viability of smaller enterprises, as with the Rugmark process to certify the absence of child labor on exported rugs discussed in Tom O'Neill's chapter. Conversely, social movements that have been promoting "fair trade" instead of free trade can sometimes provide new opportunities for small producers, as B. Lynne Milgram's chapter on craftworkers in the Philippines argues.

The advantages of smaller businesses may involve the use of family labor and other kin-based resources (e.g., using the home for production and informal loans in situations where formal finance is unavailable). Exploitation, both of household dependents and workers, is certainly not uncommon, as the chapters by Frances Abrahamer Rothstein, Hill Gates, and Gavin Smith and Susana Narotzky make clear. Rothstein in particular argues that the flexibility of the small and medium Mexican firms she has studied is largely the result of the vulnerability and exploitation of their workers and subcontractors, as well as their own self-exploitation. Thus, while small does not necessarily mean "doomed to disappear," it may not be "beautiful."

We define petty capitalists here as "individuals or households who employ a small number of workers but are themselves actively involved in the labor process." We suggest that the category of "petty capitalist" is more useful for an ethnographic approach that emphasizes the meaningful experience of actors than other popular terms like *entrepreneur* or *family business*. A category such as "entrepreneur" that includes both a flower vendor in a street market and Bill Gates has certain analytic limitations. "Family business" similarly covers a vast range in terms of size of enterprise, but it also makes the assumption that kinship is the underlying basis for organization, which may be common but not universal for petty capitalist enterprises. By concentrating on enterprises where the proprietors are actively engaged in the labor process, even if only to the extent, for example, of producing prototypes or setting up the equipment during product shifts, the assumption about the sharp boundary between capital and labor, so common in the discussion of globalization, is brought into question. By being productively engaged on the workshop floor, the petty capitalist may be able to emphasize the commonality of purpose with workers, and also has considerable advantages in surveillance of the labor process (Bowles and Gintis 1990). Seen positively, reduced separation between labor and management creates opportunities for gradual improvement of production processes through mobilization of tacit knowledge available to workers, and for flexible resolution of conflicting demands characteristic of a business environment. Michael Dell, founder of Dell Computing, has stated that one of his goals has been to maintain the culture of a start-up even with thousands of employees. Seen negatively, petty capitalists can take advantage of their closeness to the production process to heighten their control over, and exploitation of, their workers. Petty capitalists are an intermediate category, bounded by petty producers and subsistence producers on one side, and by "real" capitalists on the other. Such a position is inherently unstable, since improved fortunes may lead to the shedding of the "petty" status, while a decline in fortunes may result in proletarianization or impoverishment. People's strategies and life trajectories move them back and forth between the categories.

Many approaches to entrepreneurship and small business take a position of either promotion of the merits, or debunking of these alleged merits as ideological cover for heightened labor exploitation. In this volume, we do not adopt a common position on this, but instead suggest that there is sufficient internal diversity among petty capitalist enterprises to support both polar positions. Instead, by drawing on expertise from a variety of different contexts, the many distinct facets of smaller enterprises come into comparative focus.

## 2

There is a vast literature on petty capitalists, some of it produced by authors included in this volume; whether or not those studies refer to them with that label, or as petty producers, petty bourgeoisie, entrepreneurs, or peasants. We do not attempt to surpass or synthesize these traditions. Instead, we pursue a more modest goal: to build on this impressive scholarship, and to make a contribution to seeing how petty capitalist practices and enterprises have changed in an era where even small businesses must either sell on global markets or defend themselves from foreign competitors. Eric B. Wolf (1982) and Sidney W. Mintz (1998) among others, remind us that globalization is far from new. Still, the easing of international trade, transportation, and communication through political and technological developments has meant that the world has indeed shrunk for small business operators. In the past, it was only certain kinds of petty capitalists, particularly long-distance traders, who could produce directly for world markets. In most cases, petty producers of coffee, grain, cloth, or crafts were dominated either by states or by merchants who controlled access to markets and investment capital (or both).

Ethnographic studies of peasants and urban residents in anthropology increased dramatically after World War II, due in large part to the collapse of the prewar intellectual division of labor in a context of decolonization. It would hardly have been politically correct for college textbooks to continue to refer to anthropology as the study of primitive societies. Redefining itself as the study of humanity in its full diversity across time and space, anthropologists could no longer justify studying only the least developed, least urban cultures on the planet. Ethnographers began to explore how non-Western people made a living in part through involvement in market processes, particularly in the form of the informal sector in cities (J. Smart 1989) and in peasant production in the countryside (Cook and Binford 1990), as well as through involvement as wage laborers in colonial plantations and mines. Much early work on these topics tended to adopt, explicitly or implicitly, modernization assumptions common in development studies at the time, so that small, locally run production was seen as transitional and its replacement by "rational," bureaucratically managed firms just a matter of time and cultural adaptation.

Dissatisfaction with such approaches spawned more radical, political economy alternatives: dependency theory, world-systems theory, and Marxist analysis. All of these approaches departed from prewar anthropological perspectives in emphasizing interactions between different societies and differential access to surplus production within societies (class). Where they differed primarily was in their relative emphasis on the importance of intersocietal influence (dependency and world-systems approaches) and internal dynamics (Marxist approaches).

Classic Marxist analyses of small producers, such as Lenin's, argued that these forms of production were inherently unstable and transitional, since even minor demographic or economic differences would result in some producers being more successful than others, with the result that some would become merchants or capitalists while others would lose their means of production. The failure of differentiation to produce a clear-cut polarization into capitalist and proletarian classes generated renewed interest in peasant economies. By the 1970s, there was a sophisticated debate about the nature of noncapitalist forms of production, and a proliferation of excellent ethnographic studies. Much of this work concentrated on producers who controlled their means of production, produced at least in part for the market, but who had no employees beyond the confines of their household, relying instead on "self-exploitation." As Henry Bernstein pointed out, however, as a result of feminist analyses that have "demolished hitherto residual, unproblematised, and unitary notions of family and household...the concept of self-exploitation remains unambiguous only in relation to those enterprises in which capital and labour are combined in a single person" (1986:22).

Patriarchal relations create ambivalences and conflicts between capital and labor even in enterprises that only include household members. Access to unpaid family labor has often been seen as a main reason for the survival of petty production and petty capitalism. However, when markets for wage labor exist in the same area, even the use of family labor is influenced by considerations of its market value elsewhere. In Winnie Lem's study of French wine growers she found that "Ideas surrounding the value of labor power...have penetrated to the heart of the domestic sphere" (1999:110), resulting in resistance by children and wives against pressure to work in the family firm. Divisions of interests within families means that control over labor remains a concern even within family firms, as the chapters by Rothstein and Simone Ghezzi demonstrate. More generally, petty commodity production has never been the sole or dominant mode of production. Despite having existed for thousands of years, it has been a minority or subordinate form of livelihood, usually existing in conjunction with tributary or capitalist relations of production (Gates 1996). The interaction between petty production/capitalism and its more powerful neighbors has a tremendous impact on the organization and management of these enterprises, and to a large extent accounts for their diverse forms. Interaction with dominant fractions of the economy has as much, or more, influence on how petty capitalists operate than does anything inherent in the form of production itself. It is for this reason that we insist on paying attention to history and local context. Even less than capitalism itself, petty capitalism is not always the same kind of entity or process. It is generally less than helpful even to talk about petty capital*ism* since it implies some kind of coherence, when instead petty capitalist practices are always distributed within, and interpenetrated by, other ways of doing things. It is for this reason that the articulationist approach within Marxian anthropology ultimately failed. Modes of production do not articulate with each other; instead relations of production and the actions of individuals and collectivities are involved with the multiple ways of livelihood found in any social formation, but particularly in an interconnected world-system.

Edmund R. Leach's comments on Burma foreshadowed a shift in worldview that is relevant for understanding petty capitalists: "In situations such as we find in the Kachin Hills Area, any particular individual can be thought of as having a status position in several different social systems at one and the same time.... such systems present themselves as alternatives or inconsistencies in the scheme of values by which he orders his life" (1964:8, orig. 1954). Petty capitalists may draw on and broker social and cultural resources to allow them to take advantage of opportunities that are not available or are more risky for larger concerns. They may be on a trajectory toward wealth and control over large workforces, such as some of the entrepreneurs in the chapter by Jinn-Yuh Hsu, or forced into it by losing a secure salaried position, or may at different times in a year be both employee and employer. The chapters in this volume illustrate the opportunities and pitfalls created by ambiguous positioning between social systems and class positions.

Prior to the last few decades, for the most part petty producers and petty capitalists were seen as threatened with extinction or marginalization. There was a continual preoccupation with survival: whether or not the sector could persist, or was fated to fade away in the transition to monopoly capitalism or to bureaucratic rationality. With the publication of two books in the 1980s, the emphasis started to shift toward seeing small enterprises as dynamic contributors to economic growth, and growing rather than shrinking in importance. Michael Piore and Charles Sabel (1984) perceived that a *New Industrial Divide* was generating an era of flexible specialization in which regional ensembles of interconnected small firms reliant on artisanship would be increasingly important in comparison to mass production. David Harvey's (1989) *Condition of Postmodernity* drew wide attention to the alleged shift from Fordism (and its attendant hypertrophism of enterprises and government) toward flexible accumulation, with smaller, more flexible ways of producing and organizing societies. Petty producers and petty capitalists are key parts of these new ensembles, in the form of small and medium enterprises that sub-contract work for larger firms, and through the phenomenon of neo-artisanal production "where technological innovations allow workers to produce a varied output of goods and services as speci-fied by purchasers" (Eberts and Norcliffe 1998:122).

These shifts create more opportunities for small enterprises. Alan Scott and Michael Storper argue that in comparison to mass production

> flexible production systems are characterized by progres-sive vertical disintegration of production with numerous producers (of different sizes) caught up in tightly knit net-work structures.... In these networks, groups of industrial establishments with especially dense interrelations tend to locate close to one another to facilitate exchanges of goods and information, and to take advantage of external economies in labor markets and infrastructure. (1992:7–8)

While technological changes such as improved transportation, communication, and computer systems have facilitated the rise of the "global factory" (Rothstein and Blim 1992), where production is widely distributed across national boundaries, some of the processes are also related to the core features of labor manage-ment. Samuel Bowles and Harold Gintis (1990) argue that capital-ist economies are profoundly influenced by conflicts inherent in the transformation of contracted labor-power into actual labor of a desired quantity and quality. This transformation is normally taken for granted, but in reality is a major concern in labor rela-tions and an important source of transaction costs. Issues of labor discipline and surveillance are necessarily grounded in particular workplaces as a result of the transaction costs involved in utilizing third-party guarantors of labor contracts to ensure the acceptable completion of work (Smart and Smart 1993). As global capitalist competition intensified from the oil crisis in 1973 (which exacer-bated a postwar trend toward lower corporate profit levels), reduc-ing labor costs and increasing fast and flexible response to market demand became key areas of innovation. For example, between December 1989 and July 1997, the self-employed share of total employment in Canada increased from 13.8% to 18.1% (Smart 2001). Technology has complex effects on petty enterprise.

Economies of scale operate against it, and raise barriers to entry, but information and transportation technologies make it easier for them to operate over distance in ways that were not imaginable two hundred years ago.

There has been considerable debate about the implications of these shifts. The more positive views of Piore and Sabel have tended to be replaced by perspectives that see flexibilization as a new form of sweatshopping, with the costs of adjustment thrust upon workers and communities (Nash 1989). Our view of petty capitalists in this volume is neither dismissive nor romantic. There are both positive and negative aspects of their involvement in production. Viewed optimistically, petty employers are more likely to recognize flaws in the process than if they simply give orders. By working side by side, there may develop a sense of "us" working together to compete or just to survive. Conversely, such working conditions make surveillance of workers, and perhaps their exploitation, easier and more immediate (Narotzky 1997a). More generally, the characteristics of petty capitalist enterprises vary across time and space: given the very strong influence of the broader economy and society on their operation, sustainable generalizations are difficult to achieve.

Our own interest in petty capitalists operating on global markets has derived from research on Hong Kong's informal sector and on small Hong Kong-run industrial enterprises in China. Hong Kong developed an industrial structure composed largely of many small companies, primarily producing for export. In 1977, 92.1% of the total manufacturing establishments and 40.2% of the employment in manufacturing were in enterprises employing less than 50 workers (Sit, Wong, and Kiong 1979:10). The average number of employees per manufacturing enterprise dropped from 30.04 in 1959 to 27.65 in 1973 (Lin, Mok, and Ho 1980:94), and to 18.5 by 1984. These small businesses are usually either subcontractors or dependent on orders from import-export firms,[1] and act as a buffer between volatile market demand and large, well-established businesses. The proportion of employers and the self-employed in the labor force has been surprisingly stable over decades.

The continual re-creation of the entrepreneurial stock and the preservation of an economy based on small and medium firms is related to a context where employees have few protections and where unions have been generally ineffective. Immigrants from China were more likely to become proprietors in the manufacturing sector than in commerce, because their backgrounds put them at a linguistic disadvantage in service sectors. Making the transition from employee to employer, however, requires assets such as capital and connections, as noted in Milgram's chapter; and thus effective utilization of networks is critical for those with small amounts of capital themselves (Chiu 1998). A similar set of processes were critical in making possible the establishment of enterprises in China by entrepreneurs from Hong Kong's lower middle class (Smart and Smart 1991, 2000). When little capital and much skilled labor is required, economies of scale have little significance so that large and small manufacturers can operate side by side (Lin & Mok 1985:227). Low capital-intensivity also facilitates changes of product lines in response to market conditions, which is especially important in markets where fashions change quickly.

Tony Yu argues that Hong Kong's entrepreneurs are of the Kirznerian rather than Schumpeterian variety. Schumpeterian, or creative, entrepreneurs disrupt industries by developing new products, processes, or financial strategies. Kirznerian, or adaptive, entrepreneurs are imitative followers, adopt rather than develop technology and products, and frequently are small firms that produce goods to be sold under another company's brand (see the chapter by the Buechlers). In order to cope with strong global competition, "producers adopt Kirznerian entrepreneurial strategies including small business operation, original equipment manufacturer (OEM) business, product imitation, spatial arbitrage and subcontracting. Such strategies provide the firms with flexibility and adaptability to cater to rapidly changing global markets" (1997:27). A variety of conditions encouraged adaptive entrepreneurship in Hong Kong, including the small domestic market, political uncertainty, as well as social and cultural factors that foster "entrepreneurial familism" (Yu 1997:29, see Smart and Smart 2000 for a critical discussion of the latter claim).

By the mid-1970s, low unemployment combined with high rents to raise labor and other production costs above regional competitors. At about the same time, China's economic reforms started opening China to capitalist investment. Access to cheap labor and land across the border encouraged a Kirznerian adaptive response, rather than upgrading technology and attempting more Schumpeterian approaches (A. Smart 2001b). Small and medium Hong Kong entrepreneurs have been active investors in China. Particularly in the first decade after opening in 1979, and even at present to a lesser extent, the rules for doing business in China were far from clear and reliable. Small and medium Hong Kong enterprises were the first to commit themselves to the risks of investing under these circumstances and still retain a substantial importance (Lever, Tracy Ip, and Ivaey 1996). They took advantage of social connections, since many of them were first-generation migrants from China. Our research into how poorly educated individuals with few financial assets could start factories in China began a decade's research into how this was accomplished, how they dealt with the uncertain property rights and sociopolitical differences between the two systems, and what the effects of this investment was on the receiving communities. An interest in how petty capitalists resemble and differ from this pattern in an era of increasing global interconnectedness sparked the decision to edit this volume.

**3**

This volume is something of a sequel to *Anthropology and the Global Factory,* edited by Fran Rothstein and Michael Blim in 1992. Of this volume's authors, Rothstein, Blim, Hans and Judith-Maria Buechler and Alan and Josephine Smart all contributed chapters. As well, many of the themes of that volume are echoed here, although we do not attempt to cover as wide a range of topics. Rothstein wrote that the concept of a global factory "incorporates the fluidity and flexibility that characterizes contemporary processes and units" (1992:239) and its study concerns all of the contributors to our volume. In addition, the authors in the 1992 volume "all take their cues from the particular situation or situations in which they have lived and studied," as well as attending to approaches to political economy that span all the social science disciplines. One difference is that two chapters of this volume are written by geographers, a discipline that has become increasingly influential in ethnographic research and theory. While all of the chapters both build on ethnographic research and political economic analysis, Adrian Smith's chapter is the furthest on the political economy pole of the spectrum, although it implicitly reflects the detailed case studies he has conducted in Slovakia.

This commonality in research approach means that the chapters in this volume are not only supported by extensive fieldwork, but also deal to a considerable degree with categories that are "experience-near" for people doing petty business: questions of loyalty, trust, exploitation, and market conditions. We suggest that an ethnographic approach is particularly useful for a topic such as small fish doing business in transnational or global arenas. This is because many of the processes described in these well-researched studies are hard to identify, at least in part because they don't coincide with the informational categories of nation-states. Since quantitative information such as censuses and surveys of economic conditions are usually compiled to represent nation-states or their constituent units it means that things like entrepreneurs' linkages with Fair Trade organizations, or Hong Kong petty capitalists doing business in their home villages in China are hard to even notice without an ethnographic approach. In this, they partake to a considerable extent of the methodological problems attendant on studying transnational networks, diasporas, and the ways in which they may enable transnational business (A. Smart 1999; Lessinger 1992).

Although we emphasized the utility of exploring "experience-near" categories, the chapter by Smith and Narotzky stresses the dangers involved in such a perspective. Anthropology and regional development discourses have converged on an emphasis on everyday life and local culture, and the contributions that they make to the constitution of effective networked clusters of small firms facilitated by high levels of social capital. They argue that emphasis on the embeddedness of economic practices in local culture and everyday concepts such as trust may obscure as much as it reveals, because local culture itself may serve to cover over conflicts, exploitation, and past events, in their case the Spanish Civil War. Instead of working with "ahistorical and class-neutral calculations of entrepreneur-like social agents," they deploy a careful examination of historical process to understand how an entrepreneurial culture came to be. Other chapters also demonstrate a careful attention to local histories, for example, the legacies of socialism addressed by Adrian Smith and Hans and Judith-Maria Buechler. The Buechlers insist as well that this history not be seen as monolithic, an effort to overcome the generic mind-set of communist socialization, since the specific situations of firms and individuals under socialism influenced their responses in the postsocialist transition.

The chapter by Gates provides an ambitious use of the historical imagination, sketching the varying relations between petty commodity production (PCP) and its accommodation with surrounding political economies and endeavoring to locate the sources of this "enduring alternative." Attempting this task is particularly appropriate for her, since her book *China's Motor* (1996) reinterpreted the last thousand years of Chinese history in terms of the interaction between petty capitalism and the dominant imperial tributary mode of production. After an impressive review of the varying forms taken by PCP due to the broader context, she argues that our difficulties in conceptualizing this chameleon-like form of production are due to "an empty center" that requires a better understanding of human nature than "the passionless plasticity that has been attributed to us by extreme constructionists." (55) She reviews recent developments in demography and human biology to argue that through the medium of nurture and affect, households will form economic units whenever external conditions permit. The result is that "the shared life and labor of PCP meet affective needs that larger institutions are rarely structured to attain." (55) Her argument will no doubt be controversial, but she is careful to avoid genetic determinism or an ethnocentric position on the nature of the family. One issue is that petty capitalists do not always rely on solitary kinship ties, but can sometimes rely more on non-kin alliances and networks. For example, Hsu Jinnyuh's chapter finds that small high-technology companies in Taiwan are based more on networks of classmates and friends than kin, since family members are not likely to have the specialized skills or contacts that are required.

Smith and Narotzky examine the Vega Baja region of Spain, an area that shares many similarities with the classic industrial districts focused on by Piore and Sabel and by others involved with the flexible specialization perspective. They note that the implications of such arguments for regional development have had an intense impact on policy formation, particularly in the European Union (see also Buechler and Buechler 1992b). Industrial districts are not only seen in the literature as agglomerations of small firms usually specialized in one kind of product, but also as having a characteristic form of organization, cemented by social relationships and a common social culture which facilitates diffusion of innovation. This emphasis on commonality, on social capital, on an entrepreneurialism that unites employers, employees, and politicians, downplays the heterogeneity and difference that they find a particularly striking feature of the region (G. Smith 1994).

Smith and Narotzky find that rather than a common experience, the life histories of workers varied across a spectrum between fixity in place and movement through local space.

Tenants (*aniaga*s) had long-term dependency relationships with landlords, whereas day laborers (*jornalero*s) worked on a daily basis for a variety of employers. Security for the *jornalero*s relied on movement through the region, putting together a variety of strategies to survive, whereas *aniaga* families tried to ensure the maintenance of their ties with their patron. The Spanish Civil War and the Franco era exacerbated these divisions. Both lifestyles relied on networks and relationships, but in one case these were horizontal networks where vulnerable individuals sought opportunities and niches and learned a wide variety of skills, and the other emphasized vertical linkages characterized by deference, paternalism, and exploitation. The crucial point here is that the two experiences and patterns are fused in the dominant ideas of flexible industrial districts, yet they do not arise out of common culture, but precisely out of a divided and conflictual class landscape. These conflicts continue today, as movement attempts to limit the exploitation that dependency on an employer facilitates.

One issue that is nearly unavoidable in discussions of petty capitalists is how to evaluate these small firms. Should they be encouraged and fostered as sources of dynamic creativity and freedom from the deadening bureaucracy of large organizations? Or are they made viable only by engaging in higher levels of exploitations than their larger competitors can get away with or by playing fast and loose with environmental or labor laws (Harrison and Kuttner 1997)? The chapter by Rothstein addresses this issue carefully, asking the crucial question of "flexibility for whom?" Subcontracting has become widely associated with offshore sweatshops with harsh working conditions and high levels of exploitation, and activists call for boycotts against companies such as Nike that take advantage of the global assembly line in this way. Rothstein notes that Piore and Sabel argue that sweating is not inherent in flexible production, and that the politics of industrial districts can restrict forms of competition to those that encourage innovation, not just exploitation. She argues that in many cases innovation and sweating are not alternatives, but paired sources of advantage. Drawing on research in a rural community in central Mexico, she concludes that flexibility at the local level is "largely an illusion which hides a reality of greater control by fewer people at the global level." Despite having a population of only eight thousand people, hundreds of small garment workshops opened in the 1990s, most of them doing subcontract piecework for larger enterprises.

Rothstein emphasizes the ambiguous class position of most employers, which results in some mobility in and out of the status. Although owners in general do better out of the arrangements, they are also at the mercy of wholesalers and retailers that they produce for. They participate in a classic buyer-driven commodity chain, in which the producers are small and numerous and have little control over the process. Flexibility, she argues, is primarily a way in which local people work harder and with even less control over the process than in the past. Seen from the perspective of our research in Hong Kong, we wonder to what extent we can generalize from the case of San Cosme. A different situation is seen with the petty capitalists in 1950s Hong Kong, who were just as vulnerable to buyer-driven commodity chains and could not resort to subsistence agricultural strategies. Yet, a complex economy with few safeguards and protections continued to expand and increase the colony's prosperity. There were sweatshops on an epic scale, small factories crammed into three-hundred square-foot apartments or in smaller public housing units, yet small manufacturers managed to continually increase production until the mid-1980s, when most of the work was transferred offshore, most of it to China.

As Rothstein points out, offshore producers are reliant on market demands over which they have no control. Yet, if the small fish are able to change over to supply new markets, they can overcome their reliance, by only being provisionally committed to particular products. To maintain this kind of flexibility, however, sunk capital costs must be kept relatively low, privileging labor-intensive production. If petty capitalists, and local economies can "ride the wave" of changing markets, they can regain a degree of control, in the same way that the Vega Baja *jornaleros* learned skills through the necessity of movement through different opportunities to make a living. Nothing guarantees, though, the survival of individual entrepreneurs, even if the small and medium sector persists through all the crises.

In his scathing critique of regionalist neo-orthodoxy, John Lovering (1999) points out that a rather small number of examples of flexible specialization are repeated again and again. The archetypes are particular regions in Italy (see the chapter by Ghezzi), Germany, Silicon Valley (see the chapter by Hsu) and to a lesser extent South China (Christerson and Lever-Tracy 1997). These success stories have produced a policy paradigm (and consultancy industry) that has attempted to promote similar forms of regional dynamism in less prosperous areas. Adrian Smith's chapter on

Slovakia explicitly engages with these regionalist ideas (e.g., Smith and Narotzky's chapter) and criticizes them for various theoretical and empirical inadequacies. The strength of this chapter is particularly seen in the cogency of the argument and in the careful evaluation of European Union (EU) policies that promote small and medium enterprises (SMEs) in the former socialist states of East-Central Europe. Policy emphasis on small firms and flexibility is particularly central to transition policy because the failure of socialist economies is widely seen in terms of the lack of flexibility and responsiveness in the large, centrally planned production complexes. Katherine Verdery (1993) for example, argues that while socialist economies were already losing the competition with the West, the shift to flexible accumulation practices and its attendant speeding up of competition and change sealed their fate (for a dissenting analysis of the applicability of this account to all socialist economies, see A. Smart 1998 on China).

Adrian Smith concludes that where local clusters of small and medium firms have been most successful, it has been in locations where former state enterprises were located. The production traditions in these areas provide the basis for a proliferation of new firms, as state managers leave and start new establishments. Thus, echoing the historical emphasis just discussed, the legacies of socialism clearly influence small firm development, and not only in negative ways. One result is that small and medium enterprises with a reasonable prospect of survival are located in only a few areas, particularly near Bratislava. The implication is that development policies cannot ignore local conditions and histories: one size does not fit all, and a crucial lesson would seem to be that in order to have a chance at good results, policies must find ways to build on the past in constructive ways. Another reason that he offers for skepticism is the dependence of small firms on their subcontracting links with more powerful firms outside the region. In his examination of the garment industry, he echoes Rothstein in emphasizing the impact of the buyer-driven nature of the commodity chains in this sector, and the danger that buyers will shift their contracts to lower-cost competitors elsewhere. His evaluation is that while petty capitalist production provides partial and temporary mechanisms for economic development, whether or not they have the potential for upgrading production remains an open question.

Simone Ghezzi situates his study in the context of differences between analyses that emphasize deterritorialization made possible by time-space compression and those that highlight the revital-ization of regional production complexes. While both discourses are associated with ideas of flexible accumulation, one emphasizes locality while the other stresses the increasing mobility of capital and its disengagement from local responsibilities. The Brianza region of northern Italy is a classic example of an industrial dis-trict, with an emphasis on small firms in woodworking, metal-working, and plastics. The success of the region, in the context of increasing global competition, cannot be separated from the process of exploitation, Ghezzi argues. In order to remain competi-tive everyone, owners, family members, and their employees alike, must work hard. (Interestingly, he specifically mentions that firms that used to outsource production in the Brianza have established firms in Eastern Europe, taking advantage of the EU development programs that Adrian Smith discusses.) He explains how "working hard" in a context of petty capitalism has tended to devalorize the work of women (see also Blim 2001). The crisis of larger firms in the region in the 1950s both provided the context for the upsurge of small workshops and for the reduced status of women. Despite the fact that women work as hard in these family businesses as do men, much of their work is seen as "unproductive" despite being indispensable. Working hard is also crucial in a context where increasing the quality of products is a key to survival. "Quality" has become a preoccupation and thus an "experience-near" con-cept, but ironically the meaning of quality has become associated with external demands for standardized guarantees, particularly the ISO 9001 certification. The interface between global harmo-nization of standards and petty capitalist production processes is a particularly fascinating issue, addressed further in the discussion of the chapters by Tom O'Neill and B. Lynne Milgram.

Hans and Judith-Maria Buechler examine a range of firms in the former eastern Germany (GDR or the German Democratic Republic), some of which are classic petty capitalist enterprises while others would not fit our definition, due to their size or because they are subsidiaries of larger conglomerates (although some actually became small enterprises as a result of traumatic restructuring). However, by systematically comparing this spec-trum of firm sizes, they are able to identify both commonalities and differences and thereby enhance our understanding of the dynamics of petty capitalist firms. They analyze the trajectory after reunification of firms that had operated under the GDR, examining how the nature of the industry and the strategies of the operators influence the outcomes. Their general conclusion is that it is misleading to focus too narrowly on contrasts between economic systems as a whole (capitalism vs. communism) or firm size, because similarities across the divisions and diversity within a type are just as apparent as the converse. Constraints within markets, and the impact of external actors such as foreign investors, need to be examined carefully to see how firm owners respond and their chances of success.

Most of the chapters in this volume are concerned with the "old" economy, even if information technology is used in certain cases to improve the competitiveness of the small firms that are discussed. This makes it easier to dismiss the relevance of such petty enterprises. Hsu Jinn-yuh's chapter is particularly useful in that it deals with small enterprises (in terms of numbers of employees, if not necessarily the quantity of capital invested) whose owners can still be seen as petty capitalists (in our sense of active involvement in the production process), but operating in the "new" economy, producing semiconductors. If petty capitalists can operate in this kind of sector, they are less likely to be dismissed as remnants of the past. However, it also makes it possible to examine how petty capitalist practices adapt to new conditions of work and doing business. One question addressed by Hsu is whether or not it is sensible to think of small Integrated Circuit (IC) firms as at all related to other forms of petty commodity production or petty capitalism. The dynamics are clearly different. Most high-tech firms, even if they start small, are not likely to stay small: either they grow or they fail. However, a small enterprise component can still survive, if new start-ups continue to be generated. Hsu argues that the conditions for this continue to exist, fostered in part by the shift away from economies of scale (which privilege the largest firms) toward economies of scope (which encourage vertical disintegration and alliances). Hsu also argues that some of the legacies of a petty commodity production style persist even in large Taiwanese technology firms, particularly the emphasis on trust and personalistic relations of production that facilitate informal technical cooperation between firms, and build on the tacit knowledge embedded in learning communities. In contrast to most of the other chapters in this volume, however, the key lines of cooperation are not defined by kinship, but are created through common experiences in school and in former workplaces. Family members usually do not have the specialized knowledge and contacts required in this field. Of great interest is the contribution that Taiwanese that have returned from working in Silicon Valley have made to building the semiconductor industry in Taiwan and in constructing alliances that closely link the two areas.

Hsu also demonstrates that even in an industry of the future, history is central. There is a surprising parallel in his account to Adrian Smith's finding that SMEs tended to be most successful where they spun off out of the large production complexes of the socialist era. Hsu describes how many of the start-up firms, and key personal ties, can be traced back to state-owned firms; he also describes how government investments eventually created an environment in which private initiatives in high-tech could thrive.

Donald M. Nonini also provides a variety of insights into interaction between governments and petty capitalists in his chapter on Malaysia. The specifics of this interaction are refracted through the medium of ethnicity, providing a dynamic that does not appear in any of the other chapters in this volume. Reflecting colonial history, the small business sector became identified with the Chinese minority, and government policies attempted to promote the economic development of the Malay, or Bumiputra, majority, usually at the expense of the Chinese. Nonini's analysis reveals the complex history by which the interaction between government actions and discourses (or governmentality, to follow his Foucauldian usage) and the organization of petty capitalist activities. One sharp contrast with Hsu's chapter is that the interaction between the Malaysian state and petty enterprises actively discouraged them from involvement in high-tech ventures, while Bumiputra and foreign investment in these areas were subsidized. He suggests that the relationship between the state and petty capitalists should be seen as involving predation that has encouraged the proliferation of numerous small firms rather than their expansion, because larger enterprises are subject to greater restrictions and extractions. He points out that this pattern has demographic implications (echoing Hill Gates's call to pay more attention to the demography of petty capitalism) since the petty capitalist sector tends to produce more progeny than capital accumulation allows for reproduction employers. This promotes career trajectories of professionalization, but for the Chinese this route is also discouraged by the state, resulting in pressures toward study abroad and emigration. Thus, despite the considerable hostility between petty capitalists and the Malaysian state, the organization of the sector cannot be understood without attending to these interactions.

Other chapters suggest the same, although the dynamics of the interaction differ considerably.

Regulation of business practices is not confined to the domestic actions of governments. The chapters by Milgram and O'Neill illustrate the impact that supranational organizations and transnational nongovernment organizations can have on petty enterprises. Ghezzi's account of the demand that Italian firms adopt the ISO 9001 quality certification process shows a comparable process of transnational standards being imposed on and influencing local practices.

O'Neill examines the impact of the international campaign against child labor on small-scale carpet production in Nepal. This resulted in a branding system named Rugmark, which certifies enterprises as "child labor free." Certification was demanded by the major importers, particularly European importers, who control the market in what is clearly another "buyer-driven commodity chain" (see the chapter by Rothstein). Building on careful analysis of the organization of carpet production, he demonstrates how the inspection and registration regime has had the effect of making the position of small producers even more precarious and reducing their market share. While they had previously been largely dependent on subcontracting for carpet exporters, they also had alternative routes to exports, the stock trade, but this was largely closed off by the certification system. O'Neill points out that the decline of small-scale enterprises is unusual in comparison to other sectors within the Nepalese economy, where petty enterprise and the informal sector continue to proliferate, and where child labor continues to be common. It was the international exposure of the carpet trade that made the small producers vulnerable to the imposition of a transnational social labeling system that imposed costs that contributed to the loss of viability for smaller producers.

Milgram examines another social labeling system with rather different effects on small producers in the Phillipine, the "fair trade" movement. By developing links with the Alternative Trade Organizations that promote fair trade rather than free trade, artisans and petty capitalists in the rural Phillipines have been able to open channels that allow them to enter the global craft market "more on their own terms." Although several other chapters, particularly those by Ghezzi and Rothstein, examine the position of women within petty capitalist enterprises, Milgram here focuses specifically on female producers. National rural enterprise development programs that targeted handicraft promotion largely failed to assist petty producers and instead primarily benefited merchants who acted as brokers of the producers' goods. By contrast, networks between producers' cooperatives and Alternative Trade Organizations that assist in the marketing of "fair trade" goods have been more effective at assisting petty producers and small entrepreneurs. Fair trade ideologies emphasize the responsibility of consumers to pay reasonable prices to producers and the need to bypass the middlemen who often reap the greatest rewards from Third World handicrafts, coffee, and other goods. Although acknowledging some limitations, Milgram sees these transnational linkages as empowering rural producers. Despite the sharp differences between the goods and the actors, there are some similarities here with Hsu's account of the Taiwan/Silicon Valley interface in that personal ties serve to enable new practices. On the other hand, the outcomes of the social labeling process here contrasts sharply with O'Neill's study: small producers are boosted in the Philippines while losing out in Nepal.

All of these chapters contain many more points of interest and contributions to our understanding of the place of petty capitalists in the contemporary world than we have been able to highlight here. There are also more commonalities and points of convergence, as well as points of intriguing differences, than we could draw out. We hope that at least we have managed to demonstrate that petty capitalists do indeed have something to offer, both practically and intellectually, as a way of focusing on the transformations of recent decades, and the way in which this "enduring alternative" continues to modify its operations in order to take advantage of opportunities and niches within a world where massive corporations are usually seen as the main economic forces of globalization. However, as many of the chapters have emphasized, petty capitalists are more than just economic agents. They are members of households and of communities. They are fathers or husbands or sons, wives or mothers or daughters, classmates, neighbors, and friends. The survival of their businesses may require profits, but their goals may also involve maintaining traditions, avoiding the humiliation of being an employee, helping to build a locality or producing new products, or avoiding the exactions of more powerful individuals and institutions. Small enterprises possess a dynamic that is distinct from that of larger companies, at least in part, and that plays its own role in the constitution of the contemporary interconnected world. More so than large conglomerates, petty businesses are rooted in local places, even while they may be empowered by their participation in transnational networks and spaces. Yet their voices are largely silent, even while the merits of SMEs are touted widely by policy wonks and public intellectuals in the European Union and elsewhere. By attending to the fascinating stories in this volume we see some of the ways in which the smaller fish of the world are swimming in global, not just local, ponds.

## Notes

Keely Breibish and Teresa, Stevens provided excellent editorial assistance. Mary Adair prepared the index.

1. Contrary, perhaps, to expectation, most import-export firms are small in size as well, although there are large and influential exceptions such as Li and Fung. In 1991, there were 69,066 such enterprises, with an average of 5.35 workers per firm; by 1998, 92,604 firms had an average of 5.1 workers (Census and Statistics Department 1999:93).

# 2

# Petty Production:
# The Enduring Alternative

## Hill Gates

Petty commodity production (PCP) has flourished in many contexts throughout human history. It sometimes emerged entirely outside class society, as in the producer-trader networks of Melanesia (Malinowski 1922; Sahlins 1972). It was a characteristic element of the political economy of most preindustrial agrarian states (McCorriston 1997; Bennett 1996; Gates 1996). Petty producers maintained niches throughout Europe's long transition from feudalism to capitalism (e.g., Gulliver and Silverman 1995). Under capitalism, early and late, it has been regularly reinvented as a survival strategy (Hart 1973; Littlefield and Reynolds 1990; Clark 1994). And PCP has been the essential platform under East Asian development that successfully competes in the global corporate market (Cole 1971; Tadao 1983; Odaka Keihosuke, and Fumihiko. 1987; A. Smart 1995; J. Smart 1999; Chen Hsin-hsing 1999; Lee Anru 2004). For a contemporary high-tech cousin of PCP, we might choose the dotcom. Even in the hard times of this new century, high-tech firms can be founded on informal capital by small, highly personalistic work teams to make handcrafted products for well-targeted markets (Madrick 1999; Hsu, this volume).

No investigation of PCP can ignore three core attributes. The first of these, its personalistic relations of production, receives special treatment in this volume as the authors focus on petty capitalists who are both owners and production workers.[1] Other attributes of PCP viewed broadly and historically are the small

scale of its instititutions and its historical tendency to accommodate to, rather than to transform the mode in which, it is embedded. A fourth attribute is the sometimes-neglected question of the
demographic effects of petty production.

Do these parameters define a meaningful reality, a useful concept? Petty commodity production appears in such a broad range
of historical, ecological, cultural, political-economic, and technological contexts that it might well be a theoretical mirage, each exem-
plar of which "means" and operates quite differently. PCP would
then vanish. I do not think that PCP is a false category, but I
argue that we must make a greater effort to explain why this pattern (if it is one!) is so enduring, so accessible to reinvention, so
protean in its accommodation to varying contexts.

PCP is a politically as well as a theoretically troublesome concept. By its practitioners, even those who own no means of production, it is generally perceived as a desirable, even virtuous way of
life. As a hopeful strategy for the impoverished and a filler of tiny
but significant economic niches, PCP is generally tolerated, and
often encouraged, by those whose political-economic power encompasses it. Successful practitioners of PCP, however, draw contempt
both from power-holders—for their presumption and their aes-
thetic solecisms—and from the left—for political unreliability.

While it is structurally loose, the recurring parallels and
perenniality of local PCPs depend on universal tendencies at the
heart of family formation. Arguments from human nature remain
contentious in anthropology. By rethinking PCP in the light of current knowledge of human biology, however, we develop a more
complete historical materialist approach. Production of any kind is
an aspect of what Karl Marx called labor:

> a process between man and nature, a process by which
> man, though his own actions, mediates, regulates, and con-
> trols the metabolism between himself and nature. He con-
> fronts the materials of nature as a force of nature. He sets
> in motion the natural forces which belong to his own body,
> his arms, legs, head and hands, in order to appropriate the
> materials of nature in a form adapted to his own needs.
> Through this movement he acts upon external nature and
> changes it, and in this way he simultaneously changes his
> own nature. (1977:283-284).

Marx would almost certainly be delighted to learn of the
advances in developmental psychology and human biology that

today enrich his sketch of the human animal (Bateson and Martin 2000; Goodman and Leatherman 1998; Maccoby 1998; Wolf and Durham, in press). Many sophisticated leftist thinkers now cautiously investigate human nature rather than condemning the concept (e.g., Geras 1983; Roseberry 1998; Sayers 1998). Michael Hardt and Antonio Negri's *Empire* (2000), a Marxist revision of recent analyses of the postmodern, depends for its coherence on attention to cognitive and affective capacities that we all share.

## Analytic Perspectives on PCP

In the modern West, PCP has been seen as a an endangered species of political economy. The label "semiproletarian" was invented to describe the slippage of some petty producers into part wage-work, part self-subsistence (Roberts 1978), or to emphasize the insignificance of ownership by small firms deeply subordinated to capitalist outsourcers. After World War II, as mom-and-pop shops lost out to corporate chains in capitalist economies, PCP began to be seen as analytically trivial.

In the mid-1970s, PCP became salient again. East Asian competitive successes in industrial goods drew scholarly attention to the variants of capitalism under which these successes became possible (Gates 1979; Morawetz 1981; Deyo 1989). The rubric Alan Smart (1995) calls "local capitalisms" develops this tradition very effectively. A key element in East Asia's new version of capitalism was its undergirdment by PCP. Corporate brand names implied corporate production, but in reality labeled only corporate assembly, marketing, and export systems. Much actual production was by small, private, often family-owned firms with relations of production distinct from those of public and private corporations. The importance of the petty producer platform under global success was reemphasized when North Italians too began to shine in global competition through small-scale, flexible, and often family-centered firms (Piore and Sabel 1984; Blim 1990). Even neoliberal economists took note of experiments like the Grameen bank; Islamic *hawala* and East Asian informal finance institutions began to appear in the pages of the *Wall Street Journal*.

Grappling with increasing U.S. balance of payments deficits, analysts began to write of "flexible accumulation" (Harvey 1989) as a new moment in late capitalism. Much of this flexibility came from the high skills and low capitalization of petty firms. As Frances Abrahamer Rothenstein emphasizes in this volume, however, "flexibility for whom?" soon became the key question. PCP was further highlighted by left-feminist analysts who briskly deconstructed the benign image of egalitarian producer households, revealing strong internal hierarchies of power and consumption and rebuking tendencies to romanticize the family firm (e.g., Collins 1991; Lem 1991). The combination of PCP in international production and its locus at the intersection of kinship and gender divisions of labor prompted an enormous amount of fruitful empirical research (e.g., Ghezzi, Milgram, and O'Neill, this volume).

Following the cultural turn of the 1980s and '90s, regulation theorists offered an updated and relabeled mode of production approach emphasizing the holism of the process through which labor is regulated, giving special attention to the state and to Gramscian broad-spectrum hegemony (Boyer 1990). By underlining the necessary integration of political-economies with their cultural matrices, they refreshed classical mode of production analysis. "Regionalism" too, appeared, developing left theory through nuance rather than rejection.

PCP is not associated with only one or two of the Marx/Engels modes of production (S. Amin 1972; E. R. Wolf 1982; Sacks 1982; Haldon 1993). Nearly any MOP (Mode of Production) can tolerate some small-scale production for exchange, although both Mao and the Inca tried briefly to extirpate it. As "petty" production, PCP is defined as a set of relationships always subordinated to another mode, which sets broad political-economic and cultural limits on it. I see five main contexts within which PCP has been analyzed. Each is generated by positioning PCP in a dominant political-economic structure, by its timing vis-à-vis capitalist industrialism, and by the contingencies of regional histories. They are (1) domestic mode of production; (2) petty capitalism under tributary modes; (3) proto-industrialism; (4) petty bourgeois/old middle class; and (5) informal (off-the-books/black/underground) economies.

Many analysts today would include a sixth variant, the PCP that puts the flexibility in flexible accumulation, and, together with improved information transfer technology, significantly raises productivity. I disagree. The shift from the high industrial capitalism of the early and middle twentieth century to a postmodern or late capitalism has been seriously overemphasized: an example of the narcissism of small differences. In what is perhaps the most coherent recent interpretation of this shift, Michael Hardt and Antonio Negri stress the idea of an inversion of the Fordist structure of communication between production and consumption. Ideally, according to this model, production planning will communicate with markets constantly and immediately. Factories will maintain zero stock, and commodities will be produced just in time according to the present demand of the existing markets. This model thus involves not simply a more rapid feedback loop but an inversion of the relationship because, at least in theory, the production decision actually comes after and in reaction to the market decision. In the most extreme cases the commodity is not produced until the consumer has already chosen and purchased it. In general, however, it would be more accurate to conceive the model as striving toward a continual interactivity or rapid communication between production and consumption. This industrial context provides a first sense in which communication and information have come to play a newly central role in production. (2000:290)

Just such a position has been widely entertained in the last two decades. Neoliberal and left analysts alike began to hope that crises of overaccumulation were a thing of the past and that the business cycle had finally been tamed. The Empire was to be steered by the invisible hand, and states smudged out of significance by transnationalism. Now, stock market crashes, worldwide depression, and the resurgence of American militarism to nineteenth century levels have demonstrated the weakness of political-economic postmodernity, of theories that overemphasized change rather than continuity in capitalism. Instead,

> ...there has indeed been an important technological transformation in America, but not necessarily one that will lead to more rapid productivity growth. The new economy is a return to a contemporary version of a crafts economy, where the most valued contribution is the skill of the worker. The new crafts workers are business managers, consultants and marketing and financial experts as well as scientific and technical researchers and computer specialists. Or to put it differently, in an age where information is so widely available, it is not the information that is valuable but what is done with it. (Madrick 1999:50)

His emphasis on human skills that modulate what technology (even the new stuff) can do unaided returns us to contemplation of petty production from the point of view of its human inputs and social/affective relations of production. Let us reexamine the five variants of PCP that have produced most of the sturdy empirical studies of our subject, attending to these human inputs as well as to the often contradictory pressures of production modes.

## The Domestic Mode of Production

The idea of a domestic mode of production has been current in leftist discourse since Aleksandr Chayanov, who admired the Russian peasant extended household commune existing prior and external to czarist rule. The *zadruga* was loosely linked to others in an egalitarian exchange of use values, and thus the sole social unit necessary for anarchism. In this perspective, petty commodity production, obviously necessary even to very simple standards of living, did not undermine households as social units. Variations in wealth did not induce capitalist relations, but were structurally unimportant by-products of the domestic cycle and its dependency ratios.

Marshall Sahlins resuscitated the DMP in which people underproduce in the sense that they "seem not to realize their own economic capacities. Labor power is underused, technological means are not fully engaged, natural resources are left untapped...production is low relative to existing possibilities....Almost every family living solely by its own means sooner or later discovers it has not the means to live. And while the household is thus periodically failing to provision itself, it makes no provision (surplus) either for a public economy 'including extrafamilial institutions' perhaps just as urgent for survival as the daily food supply" (1972:41). Societies dominated by a domestic mode of production are either an anarchist illusion, or extremely rare and short-lived, for household survival requires the existence, however limited and fragmentary, of a *political* economy to motivate surplus reproduction, production, and more extrafamilial forms of exchange (1972:101). Even among household producers on state fringes (e.g., the *zadruga*) and in the stateless societies that anthropologists once specialized in, household autarchy was sporadic at most.

With the emergence of class societies, most petty producers have been "peasants." Their adaptations were famously labeled by

Eric Wolf, who described them as rural cultivators, together with other extractive and handicraft producers, "whose surpluses are transferred to a dominant group of rulers that uses the surpluses both to underwrite its own standard of living and to distribute the remainder to groups in society that do not [produce basic goods] but must be fed for their specific goods and services in return" (1966:3–4). He stressed their necessary connection with other sectors of society:

> The peasant is not engaged in agriculture alone. Cultivation may produce the calories a man needs, but he also has to dress himself, build houses, make containers, and manufacture the tools utilized in cultivation. Moreover, agricultural produce and livestock products must be processed, grain turned into bread, olives into oil, milk into butter, hides into leather. (1966:37)

And he emphasizes the forced production of surpluses for rent and taxes. Peasants cannot be understood without reference to their exchanges with market and state; an identical logic applies to artisanal and urban petty commodity producers.

While most anthropologists have agreed that a stand-alone DMP is not feasible, some have been attracted by Chayanov's insights (e.g., Durrenberger 1984; McGough 1984). Sometimes the DMP is used to insulate households (and the analyst's work) from wider problems of class (Greenhalgh 1986), or to take up the slack in an argument that depends on the illogical separation of political and economic phenomena (Sangren 1985).

## Petty Capitalism under Tributary Modes

During China's imperial eras, what I define as petty capitalism was developed as an exceptionally sophisticated type of PCP that manufactured for domestic use and for an immense precolonial Euro/Afro/Asian trade. From the early states of the Eastern Mediterranean and South Asia, tendrils of exchange reached China across Central Asia, and for the last thousand years via Southeast Asia and the Indian Ocean (Abu-Lughod 1989). Among their many export commodities were superb textiles: cottons from India, silks from China, and delicate Southeast Asian summer cloth of exotic fibers, "so transparent that it concealed nothing"

(Reid 1988:86). The finest of these were made by skilled craftspeople, often in bonded service to some local ruler. Given these relations of production, this was not PCP. But such long-distance trade in fine goods implies much larger domestic markets for simpler products. Commonplace fabrics made from reeled floss, twisted bast, and spun yarn was the task of unimaginable numbers of petty producer girls and women. Despite millennial labor demand, parental authority over women and children were strengthened rather than loosened. Local combinations of religious and secular authority privileged tributary exchanges, including those of kinship and gender, over those of the market. History's most extraordinary constraints on women—claustration, (confinement to a cloister) veiling, footbinding, suttee, (self-cremation of a widow on her husband's pyre) and perhaps female circumcision—were invented in this great arc of agrarian-handicraft empires that Judith K. Brown calls "the mother-in-law belt"[2] (1997).

Chinese rulers especially perfected the regulation of, and predation on, their producers by making kinship the last link in their political-economic chain of command, by tying secure property rights to household statuses, by creating judicial institutions to enforce kinship law, and by delegating patriarchal authority over employees and bond servants to household heads. Behind silk-reelers stood parents, and behind parents, local magistrates imbued with Confucian concern for kinship/gender order and female industriousness (Mann 1997; Gates 1996). In consequence, Chinese petty capitalists were (and to some degree, still are) agents in markets constrained and tapped for surplus by an eclectically mercantile and physiocratic ruling class. They create an interesting variant of PCP, I think, because the relations of household production are so meticulously specified and disciplined by successive Chinese dynasties. Through such modernism *avant la lettre*, China maintained an enormous and expanding manufacturing population; repelled or transformed all other political-economic structures that probed its borders; supported an immensely cultivated elite stratum and a rich, resourceful popular culture; and through its massive productivity, was arguably the center of the world economy from 1000 P.E. to the 1850s (A. G. Frank 1998). The Chinese Empire shows us the global impact of PCP when its pettiness is harnessed to worldwide commerce and to an elite outlook alert to the longue duree.

Demographically, the Chinese political economy was a huge Darwinian success, steadily ramping up numbers over its final thousand years. Production intensification was not limited to agriculture; the Chinese underwent not only agricultural involution, but became a pan-sectoral "high level equilibrium trap" (Elvin 1973; Huang 1990) in which massive labor inputs added value to such unpromising raw materials as insect by-products and sugarcane waste. Children were labor assets not just to peasant farming, but to international trade. It has recently been argued that Qing couples began to limit births as a labor/resource balancing strategy (J. Z. Lee 2000; but see A. P. Wolf 2001). If so, they limited them at levels that continued to push the population growth curve up logarithmically, supplying workers for large global and immense domestic markets.

The structural stability of this political economy was remarkable, although change occurred as well. Its egregious age and gender inequalities increased during the last dynasties (Sommer 2000) but caste-like class relations faded, supporting modest levels of popular egalitarianism. Through Ming and Qing eras (1368-1911), rulers managed the market for distinctly noncapitalist ends; even Maoist rule combined socialism with many tributary elements.

As China edged into world trade after 1978, its low-end petty commodity producers became the economy's strongest sector—the small-to-medium and township—village enterprises. Its high-tech start-ups (e.g., the now-powerful Legend software company) were initiated and nurtured directly by the state sector. In Taiwan, where a huge state-and-party sector is still more structurally analogous with China than is generally recognized, high-tech SME successes by partnerships of intimates have similarly been cultivated into competitiveness by the state, as we see in Hsu (this volume). In the post-Soviet sphere, by contrast with post-Maoist China, small and medium enterprises (SMEs) have had very mixed success (e.g., Buechler and Buechler, and Smith, this volume). One might hypothesize that at least a part of the difference with China results from the very different use of kinship in Soviet governmentality.

## Protoindustrialization

Analysts associated with protoindustrialism (PI) began to rethink Europe's transition from feudalism to capitalism through the lens of demography after family reconstruction studies (Wrigley and Schofield 1989) suggested that expanding preindustrial production stimulated population growth (e.g., Mendels 1981). Signally important in this literature was the discovery of a hitherto unrecognized European marriage and labor regime (Laslett 1977; Hajnal 1965, 1982). Women in Northwest Europe's hearth of capitalism had long distributed their labors of production and reproduction in unique fashion. By not marrying at all (some 15 percent) or marrying a decade past puberty in their late twenties, these women preempted a huge proportion of their societies' fertility potential. No other known population does this. In precontracepting societies from the Amazon to the Yangzi, almost all women marry, and girls begin their sexual lives (married or not) at around puberty. Thus, generally, they take full advantage of their reproductive potential during their most fertile years.

By contrast, early modern Europeans had a "nuptiality valve" for their large pool of unrealized potential fertility. A shift from traditional late marriage for women to marriage at an earlier age was possible should their conditions of family formation change. Some economic historians, examining the correlation between intensive preindustrial commodity production and marriage age found that in boom times for cottage industry, new households formed earlier, increasing lifetime fertility and regional population growth rates. Population outstripped access to means of production, driving proletarianization and thus Europe's transition to capitalism.

Alas for this elegant contribution to women's history and transition theory, subsequent research fails to support a consistent pattern among these variables; PI defeats any simplistic application of stage theory. The sprouts of capitalism in Europe did not grow only in protoindustrial soil, although some local craft traditions were industrialized (Hafter 1995). Some PI areas faded into overintensification and social misery (Ogilvie 1993; Hendrickx 1997). And surprisingly, according to Manuel Castells and Yuko Aoyama, some late twentieth-century Italian small producers leaped "from proto-industrialism to proto-informationalism" (1994:27)—by which they mean an information-driven, post-Fordist political economy. Further contrasts may be unearthed from the historical study of Eastern European protoindustrialization. The Habsburg regime and marriage-control policies (Rebel 1989, 1991) managed their emerging markets in ways reminiscent of tributary China rather than incipient-capitalist England or the Netherlands. East and West were richly interlaced in the past thousand years, as recent reevaluations of European history have made abundantly clear (e.g., Goody 1996; Frank 1998). Comparative historical studies of household formation, division of labor, and demographic tendencies in such contrasting regions as China and Northwestern Europe are beginning to enrich our understanding of PCP as well (Engelen and Wolf, in press).

## Petty Bourgeoisies

"Petty capitalism" as I have defined it here depends on its embeddedness in Asian political economies of flourishing trade and powerful cosmic/state/kinship modes of production; "protoindustrialism" is both Eurocentered and time-bound: capitalist industrialization changed most, if not all, of its conditions of existence. But some PI households, their communities, and their class cultures "weathered the storm" (Seccombe 1993) of the capitalist transition in Europe. It may be helpful to reserve the label "petty bourgeoisie" for just such islands of resistance to direct proletarianization who carry forward an elaborated heritage of ideologies and institutions from a time when these occupied much larger local social spaces. The previous comment by Castells and Aoyama connecting "proto-industrialism" and "proto-informationalism" in Italy as phases in a single process reminds us how difficult it would be to construct a watertight typology of PCP variants rather than (as here) to underline clusters of areal/temporal/disciplinary research. The apparently new "petty bourgeoisie" emerging in post-Soviet societies present particular challenges to analysts. While it necessarily responds to intrusive foreign and local capitalisms, it also carries a legacy of existing resource distribution from the socialist (-tributary?) period, and another from presocialist forebears across the generationally brief socialist era.

The petty bourgeoisie as it persisted into mainstream European capitalism typically reproduced itself as households and networks continuous with the past in personnel as well as in material and cultural legacies. The term *old middle class* of owner-producers (as opposed to the *new middle classes* of a credentialed salariat) speaks directly to this link with the past. The butt of aristocratic, bourgeois, and radical critique, the petty bourgeoisie has been an extremely important cultural subject. What changed, and what remained the same, as PI producers accommodated to the world that capitalism was building around them? Massive literatures in European social history offer many answers; I will suggest only three.

First, petty bourgeois producers have endured only in niches that machine-aided mass wage-labor did not readily occupy. Even commercial services lost ground quickly in the twentieth century to department stores and to mail-order commerce. Sustainable specialties narrowed dramatically, tilting toward personal and commercial services and artisan production of conspicuous luxuries.

Second, along with their menfolk, petty bourgeois women arguably lost less of their early modern powers and liberties to industrial capitalism than most European women. As partners in their family firms (even when partnership was not culturally recognized), women contributed mightily to them, often as their husbands sought waged or salaried work elsewhere. Women's reproductive, manual, cognitive, and affective labor in PCP creates more social power, even when veiled in patriarchy and limited to the household sphere, than waged (perhaps even salaried) work can do. Squeezed by capitalist and state pressures, the petty bourgeoisie builds on PI industriousness and overcomes any tendency to PCP "underproductivity" with an almost gender-neutral mobilization of its labor power.

A third petty bourgeois characteristic that confirms their continuity with precapitalist forms of PCP lies in the cultural realm. Nineteenth- and twentieth-century petty bourgeois households were snubbed most viciously, perhaps, for old-fashioned, sometimes oddly aristocratic pretentions: for "getting above themselves." Marx trashed them for political unreliability because "the petty bourgeoisie... [is] a *transition class*, in which the interests of two classes [bourgeoisie and proletariat—H.G.] are simultaneously mutually blunted" 1979:133). He reserved his sharpest invective, however, for their style:

> The petty bourgeoisie, great in boasting, is very impotent for action and very shy in risking anything. The *mesquin* [miserly] character of its commercial transactions and its credit operations is eminently apt to stamp its character with a want of energy and enterprise; it is, then, to be expected that similar qualities will mark its political career. (1979:89)

One might expect that these class-confused and chicken-hearted folk would keep a low public profile, but this is not our cultural stereotype. Not only are they "great in boasting," they are vastly concerned with face or respectibility in every aspect of life, keeping the aspidistra flying behind (machine!) lace curtains, and lusting after respectability. As a bred-and-born daughter of the PB, I claim native intuition here. We do not imitate the dull bourgeoisie that stands directly above us. We go straight for the Queen Mum, for the Duchess of Kent, for Princess Margaret, for Lady Di: for the hegemons of the feudal era where our ancestral PCP was formed.

## Informal Economy

In 1973, Keith Hart wrote of an "informal economy" of self-employed people running small businesses with low profits, no access to credit from finance capital, often as a substitute for desirable but unavailable wage labor. Informal economy existed as a realm residual to formal economies driven by corporate capitalism and state circulation of wealth. In 1992, he reemphasized the importance of states for unindustrialized societies. With low capitalist production, informal producers draw much of their earnings from tax evasion and sales to the state functionaries who make up the bulk of effective consumers in such contexts. The fundamental question underlying the informal sector debate concerns "the ability or inability of small-scale enterprises to generate not only employment but also autonomous economic growth" and hence guide policy; whether "growth in this sector—evolutionary or involutionary" illuminated the "relationship between large-and small-scale enterprises with the dualist approach assuming it is benign, and the petty commodity production approach assuming it is exploitative" (Moser 1994:12). While the "dualist approach" in such contexts once implied alignment of the analyst with a neoliberal position, concern for exploitation pointed other analysts toward seeing informal activities as what Rhoda H. Halperin and Sara Sturdevant call "anti-economy" (1990:324), Josephine Smart identifies as "active resistance to proletarianization" (1990:271), and I see also as a way to contest tributary and various twentieth-century socialist modes.

In complex societies, such evasions inevitably leak into illegality, on which a literature of underground economy has been founded (e.g., Mattera 1985). Whether tax evasion and the like are viewed as resistance to predation or uncitizenlike illegality is, of course, a matter of whose side one is on.

Attempts to get a theoretical grip on informal economy and its connection with other variants of PCP remain in what M. Estellie Smith dubs the preparadigmatic state of the field (1990:9). Halperin and Sturdevant's "Cross-Cultural Treatment of the Informal Economy" breaks new anthropological ground by attempting to deconstruct it as an "heuristic device designed to handle variability, pluralism and change in economic systems" (1990:333). This accords with the untidiness of my effort here to summarize the multiple contexts and historical transitions that accommodate PCP, but leaves us still groping for a common thread.

## Kinship/Gender as Relations of Production

The social and cultural concomitants of financing, production, distribution, and consumption of goods and services by petty producers are complex. In whatever "culture," nation, region, household, or individual, any halfway competent anthropologist can find and label an infinity of difference. Reducing local surface complexity to a parsimonious set of reliable generalizations is far more difficult. An important starting-place for such a project lies in recognizing the power that relations of production assume when they are cast in the idiom of kinship and gender. Seeing kinship/gender in this way has proved its worth to many scholars, often characterized in mode of production language: the Morgan/Marx/Engels formation "primitive communism," various interpretations of lineage and domestic modes, the kin corporate mode that updated, feminized, and generalized these (well exemplified in Sacks 1982), and many other explorations of the production/reproduction aspect of kinship/gender. Petty producer relations of production are not limited to kin relations; petty producers are notoriously opportunistic, using wage laborers, apprentices, and bonded workers as well as family members and trusted intimates. The distinction between self-employed and subordinated kin has received insightful attention. But most analysts agree that local forms of kinship—real, fictive, or merely as paternalist metaphor—are core relations of production in PCP.

We gain ground in understanding petty producers by exploring a slowly maturing materialist approach that views kinship/gender differences across the world as largely constructed by local conditions of labor. Sir Edmund Leach once opined that "kinship systems have no 'reality' at all except in relation to land and property.

What the social anthropologist calls kinship structure is just a way of talking about property relations which can also be talked about in other ways" (1961:305). In *Human Families*, (1998) Stevan Harrell takes a similar stance, greatly enriching the study of kinship by insisting that its local forms have emerged to meet both material needs and those that derive from our common species nature: for autonomy and sociability, for sexual expression, and for affect in many forms. Harrell's magisterial book is not about extended "kinship in general" but about its key institution, families: "The family is a special type of kinship group, one consisting of close relatives in close cooperation in daily life. In many cases, the principles of family organization, or the activities of the family, are not the principles of organization or the activities of the larger kin groups in which families are embedded." Furthermore, families "in any community cannot be understood only paradigmatically, in comparison to families in other communities, but must also be understood syntagmatically, in relation to other groups in which its members participate." And "the emphasis is on the family as a group of people that do certain things with, for, or to each other. . . . What do people do as members of families? and Who does these things with and for whom?" (1998:5).

Kin help each other put rice in the bowl or thatch on the roof. But Harrell is no simple materialist. He insists that people also need others as partners in sexual, affective, and cooperative acts. These needs are socially and culturally inflected—obviously—but they are "constructed" on a common biologically based human nature. All these needs can be met in families of genetically unrelated individuals, not only in the minimalist hierarchies of inclusive fitness. As recent work on incest avoidance (A. P. Wolf 1995; A. P. Wolf and Durham, in press) and mothering (Hrdy 1999) have demonstrated, evolution selects for human behaviors that are *commonly* developed in the context of a genetically related kin group, but that *will* develop in whatever socially defined "family" (or household) an infant is reared in. These anthropologists are moving, cautiously, into the near-virgin territory of the empirical understanding of human nature including evolved species-specific forms of affect.

## Affect and Relations of Production

"Human nature exists," writes Melvin Konner (2002:xiii), and I concur. The problem remains, however, that we do not yet know much about what human nature is. Every human community has folklore about it, whether its tribal elder authors are Dreamtime Ancestors, Confucius, or Rush Limbaugh. Like folk medicine, some human nature lore fits reality; some is just medicinal lizards on a stick.

Although human nature exists, the way in which it is characterized is necessarily framed by the historical circumstances of those studying it. Twentieth-century anthropologists seeking recognition of, and respect for, cultural diversity hammered out socially necessary cultural constructionist arguments as ripostes to sexism, racism, and xenophobia. Twenty-first century social analysts now search as diligently for the commonalities that identify us as a single species on a single planet with needs for global justice and survival. The anthropological legacy we carry forward must stress the unities without abandoning the diversities. To assume the existence of a common human nature is not to assume the accuracy of my, or Michel Foucault's, or Mohammed's, or your guess at what it will be discovered to be. Most of the work of untangling reliable generalizations from folkloric doodah remains to be done.

Work on human biology has begun to resolve one difficulty that has particularly befuddled anthropologists. The Cartesian dualism of Nature versus Culture is yielding to a more sophisticated dialectic well summed up by Sarah B. Hrdy:

> Phenotypes [actually existing organisms—H.G.] are produced by interactions between genes and other environmental or parental influences. They can be affected by all kinds of variables—how much cytoplasm the mother delivers in the egg, what other chemicals she adds, what time of year it is, what the mother is eating at the time, diseases she might have, even her own recent social history.... [This is not to say] that genes don't matter but rather than their powers are inseparable from context, including both external context and the developmental context, since genes act by influencing a responsive structure that is already there. This is true at every level, from immune system defenses at the cellular level to character at the personality level. It is as absurd to talk about behavior being "genetically determined" as it is to claim that genes have nothing to do with behavior. (1999:56-57)

Such a developmentalist approach is standard for biologists (e.g., Bateson and Martin 2000), and increasingly guides psychologists (e.g., Maccoby 1998). An elegant example of developmentalist analysis by a biological anthropologist is that of James J. McKenna on co-sleeping—babies sharing a bed with their parents (or with any regular caretaker) (McKenna 1996; McKenna, Mosko, and Richard 1999). While they sleep, the immature sleep-wake cycle of infants is unknowingly coached into mature performance by that of the caretaker. Infants turn toward the older person's carbon dioxide exhalations, synchronizing their heartbeats and sleep-arousal cycles. Babies learn to wake and to escape the danger of sinking into deep unconsciousness and death. We may reasonably presume that they are learning other lessons as well. Cultural practices affect this evolutionarily normative behavior: infants sleeping alone appear to have higher rates of Sudden Infant Death Syndrome; co-sleeping in too-soft beds may result in infant smothering; the way babies sleep may affect their arousal threshholds as mature sleepers, creating variation in behavior easily misperceived as purely cultural. Culture diversifies child-rearing, while biology sets limits to the range of survivable customs, and individuals are formed whose behavior could not be deduced from either culture or genotype.

Research into the human biology/behavior interface reinforce this view that the culture/nature dichotomy is a false guide. Brain studies especially reject the mind/body distinction (Damasio 1999; LeDoux 2002). The philosopher Thomas Nagel, reviewing research on consciousness, summarizes an important position: "An inquiry into conscious experience cannot be based merely on the observation of external behavior; but it also cannot be carried out in abstraction from our physical nature. The understanding of the inner life of the person who is conscious must include the physical body from the start" (2002:74).

A striking example of this occurs in the operation of

the neurological apparatus of vision called the dorsal system. The dorsal system allows visual input to play a part in the control of action without going through consciousness. When you run on a beach, for example, you avoid stepping on stones in your path, not because you perceive them but before you perceive them, in virtue of a direct contribution of visual information to the control of action. In other words your eyes can guide your feet without giving you a visual experience first (2002:76).

Such evidence convinces me that between the biology/behavior inseparability of the autonomous nervous system, which everyone concedes, and the experience of perception, which can be culturally constructed in many ways, lies a connective tissue of body/mind, biology/experience, nature/culture unity common to all humans.

Most objections to the dissolution of these dichotomies take either a strong or a weak position. The strong position depends on the belief that the passage to cultural capability has rendered our species completely different from all others; our nature has become entirely plastic and our cultures have entirely free creative play. In this view, Homo sapiens transcends the natural order. There is no way to argue against this metaphysical position.

The weak position depends on the assumption that our cognitive faculties command all our other processes and characteristics. Emotional responses especially are seen as readily constructable by patterns of culture. The new interest in human biology would suggest, however, that some emotions are more constructable than others. An unusually well-documented example of research into an evolved emotional response that measurably resisted the weight of Chinese culture is that of Arthur P. Wolf (1995, and Wolf and Durham, in press). Wolf shows that incest with primary relatives is strongly opposed by an aversion that develops between children raised together from an early age.

Statistically, inbreeding between primary relatives (parent-child, sister-brother) causes inbreeding depression. Mammals have evolved to avoid it, and humans taboo it. Taking advantage of the South Chinese natural experiment of widespread childhood adoption of future daughters-in-law, Wolf has shown that the aversion develops even between genetically unrelated couples. The mechanism, early childhood association, works for unrelated pairs because, evolutionarily, children reared closely together in childhood were almost always close kin. Developing a biologically based incest aversion did not require evolution to produce a mechanism that distinguished kin from non-kin, only one that distinguishes early associates from those less familiar. Some links in this chain are still indistinct: what *exactly* triggers the aversion in children reared together? Research continues. But Wolf has demonstrated that in his very large sample, incest avoidance is dependent neither on cultural learning nor on genetic predisposition. It is a developmental outcome of a fully integrated process.

Child-caregiver bonding has been another subject of important and now well-substantiated research. Wolf's work indicates that the attachment of young humans to their caregivers—usually but not necessarily their biological parents—precludes the formation at sexual maturity of sexual attachments between them. Attachment studies, beginning with those of John Bowlby (1969, 1988), were given cross-cultural confirmation by Mary D. S. Ainsworth (1967) and have inspired much empirical research in recent years (Cassidy and Shaver 1999). Attachment is an evolutionarily selected-for genetic predisposition of young humans (and mammals generally) to seek closeness with their caregivers. The importance of this infant "agency" in its survival is hard to overestimate. Attachment behaviors by babies also elicit caregiving. Sarah Hrdy's study is especially informative on this subject (1999, esp. 536–541).

Wherever attachment has been studied, babies develop one of several different patterns depending on caregiver behavior. Curiously, neglect or even cruelty rarely extinguishes a young child's attempts to attach, as studies of abused children clearly show. Anger and fear, as well as love, may grow from the urge to attach. We may see these as situationally perverted forms of affect, but affect they surely are.

Attachment and sexual bonding appear to be allomorphs of a common physiological process (Erickson 1989, 1993; Wolf 1995), involving the hormone oxytocin. They are powerful forces in family formation and maintenance. As Stevan Harrell puts it, the need for emotional warmth is a requisite that exists "regardless of the particular nature of a social environment in which a family system exists" (1997:32). Sexual passion is notoriously subject to cultural molding, and sexual bonding may well be a less enduring emotion than a well-established child-parent relationship. William Jankowiak (1995) is a strong supporter of the universality of recognizable sexual passion.

The intense feelings—positive and negative—that are generated by attachment seem to be especially important in maintaining families as enduring cooperative entities. The power of kinship/gender relations of production is based on literally *embodied* affect, a thoroughly material condition. In the vast majority of human lives, the complex interplay between evolutionarily selected predispositions and experiences from womb to tomb takes place among those we define as kin. However exploitive they may come to be, kin relations of production are more naturalizable than any other kind as they inevitably engage with the affect of those who sleep, eat, and live together—regardless of their genetic relationships.

## Conclusion

The self-reproduction of autarchic households is not an option, but the affective relationships they typically foster can be very strong. The more complex the social formation, the more it impinges on, stresses, and provides alternatives to household organization and production. Between these two limits, PCP is constantly reinvented, and often culturally highly valued. Part of the explanation for this strong central tendency lies in emotions that enhance developmental and reproductive success. Whatever the political-economic environment, affect motivates the maintenance of early relationships. Each person's evolutionary and developmental history creates consistent and powerful pressure toward finding economic niches that can sustain those relationships. Because each human infant demands care (though not all get it), and because each sexual encounter renews emotions (good, bad, or indifferent) between adults, we are constantly motivated to live as families (of whatever composition). The pluralism associated with PCP and with our difficulties and debates about how to conceptualize it suffer from an empty center. That center must contain a more generous understanding of human beings than the passionless plasticity that has been attributed to us by extreme constructionists.

Economic cooperation among close kin is not biologically "determined," whatever that might mean. Its immediate, functional cause is not the elegant algebra of inclusive fitness. Taking shape in the interplay between genetic potential and the contingencies of individual lives, affect makes economic units of households whenever external conditions permit. Affect is a real and material factor in our human decisions, its reliable mammalian voice louder in our ears, except in great extremity, than the siren song of the market or the pious exhortations of the state. We do not internalize the latter two—so elaborately and historically constructed against our well-being—in the same embodied knowledge as affect teaches.

In any given political economy, the shared life and labor of PCP meet affective needs that larger institutions are rarely structured to engage. The kind of animal we are resists both absolute individuation and total dependency, conditions that capitalism particularly forces upon us. Humans do not—cannot—move through time as individuals, only as affectively related clusters. Close to the point of production and far from the eyes of the Emperor, PCP easily infiltrates the hard artificialities of the subject/ruler and capitalist/proletarian binaries, softening their irrationalities, compensating (sometimes perversely) for the poor fit of any and all known complex economies with human needs and desires.

PCP, for all its failings, is our default position, and may have more to offer most of the world's people than anything a Global Emperor or a Planetary CEO can imagine. The first steps many people willingly take toward stable subsistence in our economically threatening world is PCP. PCP households, and the communities they create for the larger tasks they face, do not make revolution. But they keep most of us alive to fight again.

## Notes

1. Because this chapter surveys PCP defined very broadly, I reserve the term *petty capitalism* for a subset of PCP that occurs in social formations where authoritative, extra-kin control of kin definition and kin property relations stabilize and constrain firm size. This usage will be discussed in the next section.

2. Brown's defines her felicitous term *The Mother-in-Law Belt* as "the vast, old world area stretching from western-most North Africa, across the area surrounding the Mediterranean to western Asia to the sub-continent of South Asia to [East Asia]." It spans "a variety of cultures with ancient, written traditions...observing several different 'great book religions'...there is...a uniformity among these patrilocal, patriarchal societies, when viewed from the perspective of young wives" (1997:87).

# 3

# Movers and Fixers: Historical Forms of Exploitation and the Marketing of a Regional Economy in Spain

*Gavin Smith*
*and*
*Susana Narotzky*

## The Problem Laid Out

The most influential work being done on what might broadly be described as petty capitalism in the European Union (EU) is framed within a discourse of *regional economies*.[1] Not only has a vast amount of literature now been produced on European regional economies and industrial districts, more importantly a major part of EU development policy is built upon the findings of this literature. In this chapter we attempt to demonstrate that this literature is superficial: superficial in its use of a neoclassical understanding of economy and society; superficial in its cursory and teleological use of history; and superficial in its use of "culture" as an ontologically unexplained residual category employed to save what economic modeling and modernization sociology cannot account for. Following Karl Marx we believe that an historical realist understanding of regionally clustered yet rurally dispersed firm activity is more adequately explained by shifting away from the immediacy of the daily practices of small entrepreneurs in the economy and toward *history* and the *obscuring of relations of exploitation.* We hope to show too how "culture" can become a deeply ideological and hence analytically misleading notion.

In the past twenty years social science research on small-scale economic activity in Europe has increasingly been driven by the policy institutions who provide the vast majority of funds for this kind of research (Lovering 1999; MacLeod 2001). Policy institutions in turn are enmeshed in a neoliberal discourse that Colin Gordon has described in the following terms:

> "Work for the worker" means, according to the neo-liberals, the use of resources of skill, aptitude and competence which comprise the worker's human capital, to obtain earnings which constitute the revenue on that capita.... From this point-of-view, then, *the individual producer-consumer is in a novel sense not just an enterprise, but the entrepreneur of himself or herself.* (1991:44, italics added)

All that needs to be added to this observation, in the context of the regions, is that they too must become enterprises and the entrepreneurs of themselves: hence the instrumental use of the notion "local culture."

We will use greatly attenuated material from our forthcoming book (Narotzky and Smith) in order to argue for a quite different understanding of the "regional economy" that has been the object of our studies. We have been working in an area of Spain to the south of Alicante where a variety of consumer goods are produced through a system of dispersed production. These include carpets, nets and ropes, dolls, dolls clothing, and, above all, shoes. Firms running factories employing between 150 to 250 workers outsource jobs to rural-based workshops—often of dubious legal status—of 15 to 20 workers. Homeworkers, almost entirely women, but recently joined increasingly by men, take in work from both sources, and between them run a complex network of work-distributors. This, by the way, takes place in a rural setting of intensive and (up until some ten years ago) productive irrigated agriculture. Since Gavin Smith began doing research in this area (in 1978) these kinds of phenomena have come to be described as the *social* market (Bagnasco 1981), as an *embedded* economy (Granovetter 1985), or as a *networked* society (Law 1986). When these characteristics had some kind of spatial clustering, they came to be seen as peculiarly *regional* economies. With the "Third Italy" (Bagnasco 1977) as the flagship model, these *regionalist* studies[2] have had a profound effect on policy—to the extent that the European Union is committed to a development scheme that promotes economies with regional coherence. The area of Spain that we have been studying has been so identified. Yet by giving causal weight to present-day "cultural dispositions" in a region, or unique features of its social institutions, these studies forego a thorough engagement with social contradictions and historical processes. Giacomo Becattini for example writes,

> The system of values...constitutes one of the preliminary requirements for the development of a district, and one of the essential conditions of its reproduction....This does not mean that there will be no clash of interests between the members of the district, or no perception of such clashes. Rather, they are experienced and defined in similar forms and within a framework of a sort of community-like superior interest which becomes an inner principle for the people of the district as a whole. (1992:39)

Surely a statement such as this begs the question of just how such a "community-like superior interest" came into being (if it exists at all), and this is a question that can only be answered through a thorough historical study, which will most likely reveal a complex interweaving of multiple social subjectivities that may or may not be specific to the region. When writers use locally shared cultural dispositions to explain particular features of people's conduct they avoid the complexity of regional *histories*—in the plural (see Sider and Smith 1997). We must be alert to the danger of falling into the discursive mode of entrepreneurial interest and firm efficiency while obscuring the fundamental ways in which surplus is *produced* and *extracted* and the differentiations that are induced and reinforced as a result. This renders a quite different epistemology for understanding how culture takes on relevance in the informalized world of a regional economy (Narotzky 1997b, 2000). The task mandates that we tease out the way ongoing formative practices of social agents—contradictory, conflictual, and fragmented as they may be—arise out of specific histories in which agency unfolds through narrow cracks between the tectonic plates of the logic of capitalist reproduction: that is, the *specific* ways in which value is produced and then extracted and circulated: a dialectic between movement and regulation.

## Two Indicative Vignettes

The problem is quite simple: it is that the strategizing work of actors and their own explanations of what it is they are doing are relatively easily accessible in the fieldwork setting. Moreover these everyday observations are reinforced in the public arena: from talks with mayors and union activists, to workshops held by academics and policy-officials as well as in pamphlets produced to promote the region.

*Two labor organizers....*

In the midnineties we were talking to two young men who ran a local union office. They were complaining to us about a common practice that was not helpful for building the union in the region. A non-union member man or woman working in a local factory would reach a point where they had nowhere to turn. They had been sick and had failed to get sick coverage, or they were fired without notice and not given their back-pay, and so forth. Such a person would come to one or other of these people and ask the union to help them out. On each occasion the union would take up the individual case, occasionally with success. "But they never join the union," they would say. "Why not?" we would ask. "Because in this region you have an entrepreneurial worker. You have an entrepreneurial culture." We would ask them what they meant by these expressions. At first we were greeted by sheepish grins. This was a term they had heard bandied about by social scientists and the truth is that they expected us as social scientists to simply accept it as an explanation. But when we said that we were puzzled, they explained to us:

> Here everybody in the family works. The man works for a while for wages. When he's got a little put by, he goes out and sets up a workshop. After a while maybe he needs another machine—maybe then he gets behind on payments for a shipment. So he turns to his wife, and she works some overtime and gets the money for him. Then he needs more extra work done and his wife takes it round to her friends in the neighbourhood.

Do these ventures last? we asked. "Not at all. In no time he's back out without work. He looks around. Finds some work in another workshop maybe. Then maybe his wife will set something up. Use her friends and start something small, who knows?"

*... and a mayor.*

On another occasion we were talking to the mayor of the town that acted as the center of gravity for our study of the region. We asked him why small industries were attracted to the town. "Well it's not really because of the infrastructure. Most of that came in the Franco era. We have developed a *polígono industrial* (an industrial park) and we offer tax breaks. Mostly though it's because of the workers we have here." At this point he pauses to tell us about the crucial role of the women *aparadora*s in shoe manufacturing. These are women who work on shoe uppers usually at home on their own quite-sophisticated machinery. The job requires some years of training and there is now a bottleneck because no more women are being trained. "We have no money to help train them. I try to get the firm-owners to do it, but they won't because they are afraid a trained woman will simply go elsewhere." The mayor is worried that this blockage will lead firms to go elsewhere. Later in the conversation we discuss conditions of work inside the workshops and factories. It transpires that the mayor's own wife works in one of the larger factories. Due to poor ventilation in the factory, she suffers from asthma and occasionally from chronic headaches. She also has sleep problems, resulting from both ailments and is losing muscular control in her wrists from her work. We ask the mayor if, as mayor, there is nothing he can do to help his wife. "It's part of her job," he says. "It's what comes with the job." But there are regulations covering things like ventilation, we respond. "Yes," he says, "But we need these factories here. It is they who give work to people."

What is being discussed here will come as no surprise to anybody who has worked in a regional economy, but we confine ourselves to two observations. The first is the extent to which the discourses are themselves part of a larger hegemonic field; one invoked in the regionalist literature, reproduced in policy-formulations and thence delivered for consumption at the local level. The second point relates to this. The hazardous currents of a present directed largely from well beyond the local fieldsite has the effect of fetishizing local agency. Strategies of the present are perpetually frustrated in the attempt to gain some control over the future. The hazards ahead make glancing in the rearview mirror distracting and selective: history, as the seedbed of local culture, becomes "history."

## The Locality Today, as a "Regional Economy"

Perhaps the most immediately striking feature of the Vega Baja is the heterogeneity of enterprises and of work practices.The region has responded to the huge volatility that it has faced chiefly because of its long-term reliance on external demand, by reconfiguring the way each enterprise and each worker's household is embedded in a sector of the economy. Once it was silk, then olives and wheat, then olives and wine, until we reach the 1950s when the region experienced a boom in the production and processing of hemp for the manufacture of sandals, shoes, ropes, and carpets.

By the 1960s, this mix of agricultural and industrial activities tilted toward the industrial sector, particularly shoe manufacturing. During the 1960s and early '70s large factories that relied on labor from the smaller towns and villages of the area were established in the towns of Elche and Crevillente. Many men and women migrated to these larger towns. Others went to work daily on buses provided by the factories. During peak production seasons, home-based piecework was a complementary device to increase production capacity in the more labor intensive parts of the process. Generally, foremen in the factory became intermediaries distributing outwork, using their kin and local networks to get the extra work done. Then, after Franco's death in 1975, a fairly rapid transformation occurred, as production was more thoroughly dispersed away from the unionized factories in Elche and Crevillente and into the surrounding smaller towns.

The present-day structure of industrial production in the area is comprised of large factories, small family firms, unregulated workshops, work-distributors, home-based workers, and industrial wage workers. Only factory workers tend to have some kind of legal contract. Small factories, workshops, work-distributors, and homeworkers rely heavily on family labor, kin, and neighborhood networks to access work and labor. Firms, workshops, and work-distributors try to diversify their clients and directly control market outlets when possible, shifting backward and forward and placing great stock in local knowledge. Homeworkers, lacking this flexibility, instead are highly dependent on, and loyal to, particular work-distributors. Industrial wage workers, on the other hand, find that both working conditions and the short life of firms lead them to move between different factories and workshops, and between different jobs locally, as well as within the region.

The picture that emerges is one of production processes that are structured locally in diverse forms and where people tend to shift between different labor relations that vary greatly in their stability. The main cleavage is set by the extent to which firms, workshops, or individuals are forced to depend on a single source of demand or are able to simultaneously supply different clients. This results in an emphasis on diversification on the part of petty and large entrepreneurial figures alike. For workers, the main difference arises between those who are free to be mobile and tap a wider labor market and those, like homeworkers, who are dependent on very limited sources out of necessity.

It is important to note that, except for the large factories that have flexible location practices and that are able to use information technologies to their benefit, the work-distributors, small-scale entrepreneurs, and workers are tightly bound to each other and frequently merge into or emerge from one another. There is, locally, a perceived and extremely differentiated network of shifting but necessary alliances. Moreover, the instrumental weight of personal and affective relations in the construction and maintenance of these hierarchical networks of production has its corollary in the stress produced on these affective relations, induced by the tension of differentiation within the realms of shared belonging: the family, the community, or fellow workers. Cleavages appear within work-distributor families, between the older and the younger generations, and between male and female members, who are forced to work in culturally appropriate ways, giving primacy to primordial loyalties and duties that affect their retributive claims. Cleavages appear between "good" and "ignorant" homeworkers, "uneducated" or "sloppy" ones, as well as between husbands who own a small firm and wives who work in it without being "workers." Cleavages arise between sisters in a workshop partnership on the grounds that one has the more useful commercial contacts while the other has the better know-how. Distributive and retributive problems, issues of equity, of individually as opposed to collectively grounded claims, pervade this thick network of forced solidarities, which is simultaneously a highly differentiated field of closely knit feelings of belonging.

What we are describing here are the less salubrious dimensions of the features highlighted by the "regionalist" literature as the *diferentia specifica* of a *regional* economy. Yet, as with an earlier kind of anthropological ethnography, this literature has been faulted for being mesmerized by local regional features, to the exclusion of the larger political economy (Lovering 1999) and, we would add, by the arena of political and economic policy. The larger picture includes the state, of course, but increasingly too, the European Union's regulations and public funds, so that both formal local institutions like municipalities and less formal ones like firms and other players must enter this discursive field or remain obscure and invisible. John Lovering describes such a field thus: "National, transnational, regional and local authorities, academics, consultants and journalists are devoting enormous efforts to convincing their audiences of the New Regionalist picture of the world..." (1999:379).

Municipal leaders in the Vega Baja see themselves as caught in competition with each other to attract firms. They compete by shaping a particular version of local public culture. Institutions tap into a new sense of locality that perforce is articulated with European Union-funding procedures. This means that they deenergize the dialogue that gives life to actual, ordinary, daily public culture and delegitimates variation in people's experiences. A public culture of homogeneity also has implications at a more practical social level. Local institutions of all kinds shrink from their responsibilities in respect to local citizen's protection, labor regulation, and welfare rights. Yet left without historical context it is hard to understand why specific regions have provided such fertile ground for this reconstitution of political-economic "reality." In the case of this area of Spain, we need to try to understand its emergence out of a public politics that was overtly corrupt and inherently nonconsultative, and a public culture that was long a vacuum abandoned in the privations of uncertainty and oppression during a time when "Food...eclipsed politics as the universal topic of conversation" (Richards 1998:143). Let us now look back through history, so as to bring us back to this present situation equipped with new analytic tools.

## History and Histories in a Region

It is striking as one works in this region that, while acutely sensitive to changing economic currents, public political discussion is of no interest to all but a few. Remarking on this to a friend sympathetic to the Partido Socialista Obrero Espanol (PSOE), Gavin was met by the response, "The people around here are not political." This casual remark requires enormous occlusions and selections, the result of which was that we, the field-workers, took many years to unearth the fact that during the Civil War (1936–1939) this town had been an anarchist and Socialist center. Most of the large *fincas* (estates) had been expropriated, and money had been printed for use in the area. Landlords and large tenants, faced with the unattractive alternative of working in the fields alongside their ex-employees or being drafted into the Republican army, made themselves scarce, many of them holing up in the staunchly Catholic town of Orihuela, some twenty-five kilometers away.

With the Nationalists advancing, Alicante became the last seaport from which Republicans could escape, and many from this area fled there. They were rounded up and, if not killed in transit, as many were, they were imprisoned in one of Franco's concentration camps, of which the most notorious was Albatera, just four kilometers from the town where we centered our field-work. Yet in the 1990s (and before) we had been told that people here were not "political," and throughout Gavin's years visiting this area he had spent many a Sunday picnic with families swimming in the spa waters of Albatera and eating *paellas*. The camp was never mentioned.

After the war, those landlords who did not choose to sell their property and the large tenants returned to the area. Among other things they found the church loaded with grain. The collective farms had been surprisingly efficient and a class of people quickly emerged who made their living as food and land intermediaries. Meanwhile the larger farms now had all the backing of political and military force to reestablish the relations of personal power that underwrote their operations. This strange mix of regulation and fixity articulated through personalistic power relations on the one hand and movement and maneuvre articulated through the black market on the other deserves close attention.

What emerges is a complex dialectic between the exercise of power as control over other people's conduct—stimulating certain kinds of *practices*, restricting other kinds of *practice*—and the imbrication of power within the *structured ways people feel*. The *instituted practice* of favoring one person or family over another and the *structured feeling* that it both induced and relied on became the essence of power itself. As such they become naturalized at

least for the actors involved (which was by no means all the people
in the area). They therefore cannot be unearthed *entirely* by reference to the conscious intentions of the actors. A large tenant
remarks, "By the laws of nature, to those who work for one as jornaleros, one gives *aniaga* land for when they don't have
work . . . these sharecroppers are those I seek out when I need day
labor." And we need to note particularly the opening phrase; we
need to try to understand the historical path of ordinary life that
makes it possible for such a phrase, "By the laws of nature. . . . " to
be spoken. There is ample evidence of the insecurity of life for ordinary workers in the Vega Baja, an insecurity that was both the
outcome of an unstable economy and unpredictable climate, and
the result of certain kinds of social relations that were levered
across (and made possible by) the pain of hunger in the night and
the perpetual call of disaster in the morning. And this was made
more extreme in the postwar years. This kind of uncertainty was
used as the current that sucked workers into the tether of labor
relations that used the fixing-in-place of people as the basis for
exploitation. We catch this sense especially strongly when we hear
the words of the laborer who remarked to Joan Frigolé who was
working in a region close by (the Vega Alta del Segura) "He who
simply ate, with food he was rich, because the other (the jornalero)
arrived at the point of not even eating" (Frigolé Reixach, n.d.).
This arrangement is referred to as the *aniaga* contract and is
implicitly contrasted to the contract by *jornal,* or "day-labor" contract—the *a-n* referring to *año* or "year." In such a contract, a
worker is given a minimal plot of land to be used for the basics of
household consumption. Optimally this may mean a tiny plot of
land that could be used for growing potatoes, a little wheat, and
possibly some beans, but often it may have been little more than a
space for tethering a goat or two and raising some chickens.
Though often glossed—by both writers and informants—as share-
cropped land, this is misleading. In return for the arrangement,
the worker and his family put themselves at the service of the *amo*
or "boss." This meant that the worker was always available for
day-labor work on the *amo's* land, and that he would openly
respect the *amo* as his *patrón* in public. Such a man was referred
to by the *amo* as an *hombre de confianza* (a man of trust). Trust
then, in this context, is intimately bound up with power.

Large farms would absorb as many as fifteen *aniaga* families,
but this meant neither that the farm thereby relied solely on their
labor, nor that they could expect the demands of labor on the *finca*

to provide them with a full year's work. Such farms relied heavily on day-labor recruited in the *plaza* (the main square in front of the church) each day, and *aniaga* tenants found themselves in the plaza many days seeking day-labor. Nonetheless, the degree of loyalty bound up with such an arrangement was pervasive throughout the family. Movement, both physical movement and movement thought of symbolically—for all members of the family—was controlled by the patron. We hope the symbolic dimensions of movement will become apparent as our discussion progresses. Clearly it refers to social movement both in terms of class ambitions and in terms of allegiances to other patrons and other worlds within the rural community such as schooling.[3] This gives ethnographic substance to James Clifford's comment that "Stasis and purity are ...asserted—creatively and violently—*against* historical forces of movement and contamination" (1997:7). The association of movement with contamination, especially political contamination, was fundamental and this was especially so because of the policy of "political cleansing" that became a crusade for Franco's Movimiento.[4] The language of religious purity was everywhere. Spain had to be expiated; it had to go through a cleansing, to be rid of impurities (cf. Christian 1996).

After the war, landlords and large tenants faced simultaneously a labor shortage and a floating population of day-laborers whose political sympathies were suspect. A partial solution was to gather the *aniaga* tenant and family into the personal orbit of the patron, restricting their exposure to contamination by controlling their geographic and mental "movement." Yet much of the Vega Baja, had been a stronghold of the Confederccíon Nacional del Trabajo (CNT) and the Union de General de Trabajadores (UGT). Very few agricultural laborers did not acquiesce; most were avid supporters. It was therefore by no means always clear that an *aniaga* tenant in the 1940s had been a staunch opponent of the Republic a decade earlier. Across such an equation—the labor-short large farmer and the insecure workers—the social relation was made real: the insecure tenant rewriting the history of his past, the labor-starved landlord finding in this collusion a useful form of inducement in the making of a reliable *hombre de confianza* (man of trust)—ironically a trust built upon denial.[5]

While many old workers who were once *aniaga* tenants recount stories of the rigidities and relative stability of the early Franco years, the untied *jornaleros*, if asked to talk about the period, avoid references to hierarchies of power and instead recount episodes of "maneuver" in the black market, the *estraperlo*. These *jornaleros* did not have the kind of vertical networks that would facilitate their being tied to a patron. Or they were unwilling or perhaps unable to bury the past so easily. While there were many workers who managed to find *aniaga* relationships through the 1940s and '50s, there were many more who relied entirely on mobility between jobs and employers for their livelihood.

One such was Francisco Navarro who was in a work camp after the war and then was tried and sentenced to twelve years imprisonment. He came out with the first pardon (*indulto*) in 1945. In yet another restriction on movement, released prisoners were forbidden from returning to their own towns. Yet in fact they frequently did, thereby creating a shadow world of control on which the regime relied. This meant that not only was Fransisco unable to find work because of his past, as a political criminal he was also unable to acquire the identity card that was a prerequisite for even minimal supplies of foodstuffs. As a result he and his brother were forced into the black market. The activities for *jornaleros* such as these during the period of *estraperlo* (the 1940s and '50s) highlight the complex working out of fixing people in place and their need for movement to survive.

Mobility, strongly discouraged by the local elite, was officially restricted until 1948. Travel documents were not available for those who had supported the Republic. Ironically, it was precisely the "reds," who could not get work locally because of their political position during the Republic and the war, who were forced to seek work opportunities by moving—in the *estraperlo*, or by going to other localities where they were not known, or by roaming through the countryside teaching. The control of movement was very precisely the way in which power was expressed and this had a particular effect on how the daily world was experienced. For inevitably, people needed to move and when they did, without holding permits, the risk they incurred acted as a selectively personal form of repression. Generally speaking, everyone, including the municipal authorities, knew what was happening but this meant that power could be exercised selectively.

This situation produced an alternative kind of social regulation, one that found fertile ground in the already well-developed personalized authority structures of the region. The careful dealings with neighbors that might ordinarily have resulted from the generalized poverty of basic resources in a devastated rural economy took on a special edge as official control of the production and marketing of goods meant that neighbors were also potential spies who could turn you or your family in to the authorities for activities that were essential for survival. Thus by using hunger and the regulation of food (the sole objective and thought in everyone's mind, Frigolé 1997) as a selective repressive instrument the form of regulation transformed the social relations of provisioning by forcing the production of extremely personalized networks of distribution.

In fact these people's activities in the black-market were only an extreme version of the way in which *jornaleros* sought out a living. Denied reliable access to either small plots of land or even to a minimal amount of secure employment for the *aniaga* worker, the household strategy was to maximize the opportunity of each adult member *as an individual worker* to find work. Throughout the fifties and into the sixties, as the black market was replaced by informal relations in hemp, shoe, and carpet production, *jornaleros* put together their livelihoods by moving from one opportunity to another, accumulating skills as they went. The strategies and adaptations were individual and familistic, one person's life experience and accumulated knowledge rarely being like another's. The networks of workmates through which jobs were secured produced a horizontal set of linkages. The result of this endlessly readjusting pluriactivity was that the organic unity of the household was put under huge pressure, placing a strong management role on the wife and mother.

At the risk of simplifying an extremely complicated world of labor, we suggest that the strategizing entrepreneurial workers of today, as well as the intricacies of exploitation leveraged through affectual relationships (both celebrated features of this regional economy) do not arise, as the marketers of public culture would have it,[6] out of one dominant labor experience but out of a complex of experiences that can be seen along a continuum that reflects the line between fixity in place and movement across sites. We have represented this continuum by contrasting the tied *aniaga* worker with the insecure *jornalero* though we hope it is clear that a much broader range of heterogeneity could be presented.

All class relationships are characterized by the contradictory bonding of dependency and distinction (between owner and worker) (G. Smith 1979). In these two cases we see the former being emphasized with crucial effects on the *aniaga* household and the latter being emphasized with quite different implications for the *jornalero* household. In the one case we have a worker whose movement was constrained and whose ties to hierarchical linkages provided conditions that extended exploitation to relations *within* the patriarchal household. Sons were forbidden to migrate, daughters limited in the extent to which they could take in homework, or directed to do so through contacts made only through the *amo* (the boss). This is not to say that insecurity was not present in the *aniaga* household—the entire principle of the exploitative relationship relied on the savage jackal always waiting in a darkened corner—but here it was tied to the life cycle: of boss or tenant. Changes in ownership, or the death of an *aniaga* household head, often formed the cataclysmal moments in informants' life stories.

In the *jornalero* household insecurity and uncertainty were felt much more perpetually and on a daily basis. Attempts to resolve the problem meant maximizing *individual* movement, and seeking out short-term opportunity. In such stretched households, wives and mothers tended to take on much of the resulting tension. Unlike the *aniaga* family, here, continually threatened by the centrifugal pressures of pluriactivity, the *jornalero* household becomes a site of *distinction*. It becomes a line of defense, vis à vis the exploitative relations and personalistic power that exemplify more public relationships necessary for making a living—retaining good relationships with a number of large farmers and entrepreneurs, showing deference to the mayor, cultivating the good graces of the local *guardia*, and so forth.

Let us turn for a moment to the issue of culture. A *commonly shared* culture of "those I can trust," "those who have claims on me" or "those who respect me" could only be imagined, then, at the most superficial of levels. *Aniaga* tenants and untied day-laborers by no means exhaust the kinds of relationships that occur in the Vega Baja, of course, but with just these two in mind, it is not hard to see that the perceptions of intimate culture are likely to vary from one social subject to another. The ingredients are the same—the regulation of work, insecurity, and the social value of the person—but how the ingredients are combined varies. As Eric Hobsbawm has remarked for nineteenth-century industrial Britain, the combination of military-like discipline, the purposeful generating of uncertainty, and the wage incentive, in the end did not solve the problem of managing the industrial workforce. The respect workers attached to a job well done became the crucial element in the equation, though "respectability" pulled people toward different reference groups:

> No term is harder to analyse than 'respectability' in the mid-nineteenth-century working class, for it expressed

simultaneously the penetration of middle-class values and standards, and also the attitudes without which working-class self-respect would have been difficult to achieve.... [I]n the third quarter of the nineteenth century the line between personal and collective improvement, between imitating the middle class and, as it were, defeating it with its own weapons, was often impossible to draw. (1977:263–264, italics added)

*Self*-respect was powerfully tied up with proper work but the *sources* of respect varied and affected different kinds of working people in different ways (cf. also Martínez Alier 1968).

As we have seen, these components play a crucial part in the social relations of the Vega Baja, though the way in which they work within and against one another takes on a different set of contours to those suggested by Hobsbawm for nineteenth-century England. Given what we know of the way in which authority was exercised right up to (if not beyond) the *caudillo*'s death in 1975—personalistically, selectively, and with quite open demonstrations that political office was to be used for personal benefit—we should not be surprised that for most ordinary people there was a sharp contrast between respectability and activity in the sphere of public politics. As a result the arena of public politics was not occupied by the kind of working people we have been talking about. This can be explained in part by the fact that the two figures we have introduced here each carries in herself just one of the two features Hobsbawm found to be a source of conflict in the nineteenth-century skilled worker. The fact that to be a boss's *hombre de confianza* was a sign of respect for a worker tied closely to a *patrón* is enough to make clear whence the source of respect came for *aniaga* workers, even though it came too with a certain need to show humility—to "show respect" to those in authority.

By contrast, the continual reference we heard from older untied *jornaleros* to *self*-respect is striking. Yet this was a very hard figure to carry into the public arena. Moreover, as we have seen, the organic nature of the *aniaga* household contrasted sharply with the constant centrifugal pressures felt within the *jornalero* household. As a result, self-respect came to be associated powerfully with the demonstration of responsibility (for adult men and women, often authoritarian responsibility) toward household members and close kin. Insofar as the ultimate responsibility was to put bread on the table, this meant the ineluctable conjoining of self-respect with good work (cf. Frigolé Reixad, 1991).

This in turn had an effect on public politics when it once again saw the light of day after 1978, limiting thereby the degree to which it could become the arena for the "production of culture" (cf. G. Smith 1991). For the *aniaga* worker the continuities of the past made it easy to see "representative democracy" as simply another form through which one's patron (or his designate) represented one in the public arena. But for those *jornaleros* with a strong and locally known personal or family connection to the Republican past, the issue was much more complicated. While there was a strong personally felt and locally endorsed sense that it was now the responsibility of these people not just to speak out but to take office and enact legislation consistent with *how* they had spoken out, the local feeling that public politics was synonymous with corruption remained. This in itself made entry into the public arena fraught with dangers with regard to respect. But this was not all. The national discourse throughout the 1980s and up to the present was, and is framed in terms of, national reconciliation that means the silencing of the alternative kind of society symbolized by the Republic, especially since it was strongly felt by the rank-and-file Left: Socialist, Anarchist and Communist. In short, the utopian Left were explicitly sanctioned for "speaking out" in any other language but the organic corporatism of post-Moncloa Accord Spain.

The combination of these factors made it impossible for self-respect to cross the threshold of the working person's doorstep. There remains in the nationalist Spain of the political, social, and economic elite a deep-felt shame regarding the Left as manifest in the real actions of ordinary people first in the Republic and then in their resistance to Franco's coup d'etat during the Civil War. The need for this to be silenced now as it was once "cleansed" before remains. On the other hand there is a powerful sense of self-respect among a certain fraction of working-class people in the region that is associated with the dignity of work and responsibility to one's peers. Effectively this means that the everyday world of work, of one's personal relations, and of local concerns, stands in sharp contrast to that of *lo político*.

Two factors combine here. First the conditions for entry into the arena of public political debate are framed within the discourse of national reconciliation that effectively compromises hitherto repressed ideals of privately nurtured pasts. Second, this discursive framing within notions of reconciliation, of suppressing "conflict" for the greater good, conforms not only with the current politics of neocorporatism, but evokes an older corporatism, which was violently antagonistic toward the politics of the Republic Left. The result is a vacuum, or a mime show, which makes possible a manufactured kind of political "culture."

## Conclusion

After this journey among histories, can we remain content with an understanding of the Vega Baja as a regional economy made up of strategizing petty capitalists and entrepreneurial workers sharing a common local culture? It is tempting of course to answer this question by resort to local informants, celebrating a supposedly shared sense of a depoliticized everyday, which is both experience-near and local. As we have just seen, these are indeed precisely the tropes used by the ordinary people we spent most of our time with in Spain. Yet, at the outset we proposed that a much more useful kind of problematic would be to try to discover the way in which the interconnected processes that have the reproduction of capitalist relations of exploitation in a given epoch as their goal relate dialectically to a perception of the world in terms of place-related everyday life. Insofar as this directs attention *away from* the most celebrated of actors in the contemporary world (namely entrepreneurs and capitalists large and small) and away from the present into a complex set of histories, it is unlikely to attract the policy-driven research that dominates studies of the new regionalism. Yet the conjoining of our opening vignettes—in which local political figures endeavor to embrace current policy discourse—with the histories of working people, obliges us to set the imagery of local informants into a more thorough historical realism. To begin with, this history shows a huge amount of heterogeneity. And heterogeneity means relationships *between*, practices *across*, and dialogues *among*; in short not just complexity but highly dynamic and unfinished process: conflict, agreement, repression, elimination, triumph, and so on. This is not the image we get when we read the earlier part of the quote we have already given from Becattini.

> The most important trait of the local community is its relatively homogeneous system of values and views, which is an expression of the ethic of work and activity, of the family, of reciprocity, and of change.... Parallel to this system of values, a system of institutions and rules must

have developed in such a way as to spread those values throughout the district, to support and transmit them through generations. (1992:38)

As we have seen, historically institutionalized practices have been developed in this region that were highly effective in spreading rules and values, but not evenly to all people. Yet we see here that, far from this kind of mobility being generalized throughout the region, *it was highly selective.* It was in fact the flip side to another process that acted to retain and demobilize labor for the purposes of the extraction of absolute surplus value. To a great extent the way in which this local economy used restrictions on mobility to ensure its continued reproduction was successful. At least it was successful in producing cheap agricultural goods with minimal investments in machinery and technology and did so through the division of the labor force between floating and restricted pools of labor. This was done, moreover, through the intentional manipulation of insecurity and uncertainty.

So there *is* present in the region the well-known flexible and entrepreneurial worker. There is present too the equally important internally exploiting household unit with a considerable degree of organic unity. Also present is the fixed dependent worker, now frequently a woman homeworker. Yet we also need to note that this is not a uniform pattern, that is, it is not evidence of "a uniform system of values"; indeed it was made possible precisely because it was not, nor could it be, uniformly experienced.

Much is made in the literature of the role of networks and of "affective" ties that can act as highly positive *social capital,* first for those who have it and then for the development of the region as a whole. We would endorse the stress on networks, though the fact that face-to-face communities can be understood in terms of networks surely can't be anything new to anthropologists. Yet networks here were of a number of different types. *Jornaleros'* more horizontal networks were learning institutions because they were able to penetrate inside larger enterprises through colleague-workers' knowledge, and so use contacts and information for strategizing in the pursuit of always insecure and short-run work. *Aniaga* workers' networks however, were explicitly *not* learning institutions. Moreover, as the *jornalero* horizontal networks inserted themselves into factories, so did the hierarchical *aniaga* networks devastatingly penetrate households—as many work-distributor networks do today, to produce some of the most draconian conditions of domestic exploitation—then as now.

Different though these networks are, we need to note that they both rely on the constitution of bounded space. *Jornalero* networks are household-centric reciprocal chains and, as such, they call forth their own shaping of space while *aniaga* ties explicitly secure local place while endangering and estranging the periphery.

We have noted that in the contemporary period it is not unusual to find that current practices and relationships produce cleavages—between women friends, within households, and so on. The maintenance of ties that will resist such crises requires investments—of time, of reputation, and of concern—and the value of such currency derives inherently from the past—not just the remembered or called-up past, but a much deeper and institutionalized past. We see this clearly in the differing gold standards of *respectability* as seen from the perspective of the tied worker or of the floating *jornalero*.

Finally we need to turn to the very difficult question of social regulation in the context of a regional economy. In only rare cases do the institutions of a region have the kind of formal powers that state institutions have. Indeed this is a feature celebrated in reference to the original successful region: the Third Italy (see e.g., Bagnasco's 1977 notion of the "social market"). And the idea that regulation should be taken away from the state and reside somewhere else is of course quite consistent with neoliberal ideology. Addressing this issue, writers working on regional economies have tended to emphasize the way in which present-day work habits in a region, the use of trust (*confianza*) among actors, and the presence of social capital under the rubric of local "culture" serve as a way of addressing this issue. This approach seems to obscure more than it enlightens. In fact it is only through historical examination that we are able to see how *regionally specific* forms of local regulation really operate. It is hard to imagine, for example, today's regional economy without the prior experience of the black market and the highly differentiated way in which people had access to it. It is hard too, to imagine the area without the precedent of personalistic rule and selective terror. These are all part of the creation of this regional social world; to select out "culture" as the element that makes them locally distinctive is to understand the process of culture far too simplistically.

By going back over historical ground we have sought to discover the very particular character of production-extraction-circulation compacts in the region. As their character emerged, we sought to show how the interweaving of control over people's conduct, certain kinds of daily practices, and the "the structured ways people feel" (Williams 1961, 1977) were less isolable variables having causal properties, than the intermeshing of a social world which, if not quite taken for granted, can nonetheless be referred to without added comment as "the laws of nature." It is misleading to configure such a social world in terms of the conscious intentions of actors (the interest orientation of the economistic social sciences), because what we are referring to works in a perpetual, verbally elusive, engagement with the present that becomes reified in justifications and accounting practices produced retrospectively (either by actors or by analysts).

We must therefore interrogate with a much stronger sense of critique the coincidence of policy-driven researchers' models, and the version of "local culture" marketed by the local entrepreneurs and political figures that appear to be such researchers' sole informants. Of course these models and the informant "data" that authorizes them result in the confining of participation to entrepreneurial actors and to an intentional marginalizing of the multitude from the political process. Of course they mean the *management* of the social body over and above its expressiveness, and of course this leads to the invocation of a particular meaning of the idea of culture, one that prioritizes the homogeneity of local culture over the variety of voices, and fixes its specificity in a kind of reified super organic, rather than letting it loose among the turmoil of conflictual political praxis.

Don Mitchell's reflections on the misuses of the idea of culture are especially relevant here:

> [C]ulture [can be] a concept deployed to stop flux in its tracks, creating stability and "ways of life" where before there had been change and contest. Th[is] idea of culture demand[s] a mapping of boundaries and edges, the specification of a morphology: culture ha[s] to become a bounded object that ultimately differentiate[s] the world. (1995:107).

The homogeneity of this manufactured trope of "local culture"—one that takes on a special public form because of the need for it to be marketed abroad (not quite the birch-bark bags and wooden shields of Papua-New Guinea, but requiring very much the same kind of reification)—needs to be understood in terms of its continuities with older production-extraction-circulation compacts for controling labor. Taken entirely out of the historical context of the Vega Baja, especially the years from 1939 to 1975, does such an homogenized idea of a "regional economy" really tell us enough? This period began, after all, with "political cleansing" involving the unrecorded killing of as many as two hundred thousand people in Spain and ended with the Caudillo reassuring his citizens by use of the imagery of a confident admiral steering a secure ship into the storm: "All is tied down and well tied down" (Richards 1998:148).

One person or another, one household or another, one small business or another in the Vega Baja have been persistently adaptable to climactic changes, to economic cycles, and to political zigzags—or at least those who have survived have. Indeed one could do studies of successful and blocked entrepreneurial activity and local organizational practices here that would fill Jorge Luis Borges's famous library of infinite books. But the price that is paid would never, we think, be recorded. It is to be noted that we did not begin this paragraph by saying "The people of the Vega Baja have been persistently adaptable...." Such a statement would allow us to imagine a people who adapted collectively for their best advantage; that they have never succeeded in doing. We need to recognize this not as a triumph of the new industrial order, but as a tragedy written, directed, and produced by the socially, economically, and politically powerful over a long period of history.

## Notes

1. This is a shorter version of a more extended chapter prepared for journal submission.

2. We use the term *regionalist studies* throughout this chapter to refer to work pre-eminently in economic sociology, social geography, and institutional economics. Presented in terms of a paradigmatic shift from an older tradition and given a veneer of left progressivism, the vast majority of this work relies heavily on neoclassical (not to say neoliberal) epistemology. Partly for this reason, with the exception of occasional references to Putnam, it is surprisingly compartmentalized from the work on regions being undertaken by, for example, the ECPR Standing Group on Regionalism, associated with Michael Keating and with a multidisciplinary group based mostly in Europe. Our reference therefore to "regionalist studies" could be misleading; it does not include this latter body of literature. For comprehensive discussions of the rapidly unfolding regionalist studies—now referred to as *new* regionalist studies (see Sabel 1989; Amin and Robins 1992; MacLeod 2001; Whitford 2001).

3. Schooling was formally in the hands of the state or more specifically the Movimiento, but also was the prerogative of the priest. Many

*jornaleros* however continued to receive their basic education from the roving teachers who relied entirely on hospitality for survival. Aware of these, a number of landlords ran their own schools once or twice a week in the evenings.

4. We retain this term, still used to refer to Franco's political movement and the apparatus that went with it, insidiously aligned with institutions of the state.

5. We do not mean to suggest here that there were no enthusiastic supporters of the old guard or of the Falange in the region during the Republic and during the war. There most certainly were, as we discuss at some length in our chapter. Our point however, is that there were many in the *aniaga* relationship who, for various reasons, had to be extremely discrete about their past and that this active silence became embedded in the personalistic *aniaga* relationships of control.

6. The historical evidence here is for Spain, and we are at pains to stress the importance of the *specificity* of histories. Nonetheless this evidence alone should lead us to query the kind of potted history that is produced to explain other regional cultures, based on common work experiences and shared cultural dispositions.

# 4

# Flexibility for Whom?: Small-Scale Garment Manufacturing in Rural Mexico

*Frances Abrahamer Rothstein*

This chapter, based on twenty-five years of anthropological fieldwork in San Cosme Mazatecochco, a rural community in central Mexico, describes the recent emergence of "flexible production" in San Cosme and analyzes how and for whom flexible production is flexible. After a discussion of the broader national and international context of garment production, the first part of the chapter focuses on the nature of flexible production in San Cosme. The second part of the chapter describes who in the community has been able to set up garment workshops; who works in the workshops; who controls workshop production; and why some workshops, owners, and/or merchants have been more successful. The concluding section relates local success and flexibility to regional, national, and international policies and suggests that flexible production has varied consequences at different levels of production. What is flexibility at the global level for large companies may be constraint at the local level for communities, workshops, or individuals. Furthermore, flexibility is by definition unstable; consequently what is flexible in one phase may be restriction at another stage. Finally, the analysis of San Cosme suggests that flexibility is just one aspect of a new relationship between the residents of this community and global capitalism. In this new relationship, flexibility and control at the local level are largely illusions that hide a reality of greater control by fewer people at the global level.

## Flexible Production

The concept of flexibility has been used increasingly to discuss accumulation (Harvey 1989), labor, and technology (Carlsson 1996; Vangstrup 1997) production (Taplin 1996), and specialization (Piore and Sabel 1984). Although there are important differences, most analysts focus on the idea that commitment to products and/or workers is flexible. As Arthur Stinchcombe suggests, the critical criteria is "short production runs of many different products...produced nearly as cheaply as long runs of standardized goods"[1] (1987:186).

The cheapness of flexible production has led many observers to suggest that flexible production is necessarily associated with "sweating," and exploited labor (see, e.g., N. Green 1997; Simmons and Kalantaridis 1994, 1996). Michael Piore and Charles Sabel, who have one of the most optimistic views of flexible specialization, argue that sweating is not inherent in flexible specialization. For them, competition, and thus exploitation, can be controlled by the "creation, through politics, of an industrial community that restricts the forms of competition to those favoring innovation" (1984:17). This optimistic view is not shared by all; others, especially those who see flexible production or specialization as growing with globalization and inequality are less sanguine (see, e.g., Taplin 1996).

Some of the disagreement comes from the fact that, as Nancy Green[2] points out, flexibility can exist at two levels: "the global level of an economic sector and the firm level of work organization" (1997:6). Most analyses of flexibility, she suggests, have stressed the global rather than the firm level. But, she argues, the two levels cannot be separated and we must ask, flexibility for whom? In this chapter I suggest that flexible production has enormous advantages for retailers, manufacturers, and retailer/manufacturers who face intense competition for consumers. For workers, owners, and worker-owners of the small flexible firms, however, the possibilities for gain are more illusory than real.

At the global level, the ceaseless change that characterizes the contemporary flexible production of garments is an important part of what Gereffi calls "buyer-driven" commodity chains in which large retailers, designers, and trading companies drive decentralized production networks (1994). Especially in the fashion-driven apparel industry, buyer-driven commodity chains are increasingly specifying what is produced, when, and at what price. Along with modern means of transportation and communication and the low[3] skill and capital requirements of garment production, the expanded power of buyers (whether retailers or manufacturers or, as is increasingly the case, retailer/manufacturers) constantly shifts garment production to new, more remote areas.[4] Furthermore, in the effort to constantly have new products, production has become more "flexible" (Gereffi and Hemple 1996). Rather than maintaining large inventories, retailers or manufacturers increasingly contract out apparel production. That is, they hire contractors as they need them and the contractors arrange for production of short runs. This, as Gary Gereffi (1994) among others notes, allows buyers to respond more rapidly to changing market patterns.

Until recently, such decentralized production chains or "manufacturers without factories" (F. Rothstein cited by C. Green 1998:10) were common in East Asian NICS but absent in Latin America (Gereffi and Hempel 1996). More recently, changes in trade policy, especially GATT and then NAFTA, have led to what a *Forbes Magazine* article describes as a massive shift by US clothing manufacturers from China (which had been the major exporter to the United States) to Mexico (Palmeri and Aguayo 1997). One half of apparel sold in the United States is imported; in 1980, 83% of these imports came from Asia, now it is only 41%. Meanwhile, Mexico's apparel exports to the United States have trebled since NAFTA (Palmeri and Aguayo 1997). Some of these imports are long production runs, such as underwear or outer garments, but a significant growth in small-scale garment manufacturing in Mexico (Rivero Rios and Suarez Aguilar 1994) and in the informal economy suggests that at least some of it is post-Fordist flexible production.[5] Although there has been a great deal of research on the globalization of manufacturing, most discussions of global production have focused on Fordist mass production, that is, the global assembly line.[6] These studies have shown how the movement of capital on an unprecedented scale has created a new international division of labor and with it enormous political, economic, social, and cultural changes. Another important body of literature has looked at small-scale flexible production and globalization especially in relation to the movement of people.[7]

## The Growth of Flexible Small-Scale Garment Production in San Cosme

San Cosme Mazatecocho is a community of about eight thousand people in the state of Tlaxcala in central Mexico. Until the 1940s it was a relatively homogeneous peasant community. Then, as a result of the national textile boom during the Second World War and the lack of dynamism in peasant agriculture, during the 1940s men from San Cosme began working in textile factories in Mexico City, about sixty miles away, or in Puebla, ten miles away. In the 1980s, as Mexico's import substitution industrialization was replaced by an export-oriented industrialization, the Mexican textile industry declined and many of San Cosme's *obreros* (workers) lost their jobs. The economic crisis of the early 1980s and the austerity, restructuring, and trade liberalization policies that followed meant that even those who kept their jobs faced declining wages, an increased cost of living, and fear that they would lose their jobs. One of the consequences has been the emergence of small-scale garment manufacturing within the community.

Beginning in 1989, hundreds of *talleres* or "workshops" that manufacture clothing of various sorts were started, usually by former factory workers or by workers who anticipated that their factories might close. The workshops range from a household with two machines where cut pieces that are delivered to them are sewn by family members, to a household with thirty workers and twenty-two machines that engages in every stage of production from making the fabric to selling the finished products either wholesale to middlemen or retail directly to consumers at weekly markets. Most of the *talleres* in San Cosme are small, having fewer than five workers but there are also several larger workshops with fifteen or more workers. Along with the growth of garment production, there has also been a surge in related retail activity. A weekly market consisting mostly of garments was established in the mid-1990s; a number of stores specializing in garments, fabric, and sewing supplies have opened up; and many people work as "brokers"[8] or contractors who arrange for production for others in the garment trade. The explosion of the garment trade in the community is apparent in the fact that by 1994, almost one out of every four households had members who were involved in small-scale clothing manufacturing as owners and/or workers.[9] Another 19 percent of the households had one or more merchants, many of whom were selling items produced in small manufacturing workshops.

The first workshops, which I refer to as "independent" workshops, produced mainly for regional markets. The owners of these workshops designed, cut, sewed, and marketed their products, primarily girls' dresses and women's skirts, themselves. In time, these same producers began selling to large Mexican retailers, many of whom now come to San Cosme to buy clothing. Increasingly, more San Cosmeras/os got involved in what they call *maquila*. In *maquila* workshops, workers sew precut pieces, especially collarless polo shirts and sweatpants that are brought to them by local or outside brokers. Today, the two types of workshops, *maquila* and independent, coexist, sometimes within the same household.[10]

Although in San Cosme garment production is part of the informal economy, some of the garments go to the formal sector (usually retailers) and some provide low-cost consumer items through the informal sector, usually street markets. As of 2001, most of San Cosme's production was for the Mexican market—either the formal or informal sector. More of the workshops were *maquila* shops and some production was for export to elsewhere in Latin America. Whether their production is for regional, national, or international markets, all producers in San Cosme are affected by global prices for materials, machines, and competition.

One of the important characteristics of workshop production in San Cosme, whether it is geared ultimately for the formal or informal market, and whether it is for local, regional, national, or international consumption, is constant change. Changes are made in response to varying availability and prices of supplies and demand. Not only are styles and fabrics changed frequently, but the same workshop can produce girls' dresses, women's skirts, or adult or children's polo shirts or pants. Change also characterizes the amount produced and for which market. Workshops may employ thirty people ten hours a day, seven days a week when they are busy, for example, before Christmas, and produce for large retailers, or they may only employ a few people a few hours a day when they are producing for a local street market. A woman who does *maquila* may do a hundred pieces herself in a week or, if pushed to get it done quickly, may rely on others as well. In one case, a woman had her son, her husband, a teenager who lived with the family and did domestic work, and the visiting anthropologist all assisting her when she needed to have a hundred pieces completed in a few days.

## Innovation and/or Sweating?

As Piore and Sabel point out: "Flexible specialization is a strategy of permanent innovation: accommodation to ceaseless change, rather than an effort to control it" (1984:17). Workers and owners in San Cosme have accommodated to changing market demands by producing different garments, different styles, for different markets, and at different rates. But people have had varying experiences and levels of success and, contrary to Piore and Sabel's suggestion that "sweating" is a feature of flexible specialists who fail to innovate (1984:263), innovation and sweating go hand in hand.

Although there is some variation among the workshops in steadiness of work and pay, workers in all of the workshops not only earn little, but they do not get benefits and their workplaces are not regulated by the state. Pay, even for experienced workers, is low. In 1997, one woman, for example, who had almost four years of experience working for the same workshop, was earning twenty-five pesos a day for laboring from 7:00 A.M. to 4:00 P.M., with half an hour off for lunch, six days a week.[11] She changed jobs to get higher pay by working at a piece rate. At 70 centavos a piece, making 50–60 pieces in an 8-hour day, she boosted her pay significantly to 35–42 pesos a day. Although her move meant a significant increase, it was still much less than the 2.5 times the minimum wage or 66 pesos a day required at the time for the basic food basket (Munoz and Calderon 1997).

Owners not only usually need to rely on the low-paid or unpaid labor of others but also on long hours of their own labor.[12] Since many owners also sell their own product at markets, when they are not sewing and/or managing their workshops or shopping for fabric and other supplies, they are doing business at the market. N. Green has noted the flexibility of space that characterizes homework and contracting in what have been called "kitchen and bedroom shops" (1997:231). While the location of one's work at home may enable some to generate income when they otherwise might not, for example, by combining child care and income generation, having a workshop in one's home also usually means that one's house is taken over by machines, threads, finished and unfinished garments, and workers. One woman had built a new house and furnished it with a living room set and a dining room set when she worked as a clothing vender. Then she set up her own workshop. Although the machines were in a room off the living room, in the living room her red velvet couch was covered with garments, stacks of clothes were all over, and workers streamed through the whole house six and sometimes seven days a week from morning to night. The owners' financial rewards are invariably greater than those of workers but much of their money goes back into their business and despite some relative lavishness in the houses of the most successful and larger owners, most of the owners are not doing very well. By the time the smaller owners pay for their own equipment (machines, thread, and scissors) and electricity, they are usually only just getting by.

Owners and workers also sweat due to the insecurity and unpredictability they face. By 1997 one of the largest workshops had closed because of financial problems. Several owners expressed concerns about competition from Asian imports and/or from other Mexican producers. Because of the precariousness of the market at least one workshop had switched from self-production to subcontracting. Many workshop owners, like most people in San Cosme, have household members involved in multiple economic activities. For example, one spouse may continue in her formal sector employment and also be involved in workshop activity, in the workshop, or selling workshop production, on weekends and in the evenings. Other households supplement income from garment production and/or trade by having a store, animals, and/or other income-generating activities. Most of the workshop owners and workers also raise some corn at least for their families and sometimes also for sale.

Workers, like owners, also deal with the volatility of the market by relying on multiple income strategies, by changing jobs, as in the previous case, or by trying to work for workshops that offer more consistent employment. But all the workshops let some people go during the slow periods. The woman just mentioned, for example, said she had worked only two days a week for the four months from April to August in her first job. She was hoping that her current employment would be steadier.

In sum, ceaseless change or innovation and sweating or exploitation characterize the lives of both workers and owners. Owners exploit themselves as well as paid and unpaid labor. Even workers often rely on the unpaid labor of others so that they can work for pay, as in the previous example where a woman who was doing piecework relied on the sewing help of the teenager who was working for her as a domestic laborer. In addition to hard work and long hours for themselves and those around them, workers and owners also share uncertainty and insecurity.

Although workers and owners have much in common, however (and some workers do become owners), owners generally have greater access to labor, capital, and skills that enables them to establish their workshops and to cushion themselves from some of the vagaries of the market This also means that those who are buying their products (usually retailers or poorly paid segments of the Mexican public whose consumption is being subsidized by flexible producers who make available cheap consumer items) are often benefiting from the hidden labor, skills, and investment of owners and their families as well as from the labor of paid workers.

## Access to Family and Skilled Labor

While everyone in San Cosme has access to relatively cheap labor, be it their own, other family members', and neighbors' (including neighbors in other communities), cheap labor is necessary but not sufficient for successful small-scale garment manufacturing. N. Green (1997) notes that flexible production allows those who might otherwise not work for pay to do so. Many more people in San Cosme, especially women and youths, have been pulled into paid work through workshops. In 1980 only 15% of the women were economically active. By 1994 this number had risen to 47%. Much of this change was due to the increase in workshop employment. The availability of women's and also youth labor is the basis for the low cost of labor in San Cosme. But flexible production does not only give paid work to those who otherwise have few alternatives; it also relies heavily on unpaid labor. Garment production in San Cosme is possible (i.e., even minimally profitable) in part because paid workers can be paid little and also because daughters-in-laws, daughters, wives, and sometimes male family members, can be put to work, often for long hours, without any wages.

Economists have long noted the comparative advantage that developing countries have in low-labor costs. The comparative advantage of family labor goes beyond low labor costs.[13] As Scott Lash and John Urry point out *"economies de famille,"* which they suggest characterize the families of many traditional immigrants, are a necessary part of entrepreneurial success (1987:179). A minimum requirement in San Cosme garment production seems to be a male and female, usually husband and wife, but son and mother or brother and sister pairs also occur. One partner, usually the male, handles the external contacts and the other, usually the female, handles the internal management. Individuals who are not part of such a pair seem unable to establish a workshop. One woman, for example, did not start her shop until she was back together with a husband from whom she had been separated for a number of years. In another case, a son tried to get his mother to agree to run a workshop. Although he had purchased machines and the mother sometimes did *maquila* for others, she did not want to supervise a workshop and successfully resisted. Individuals can work in the workshop of someone else or as brokers who bring work to others but no workshops in San Cosme consist only of a single owner and paid workers.

Children, often unpaid, play an important role in workshops. Many young women began sewing in a workshop when they were thirteen or fourteen years old. Younger children often pick off threads, iron, or put clothes on hangers. Children, if they do not work in a workshop, are often expected to fill in for other family members who are working in workshops by cooking, dispatching in a family store, and/or doing other domestic or productive work.[14] Even if children continue in school, the pressure to work in the *taller* or to perform household or agricultural labor may interfere with school performance.

Independent workshops need not only family labor but also skilled labor. Making the patterns (often by buying and taking apart a finished garment) is one of the specialized skills that not all families have. While they can now go into *maquila* production without such expertise, *maquila* workshops have so far generally been a less profitable alternative. Owners of workshops, either independent or *maquila*, also have slightly more education than others in the community.

Several of the most successful workshops began with very little capital (just enough to buy two machines—one "*over*" and one "*recta*"). More recently, used machines have become available. But even with used machines, a family needs to have some capital or to be in a financial position to borrow it.[15] Borrowing entails high interest or quick repayment. Independent workshops also require money to invest in fabric, and marketing the finished products at a regional market requires paying initial and weekly fees for the market stall. Most of the independent workshop owners have also invested in a car or truck to transport their products. Recently, one of the more successful workshop owners invested in a machine to make fabric.

*Maquila* workshops cost less to start and run. They are totally dependent, however, on middlemen bringing them the cut pieces and buying their finished products. Several people involved in *maquila* complained that they were unable to produce because no middlemen had brought them work. Or, as in the previous case, they may be brought too much work or pieces that are cut badly. Although all garment producers are vulnerable to market conditions, *maquila* producers are especially vulnerable to forces out of their control.[16] Those who open *talleres*, especially independent workshops, do tend to have some slight advantages in access to capital, labor and skill; however, no one is San Cosme is very well-off.[17]

## An Illusion of Mobility

David Harvey and others suggest that globalized production, flexible employment, and global markets obscure labor processes and relations. As just indicated, flexible production hides much of the labor, skill, and investment that go into small-scale manufacturing. Another consequence of this obfuscation of labor relations in San Cosme is that increasingly San Cosmeras/os are "disguised proletarians." Like petty commodity producers elsewhere, their class position places many of those involved in workshops in a peculiar place where they are capitalists and workers at the same time (Bernstein 2000). In the past San Cosmeras/os clearly identified themselves and others as *obreras/os* (workers) or as *campesinas/os* (peasants). Today, many people are "merchants" or "owners" but rather than experiencing a different class position, they are now in a more ambiguous class position.

The household location of the workshops and heavy reliance on unpaid family labor muddies the division between owners and workers. Kin who do not live in the household are usually paid the going rate and do not share in the profits. They, like non-kin, are usually called *obreros* (men workers) or *obereras* (women workers). Family members living in the household are sometimes also paid. For example, in extended households where each component family has a separate budget, the workshop may be owned by one of the component families and other household members who work there are paid. They too are usually described as workers. Family members of owning families (either single parent, nuclear, or extended families with one budget), however, are usually not called workers. Those who are more involved are called merchants and those who are less involved, for example, a son or daughter who works occasionally in the workshop or helps in selling the merchandise, are referred to by their main occupation, usually a*ma de la casa* (homemaker) or *estudiante* (student).

Families in San Cosme, as elsewhere,[18] are also characterized by variations in power and control of labor and resources including land, housing, and cash. In some manufacturing households, husbands and wives seem to share the profits and decision making of workshop production. In others, it appears that the husband controls most or all of the profits and many of the major decisions. Less frequently, usually if she is single, a woman may have control. Because few older people are actively involved in workshop production, adult offspring are usually not subjected to control by their parents (as they sometimes are when parents control land) but youths and children, who form a significant part of the workshop labor force, do not get paid if they work in their parents' workshop and benefit only indirectly from the profits. In at least some cases, daughters-in-law living with their husbands' families and working in their husbands' families' workshops are neither paid nor are they direct recipients of any of the profits.

The lack of clear division between workers and owners is also due to the fact that most of the workshops were started by "workers," usually with another family member, such as a wife or sibling. Sometimes, it was a worker (usually a textile factory worker) who lost his (or less frequently, her) job or gave up his or her job in reponse to the need for more labor in the family enterprise or, for women, to be closer to their children. Some owners continue as workers. For example, one couple began their workshop about ten years ago with the annual bonus money received by the husband who works in a relatively well-paying multinational chemical plant near San Cosme. He continues to work in the chemical plant while his wife runs the workshop that has four machines. On days when he is not working at the chemical plant, he goes with his wife to sell their merchandise. When asked what their occupations were, in 1989 he was said to be an *obrero* and she was called a *comerciante*. By 1994, however, despite his still working full-time in the chemical plant, they were both being identified as *comerciantes*.

Thus, although some of the workers in workshops identify and are identified as workers, many, despite the fact that they are working to generate profits for others (in workshops or multinational factories) and doing so because they do not control the means of production or do not control sufficient means of production, are not identified, and do not identify as workers. They may be worker-owners, such as the man in the previous example, or they may be unpaid family members. As Harvey points out:

> class conflict in family production no longer derives from
> the straight class relations between capital and labor, and
> moves onto a much more confused terrain of interfamilial
> conflicts and fights for power within a kinship or clan-like
> system of hierarchically ordered social relations.
> Struggling against capitalist exploitation in the factory is
> very different from struggling against a father or uncle
> who organizes family labor into a highly disciplined and
> competitive sweatshop that works to order for multina-
> tional capital. (1989:153)

In addition, since many of the local owners began as workers
(either in factories or *talleres*), and since hundreds of households
have established workshops, many of the workers look forward to
the day when they too will become merchants with their own
workshops. Although some will probably succeed, studies elsewhere have suggested that most workshop workers, especially
women who form the largest part of the workforce in small-scale
garment production, do not become owners (Blim 2000;
Morokvasic, cited by N. Green 1997; Greenhalgh 1994). Furthermore, even the owners in San Cosme are becoming increasingly
dependent on outside merchants, capitalists, and forces that make
their situations more precarious and constrained.

## Conclusion

Tlaxcaltecans have been involved in textile and garment production for hundreds of years (Constable 1982). But the textile and
garment trade today is part of a globalized industry that is very
different from prior patterns. The apparel industry has always
been subject to economic fluctuations and seasonal swings that
have made its market very unstable. The relatively lower capital
investment and skill needs involved in garment production have
also always meant greater competition than in other sectors. As N.
Green (1997) and Lash and Urry (1987), among others, have suggested, these characteristics have meant that flexibility and short
runs have been recurrent features of the industry since its beginning. Today, however, in the buyer-driven commodity chains in
which large retailers, designers, and trading companies control
decentralized production networks, the prospects of lower costs
and quicker response shift production (and with it much of the cost
and risk) at lightening speed.

San Cosmeras/os have participated in this flexible production by producing both cheaply and quickly. In order to do so, they not only provide poorly paid or unpaid labor, but they also absorb the costs of space, electricity, thread, and machines. As more and more countries restructure and press for NAFTA-like tariff agreements, competition from still lower-wage nations will increase. Unless workers and owners in San Cosme are willing to absorb even more of the cost of production, the community's markets may disappear. As transnational retailers increasingly compete with local venders, even regional street markets may be lost. Thus, for San Cosmeras/os, flexibility has brought them into apparel production but it may also drive them out of apparel production. "Free market" policies, which have been so successfully pushed by transnational capitalists, have given capitalists the rights and protections to roam the world seeking cheaper production with few restrictions, especially since the early 1980s. Unless their freedoms are countered by an institutional structure that gives labor, including family labor, rights comparable to what capital has managed to garner, producers such as those in San Cosme will either end up working harder and harder for less and less, or retailers will, as they have already done, move on to cheaper pastures.

## Notes

The author would like to thank Chris Bose, Nancy Breen, Myra Marx Ferree, and Carole Turbin for their encouragement and valuable suggestions. I am grateful also to the Faculty Research Committee of Towson University for their funding of this research in 1994 and 1997.

1. It is important to note that although small-scale production or petty commodity production is often flexible or part of flexibly specialized structures, flexible specialization is not the same as small-scale or petty commodity production. Any small-scale production is characterized by short production runs, but the products may be the same rather than the different products of flexible production and, as in much craft production, they need not be cheaply produced.

2. I am grateful to Carole Turbin for suggesting this reading.

3. It should be noted that the undervalued skills required are, as Elson and Pearson (1981) point out, often the result of the invisible training that women receive in childhood.

4. See Alonso (1984, 2000); Gereffi (1994); and Bonacich and Appelbaum (2000 ) for discussions of what Escobar Latapi and Martinez

Castellanos (1991) describe as a process of peripheralization in which microenterprises move from larger cities such as Guadalajara to smaller cities and towns to find lower-wage workers. Movement across national boundaries is noted in a *Wall Street Journal* article pointing out that "creative Marco Polos," rove the world looking for suppliers in countries where quotas restricting imports into the United States have not been reached (cited by Waldinger 1986:82).

5. It is very difficult to get accurate statistics on small-scale garment production. Textiles and garments are often grouped together. Furthermore, since most small-scale production units are part of the informal economy, they are not always counted. In San Cosme, for example, despite the existence of numerous talleres, no garment firms are indicated in the state industrial census for 1993 (INEGI 1994:75).

6. Excellent examples of this literature include Fernandez-Kelly (1983), Ong (1987), and Tiano (1994).

7. See, for example, Waldinger (1986), Phizacklea (1990), Kwong (1998), and Fernandez-Kelly and Sassen (1991). Among the important examples of literature focusing on small-scale garment production not involving immigrants are Beneria and Roldan (1987); Wilson (1990); Blim (1990, 1992); and Simmons and Kalanaridis (1994, 1996).

8. Fernandez-Kelly and Sassen (1991:99) note the rise of "brokers" in the garment industry in southern California. Their function was to link garment contracts with workers and contractors. The brokers in San Cosme usually link producers and retailers.

9. Unless otherwise specified, statistical data are taken from the author's household surveys done in 1971, 1980, 1984, 1989, and 1994. In 1971 every fourth household was surveyed yielding 150 households. In 1980 those same households plus and additional 50 and replacements for those households no longer occupied were randomly selected to give a total of 200. In 1984 one-fourth of the 1980 households were surveyed. In 1989 and 1994 the 200 households (with random replacements) of 1980 were again surveyed.

10. Independent production corresponds to some extent with the craft-based flexibility described by Piore and Sabel that relies on multi-skilling and autonomy whereas maquila production fits what Hsiung (1996:36) calls non-craft-based flexibility. As Hsiung, points out, in craft-based flexibility, skilled workers use technological innovation to respond more flexibly to fluctuating demand; "non-craft based flexibility achieves its competitive edge in a highly unstable international market by utilizing the labor of married women "who endure their multiple responsibilities at work and in the home 'flexibly'" (1996:36). I would stress, however, that the two kinds of flexibility may represent a continuum rather than two

discrete types with the labor of women and children being less autonomous and their flexibility being whether and how much they produce.

11. The exchange rate was approximately 7.7 pesos per U.S. dollar.

12. See also Simmons and Kalantaridis (1996:10) for a similar point and a discussion of how the entrepreneurial family "sweats" along with the other workers.

13. Simmons and Kalantaridis (1996) similarly note the competitive edge of family production in the garment industry and Greenhalgh (1994) and Hsiung (1996) argue that much of the gains from family firms in Taiwan derive from unpaid labor and from the unequal distribution of the rewards by gender , age, and relationship.

14. Similar patterns are reported by Ann Lee (2004) in Taiwan and by Agustin Escobar Latapi and Maria Martinez Castellanos (1991) in Guadalajara.

15. Future analysis will examine the gendered access to capital and labor.

16. See Taplin for an excellent discussion of how apparel firms use contracting to deal with increasingly unstable market conditions. "Because contracting by definition is generally low value-added yet labor-intensive, there is a constant downward pressure on wage rates while demands for product quality remain high. As subordinates in the network production hierarchy, contractors are very susceptible to market fluctuations and forced to pursue wage lowering/productivity enhancing practices in order to remain competitive" (1996:14).

17. It should be noted also that among "owners," the benefits are also not always distributed equally. In San Cosme, as elsewhere (see Lee 2004; Hsiung 1996; and Blim 2001), women usually benefit less than the men of their families and children, especially female children and daughters-in-law, do not always reap the same rewards as older male participants.

18. See, for example, Beneria and Roldan (1987). For a useful discussion of the exploitation of low-cost family labor and diverse interests in family firms see Greenhalgh (1994).

# 5

# Capitalism from Below?: Small Firms, Petty Capitalists, and Regional Transformations in Eastern Europe

## Adrian Smith

## Introduction

Since the collapse of the Soviet systems in East-Central Europe (ECE), a wealth of "Western" policy discourses have found their way into thinking about the post-Communist "transition to capitalism" (Bateman 1999; Gowan 1995; Pickles and Smith 1998; A. Smith 1997, 1998, 2002a, 2002b). The majority and most powerful of these discourses have been centered on the twin pillars of neoliberalism and global economic integration. Market-led transition, a rolling back of the state, and a globalization of economic life quickly became the central tenets of policies to engineer the "transition to capitalism." One of the key aspects of this discursive repositioning of economic policy has been in the realm of small firm development. It is argued that a new reliance upon small, locally agglomerated, dynamic, and flexible firms can provide an alternative to the outdated legacies of the Soviet system of centralized planning based on large, autarkic enterprises (Joffe 1990; Murray 1992; Schmitz and Musyck 1993; Hüber 1995; Lorentzen 1995; Said 1995).[1] Indeed, a romanticized picture has been constructed of a lost past of small, petty capitalist production in pre-Soviet ECE (Teichova and Cottrell 1983; Charap 1993; EBRD 1995:139). A return to such systems of economic life is, it is argued, required. In this chapter I explore the efficacy of such policies. Through an examination of the experience of Slovakia I argue that widespread attempts to support petty capitalist and small and medium enterprise (SME) development have had only partial success and have done little to overcome profound and enduring regional inequalities. I also explore the ways in which SME development and petty capitalist production, where they have occurred, have been integrated globally, through an examination of the garment sector. Such forms of global integration of SMEs and petty capitalists, while providing interesting alternatives to the dominance of regional economies by large, autarkic enterprises in Soviet societies, bring with them their own contradictions and limits. In this sense, then, the chapter examines two forms of global integration of petty capitalist organization. First, it considers the transference of "Western" discourses on SME development as part of the more general "globalization" of neoliberal economic policies to Eastern Europe. Second, it examines the uneven global integration of SMEs and the limits set by such forms of global engagement.

## Small Firms, Petty Capitalism, and Flexible Production in the "Transition to Capitalism"

Since the 1980s a vast literature has emerged on the so-called new industrial spaces and flexible specialization that has played an influential role in the construction of a discourse of local development theory and practice. It is not my purpose here to review these literatures. Rather, I seek to elaborate the key components of these arguments and explore how they have been "put to work" in the construction of an SME and petty capitalist discourse in Eastern Europe.[2]

Drawing upon the experiences of the Third Italy, Baden-Württemberg, the "high tech" spaces of the M4 motorway corridor in Britain and Silicon Valley in California, among others, an emphasis has been placed on the role of small-firm-oriented local industrial organization and agglomeration, leading to new forms of regional economic growth. First, the small firm, locally integrated clusters of the successful Third Italy economic region (mid peninsula) are seen to be one element in a model of flexible production agglomerations and local economic dynamism in traditional sectors such as clothing, textiles, leather, and footwear (Amin 1999; Brusco 1982; Garofoli 1991; Martinelli and Schoenberger 1991; Paniccia 1998; Piore and Sabel 1984; Storper 1997). Typical of such industrial districts are extensive interfirm divisions of labor with clusters of input-output relations, strong productive specialization, a plurality of local economic actors primarily in small firms, the use of "face-to-face" cooperation and consultation between firms to guarantee a locally supportive industrial structure (Garofoli 1991), a renewed craft tradition employing flexible working practices rather than Fordist standardization, and locally institutionalized practices and conventions that provide the glue holding together such complex divisions of labor (see Amin 1989; Scott 1988; Storper 1995, 1997; Whitford 2001). Second, the importance of locally integrated cooperative production between regionally dominant, often large, engineering firms and small suppliers is seen as central to the dynamic growth of the Baden-Württemberg region in Germany. Such forms of local agglomeration are said to be the result of "deep" institutional support structures enhancing the performance of firms in the regional economy (Cooke and Morgan 1993, 1998).[3] Third, "high tech" growth nodes of flexibly specialized, locally integrated electronics firms (Martinelli and Schoenberger 1991; Scott 1988)—more recently constituting the "new" cultural economy of multimedia (Scott 2000; Pratt 2001), and high-value added, advanced engineering in the motor sport industry (Pinch and Henry 2001)—also exhibit significant levels of agglomeration. Agglomeration, it is argued, not only reduces transaction costs but also enables an ongoing process of knowledge transfer and specialized labor market formation that acts to enhance the competitiveness of firms in such clusters.[4] Together, it is argued that these three different experiences of locally agglomerated industrial growth represent a new model of decentralized, disintegrated development for "advanced" capitalism and a new growth trajectory across different industrial sectors that has the potential to be replicated elsewhere if regions and their industries hope to compete in an increasingly global economy.[5]

In the context of the collapse of the Soviet systems in ECE, the experiences of the Third Italy and other such districts have been influential in considering how to move away from the dominance of "Fordist"-like, autarkic production complexes that typified industrial organization in centrally planned economies.[6] Indeed, the crisis of the Soviet model has, in part, been seen as a result of the lack of flexibility in such large production complexes. One way to ensure an effective "transition to capitalism," it is argued, is to break up large combines and to develop a new economy on the basis of private entrepreneurs and small firms (Bianchi 1992). As Giachinno Bianchi has argued, small firm development enhances flexibility (both in wage and labor deployment), labor intensification, disintegrated production and spatial agglomeration in noncompetitive environments that all "seem suitable for helping to solve transition problems in East European countries" (1992:91). The creation of such local agglomerations can enhance the restructuring of regional economies in ECE, it is argued, and can effectively benefit from a host of European Union support programs to provide know-how, assistance, and finance, focusing on sectors that have been successful in Italy and elsewhere, such as textiles, garments, furniture, knitted goods, and footwear and leather. In a similar way, Robin Murray (1992:217) has argued for the need to "regionalise economic activity" in ECE.[7] For Murray (1992:217) it is necessary to introduce "a plasticity into production," resulting in "smaller operating units, linked through the kind of networks and simple informational devices to be found in the Third Italy—registers of suppliers with details of their equipment; informal places to gather like technical colleges or collective service centers; close proximity within specialized industrial districts.

Together, such claims have constituted a vision of democratic local development in the West that can be transferred eastward into the fragile and newly emergent industrial economies of East-Central Europe. The development of petty capitalist, small-scale entrepreneurialism is seen as an endogenous solution to the large-firm legacies of Soviet planning, and a variety of support mechanisms and development programs have been established to enhance the growth of this sector. Michael Bateman, for example, provides a useful review of the plethora of SME development programs in ECE—from business innovation centers, to small firm advice centers and regional development agencies—and concludes that the "approach to small enterprise development has not been vindicated in practice, but has instead generated a bundle of serious implementation problems and lost opportunities, which are increasingly evaporating any of the supposed gains it has been said to have made to date" (1999:27). It is within the context of this more sober analysis of the potential for, and limits to, the transference of Western SME development discourses and the establishment of petty capitalist production that I approach the Slovak experience during the 1990s in the following sections.

## The Development of Small-Scale Capitalism and the State in Slovakia

One priority set early after 1989 by the Slovak (and the former Czechoslovak) governments was the development of small firms. As elsewhere in ECE, the creation of a small-scale entrepreneurial economy was seen as a required balance to the dominance of large enterprises, as a way of diversifying local economies by providing alternative employment (Brhel 1994), and as a mechanism to create more dynamic, flexible, regional economies (see, e.g., World Bank 1994:42; OECD 1999). In addition, the creation of a new class of petty capitalist entrepreneurs was seen as a way of reconfiguring the class composition of post-Soviet societies, and of denting the power of the *nomenklatura* class of Soviet societies. The establishment of an entrepreneurial petty bourgeois class was thought to be crucial to guaranteeing the democratic gains that came with the collapse of the Soviet systems.

In order to develop the SME base in Slovakia, the Ministry of the Economy in association with the EU's Phare assistance program established a National Agency for the Development of Small and Medium Enterprises (NADSME) in the early 1990s with the purpose of coordinating SME development activities and firmly establishing a discourse of necessity concerning small firm production.[8] According to NADSME (1994:11) SMEs are "'able to solve technical problems in a cost advantageous way. They can enable large enterprises to complete and supply a broad range of products without huge expenditures.... They are also able to react speedily to the individual requirements of customers... [and] they can find gaps in the market and become strong in certain market segment[s]." Furthermore, NADSME argues that SMEs can play a crucial role in the reduction of transaction costs and in increasing local economic diversification: "SMEs are an important factor in regional economic development. They safeguard the supply function in sparsely inhabited regions, villages and peripheral areas. Creating employment opportunities directly in local neighbourhoods decrease[s] transport time and expenses" (1994:11). Such thinking has also been reflected in more recent regional policy, which, under pressure for European Union (EU) accession, has emphasized the role of SME formation in overcoming the enduring and profound spatial inequalities found in Slovakia (Ministry of

Construction and Regional Development 2001; see also Hardy and Smith 2003).

The National Agency was originally established to coordinate the activities of a small set of regional business advisory centers (Regionalné poradenské a informačné centra, RPIC) created using European Union Phare program assistance and to undertake the expansion of the RPIC network.[9] The RPICs received Phare funding amounting to 89 percent of Phare SME spending in Slovakia in the first half of the 1990s (calculated from NADSME 1994). These institutions are clearly seen as central to the regional development process by the national government (1995). However, an earlier study has suggested that the system of RPICs and BICs (business innovation centers) was having a very marginal impact upon regional development and growth (A. Smith 1997). Indeed, while the number of new companies started as a result of assistance from RPICs and BICs has fluctuated, between 1994 and 1999 the peak of new firm creation occurred in 1997 (785 firms). This has more recently tailed off to 313 new firms created in 1999 (NADSME 1999:9). Indeed, a report by NADSME (2000) has pointed to a continuing decline in the number of new firms and in the level of employment in SMEs. Such results therefore raise questions over the extent to which the creation of a group of dynamic SMEs and a class of petty capitalists and entrepreneurs can be sustained, especially in austere economic circumstances and in conditions where support for SME growth is limited to largely public programs supported by European Union assistance. Bateman also makes the argument more generally that as EU funding is slowly reduced to such business support centres across ECE the emphasis of activity has shifted to the attempt to gain income to sustain employee salaries and center running costs and away from the earlier focus on new firm creation. He argues that those business innovation centers

> which are set to survive into the future are doing so by becoming indistinguishable from conventional private sector consultancies. The result is that the majority of new start enterprises, very small enterprises and the unemployed, all of which were meant to be the target group for the BICs, are increasingly being squeezed out of the client frame. Even when some of these clients indicate that they are willing to pay, the costs of such services are rising to

reflect the opportunity costs involved in their continued provision. (1999:17–18)

Indeed, recent employment data by firm size suggests that medium and large enterprises continue to be the most significant employers by far in Slovakia (Table 5.1). The number of employees in "micro" firms (fewer than ten employees), those most character-istic of petty capitalist firms, have witnessed a decline between 1997 and 1999 despite the fact that the overall number of micro firms has remained more or less constant, reflecting the somewhat marginal position of small firms in the Slovak transition.

### Table 5.1
### Number of Employees in Small, Medium and Large Firms in Slovakia, 1997–1999

| Size of enterprise | 1997 | 1998 | 1999 |
|---|---|---|---|
| 0–9 | 215104 | 152646 | 131756 |
| 10–49 | 157188 | 153969 | 153043 |
| 50–249 | 395698 | 410475 | 382852 |
| 250+ | 823657 | 872519 | 875536 |

Source: Elaborated from NADSME 2000, Figure 3.10.

While small-and medium-firm formation plays a clear role in programs for regional economic recovery throughout ECE, in Slovakia available data suggest that SME development does little to overcome enduring regional disparities (see A. Smith 1997, 1998). In Slovakia, just over 30% of SMEs (legal entities) and nearly 19% of small trade licensees in 1999 were located in the Bratislava region (NADSME 2000), which—out of the eight regional entities in Slovakia—is by far the most dynamic part of the space economy (A. Smith 1998). Indeed, the Bratislava region accounted for over twice the average per capita GDP in 1997 and an unemployment rate much lower than the national average and all other regions (Table 5.2). In more peripheral regions, such as those of East Slovakia (Prešov and Košice), the proportion of SMEs was much smaller (9% of the national total in Prešov and 13% in Košice). Even when the size of the regional workforce is taken into account, Bratislava dominates the geographic distribution of SMEs. In 1999 there were 54 SME legal entities and 149 small trade licencees per 1,000 active labor market participants in Bratislava. None of the other remaining seven Slovak regions reached the national average level of SME legal entities per 1,000 active labor market participants (NADSME 2000). The dominance of the Bratislava region is such that it accounts for more than one-quarter of total national SME employment (Table 5.3) which is approximately the same proportion of the region's share of per capita GDP.

## Table 5.2
### Key Regional Economic Indicators, Slovakia

| Region (NUTS3) | Unemployment rate, 1997 | Unemployment rate, June 2000 | GDP per capita 1997 (ECU PPS) | GDP per capita 1997 as % of EU average |
|---|---|---|---|---|
| Bratislava | 4.1 | 6.9 | 19900 | 105 |
| Trnava | 10.6 | 15.4 | 8400 | 44 |
| Trenčín | 8.3 | 13.4 | 7600 | 40 |
| Nitra | 14.3 | 22.4 | 7400 | 39 |
| Žilina | 10.9 | 17.6 | 6900 | 36 |
| Banská Bystrica | 14.9 | 22.9 | 7900 | 42 |
| Prešov | 17.8 | 24.3 | 5500 | 29 |
| Košice | 17.1 | 26.6 | 8300 | 44 |
| *Slovakia* | *12.5* | *19.1* | *8800* | *46* |

Source: ŠÚSR 1997, KS ŠÚSR v Prešove 2000, and Ministry of Construction and Regional Development of the Slovak Republic 2001.

## Table 5.3
### Distribution of SME Employment in Slovakia, 1999

| *Region* | *Percentage of total SME employment* |
|---|---|
| Bratislava | 26.9 |
| Trnava | 7.7 |
| Trenčín | 10.7 |
| Nitra | 9.8 |
| Žilina | 10.5 |
| Banská Bystrica | 13.3 |
| Prešov | 9.9 |
| Košice | 11.2 |

Source: Elaborated from NADSME (2000), Figure 3.12.

Within this context of the geographically uneven development of petty capitalism and small firms in Slovakia significant doubts must be raised as to the efficacy of policies concerning the role of SMEs in regional revival. Clearly the transfer of a discourse of SME development and petty capitalist entrepreneurialism has become part of a framing of neoliberal claims concerned with marketization and class restructuring. However, it is also necessary to explore the form of global integration of petty capitalist production where it has occurred. The following section therefore examines the way in which petty capitalist firms in the garment industry have become integrated into the global economy.

## Small-Scale Capitalism in the Slovak Garment Industry

The global garment industry is typically one dominated by a large number of small producers and a small number of large, powerful buyers and retailers (Gereffi 1999; Bonacich and Appelbaum 2000). One reason for this dominance is the low barriers to entry operating in the part of the value chain devoted to garment manufacturing. The Slovak garment industry is no exception to this global pattern. The sector employs approximately 29,000 people, although this figure is likely to be a significant underestimate because it only includes firms with more than 20 employees. Nevertheless, the clothing industry accounts for just over 10 percent of the manufacturing workforce, often concentrated in peripheral regions (see A. Smith 2003). Data supplied by the Slovak Statistical Office for four contrasting regional economies indicate the dominance of very small, petty capitalist firms in the clothing sector, which further underlines the problem of employment undercounting (Table 5.4). The Bratislava and Trnava regions constitute the economic core of "greater Bratislava." Košice and Prešov are the poorest Slovak regions. Those firms returning an employment size of 0 are owner-only firms with no other employees, which are relatively more significant in the core regions of Bratislava and Trnava. The majority of enterprises in all cases have fewer than 10 employees, although a few large, former state-owned enterprises remain significant players, especially in the more peripheral Košice and Prešov regions.

In common with the clothing industry elsewhere in ECE (Dunford, Hudson, and Smith 2001; Pickles 2002; A. Smith 2003), Slovak garment manufacturers are very export oriented. The sector comprised around 5% of total Slovak manufacturing exports and 41% of exports from light industry in 2000 (Ministry of Economy 2001).[10] As such, the clothing sector has one of the best trade balances of manufacturing sectors in Slovakia. Indeed, it is argued that if wage restraint can be maintained, the industry will provide the basis for significant export growth as European Union markets continue to open (Ministry of Economy 2001). From a survey undertaken with clothing manufacturers in four contrasting Slovak regions, nearly 80% of plants saw more than 50% of sales going to West European markets. For many firms this involved 80–100% of sales. On average, 60% of material inputs were also derived from West European countries, which reflects the role of the EU's outward-processing regime in the apparel sector (see Dunford, Hudson, and Smith, 2001; A. Smith 2003). More generally, between 1995 and 1999 Slovak clothing exports increased on average by 27% per year to account for 5.2% of total Slovak merchandise exports (calculated from WTO 1999). Alongside export growth there has been a slow but steady increase in employment in the clothing sector in Slovakia, in contrast to the general loss of industrial employment in the national economy during the 1990s.

**Table 5.4**
**Employment size profile of apparel enterprises in four Slovak regions (% of local apparel firms)**

| Employment size | Bratislava | Trnava | Košice | Prešov |
| --- | --- | --- | --- | --- |
| 0 | 32.2 | 14.8 | 7.3 | 7.9 |
| 1–9 | 35.6 | 25.9 | 43.6 | 30.7 |
| 10–49 | 22.0 | 25.9 | 21.8 | 32.7 |
| 50–99 | 6.8 | 13.0 | 7.3 | 11.9 |
| 100–199 | 1.7 | 13.0 | 5.5 | 5.0 |
| 200–499 | 0.0 | 5.6 | 9.1 | 6.9 |
| 500–999 | 1.7 | 1.8 | 1.8 | 3.0 |
| 1000–1999 | 0.0 | 0.0 | 3.6 | 2.0 |
| Total (no. of firms) | 59 | 54 | 55 | 101 |
| Unknown | 9 | 4 | 1 | 0 |

Source: Calculated from data supplied by the Slovak Statistical Office, (2000).

Many export-oriented Slovak clothing producers are involved in local clusters of production (A. Smith 2003). Two of the clearest cases are found in Prešov and Trenčín where dominant, former state-owned enterprises established a "tradition" for apparel production under the Soviet system (and before) that remains important. Indeed, as I have argued elsewhere (A. Smith 2003), such traditions have provided the basis for an expansion of the number of clothing firms and employment as managers leave state-owned enterprise and establish new plants. In this sense, then, such regional agglomerations exhibit characteristics of industrial districts elsewhere in Europe that have provided the basis for the SME scenarios just outlined. However, such clusters also develop from the specificity of experience in "transitional" economies in which the former managerial cadre in state-owned enterprises is positioned to develop networks and contacts established under the Soviet system in the creation and relative success of new firms in the 1990s. Several firms in the Prešov region provide clear examples of the reconfiguration of interpersonal networks, where former managers from the major state-owned plant were involved in establishing production and contracting networks with Western European manufacturers and buyers during the 1980s. Since 1989 several of these managers have left the now privatized plant and have established their own production operations. In one case, three former managers established a joint venture with a German purchaser and manufacturer who had previously contracted the state-owned enterprise to produce trousers and jeans for export during the 1980s. Not only did these managers become the local agent for the German plant, ensuring contracts were met among a host of often small-scale production units, they also provided logistics support and more recently have set up a production unit with the German contractor in the town oriented toward export production. Another example suggests that this case is not an isolated one. In this second case, two former managers of a smaller state-owned clothing and textile plant in Prešov established a joint venture with a Dutch contractor with whom they had worked during the 1980s to produce clothing under export contract. This joint venture, which is two-thirds owned by the Dutch partner, produces a wide range of clothing largely for export. During the 1990s such firms have become increasingly self-sustaining with the establishment by the two Slovak partners of separate design, import/export, and purchasing companies under their ownership. This diversification of activity has provided the basis on which these managers have been able to continue export-oriented contract production with the Dutch partner, but have also diversified into own brand production for both domestic and export markets.

John Pickles (2002), Pickles and Begg (2000) and Begg, Pickles, and Roukova (2000) have highlighted the significance of local agglomerations of apparel producers elsewhere in ECE, notably in the peripheral Rhodope region of southern Bulgaria. Local agglomeration in Bulgaria provides for not only dense local transactions but also enables producers to draw upon a local ethnic (Bulgarian Muslim) labor force made up primarily of women, which constitutes the basis of low-cost production. In both cases, albeit in different ways, Slovak and Bulgarian garment manufacturers rely upon a system of small, workshop-like production units that provide work for contractors elsewhere in the region or country who, in turn, supply Western buyers. Such forms of petty capitalism are highly flexible, enabling households to combine work on household plots for food production with apparel production in a family workshop (Pickles 2002). Indeed, such forms of production partially resemble the putting out system of home working evident in London's garment industry in the 1980s (Mitter 1986). Production contracting, in the East European case, is based upon the increased openness of EU (and wider) markets in the light of the EU accession process and the more general removal of trade barriers under the World Trade Organization (WTO) (see Begg, Pickles, and Smith 2003). One consequence has been the shift of production away from higher cost locations in Western Europe (see A. Smith et al. 2002), which has a parallel in North America under NAFTA (Gereffi, Spener, and Bair 2002; Gereffi 1999; Kessler 1999; Spener and Capps 2001).

Yet, such outsourcing of production has its own contradictions when based upon low-cost, low-wage production, as is the case in the clothing sector. Contractors in Slovakia use the very small-scale workshop economy as the basis for establishing flexibilities in production. For example, of the 14 firms surveyed that said that they supplied clothing as a final product or as a component for further production to other local producers, 11 employed fewer than 50 people. And of the 15 firms that supplied contractors in Europe, 11 employed more than 100 people. What we find here, then, is a local production system in which very small petty capitalist firms supply local contractors in a flexible manner, and these contractors then produce clothing and supply the production of workshops to the wider European economy. Such a system creates a very flexible form of production and such flexibilities have increased over the last ten years due to the shortening of production runs and turnover times, as the consumer markets of the West become more highly competitive. Along with an outsourcing of production, then, comes an outsourcing of the risk and impacts of increased competitiveness and tight markets in the West onto petty capitalist producers in ECE and elsewhere. In this sense, petty capitalists operating in the garment sector are very much tied into wider circuits of capital through a tier of contracting firms, as well as through the increasingly global policy mantra of SME formation.

Clearly such global engagement has dramatically transformed the industrial structures of garment-producing regions. A decade ago the clothing sector in the Slovak regions of Prešov and Trenčín was dominated by two or three large, state-owned enterprises. Today a dramatic explosion of small production units has occurred as production has been outsourced. Yet, at what cost has such a transformation occurred? Preliminary evidence suggests that low-wage production, as elsewhere in the global economy, only provides a temporary and very partial basis for competitiveness (Spener and Capps 2001; see also A. Smith 2002b). Despite the existence of some examples of successful "upgrading" of clothing production in ECE (Yoruk 2001), many managers of Slovak garment plants have suggested that cost competitiveness may only be maintained over the next five to ten years. The global "race to the bottom" in the garment sector may well leave parts of ECE, such as Slovakia, behind as buyers and retailers in core markets seek out new, cheaper production locations—a possibility ever more likely since China's membership in the World Trade Organization. While technological and product upgrading into own brand manufacturing (OBM) may provide one set of possibilities for ECE garment producers (Yoruk 2001, A. Smith 2003), evidence from the United States suggests that such upgrading may only exercise a temporary halt to relocation pressures outside of core production areas in Western global cities such as Los Angeles and New York (Spener and Capps 2001).

## Conclusion

In this chapter I have examined two forms of global engagement of petty capitalist and small firm economies in post-Soviet East-Central Europe. First, there has been a discernible shift in policy since 1989 toward the dominance of market-oriented transition, part of which has emphasized the role of small firms and local economic clusters in the rejuvenation of regional economies. Building upon Western experiences of industrial districts, such a policy emphasis has played an important role in guiding Western (especially European Union) assistance programs. However, I have also argued that the impacts of such strategies have been somewhat limited and in no way have they provided a basis for the rejuvenation of some of the most peripheral regions. Second, I have also argued that in the apparel sector, small firms that have been established are often locked into European and global production networks. Such networks position small producers in ECE as low-cost capitalist production units for Western markets. The survival prospects in the medium to long-term of such production units are, at best, limited as their cost competitiveness may become increasingly undermined by the further liberalization of world trade in the garment sector. In both of these ways, then, petty capitalist production provides partial and temporary mechanisms for economic development in the here and now. Whether such forms of production have the potential for upgrading and moving up the value chain remains an open question, although the experience of locations with increasing costs in this sector in recent years, suggests that caution is required (Bonacich and Appelbaum 2000: Spener and Capps 2001).

## Acknowledgments

This chapter arises from research undertaken as part two projects: a British Economic and Social Research Council project on "Regional Economic Performance, Governance and Cohesion in an Enlarged Europe," which was part of the One Europe or Several? research program, and a U.S. National Science Foundation project on "Reconfiguring Economies, Communities, and Regions in Post-Socialist Europe: Competitive Pressure, New Firm Creation, and Outward Processing in the Apparel Industry." I am especially grateful to my fellow collaborators on these projects: Bob Begg, Mick Dunford, Jane Hardy, Ray Hudson, John Pickles, Al Rainnie, and David Sadler. I am also grateful to our Slovak collaborators who helped in various aspects of the research: Milan Buček, Vlado Baláž, Andrea Gonová, Daniel Kollár, and Dagmar Popjaková. Parts of the results are derived from joint interviews undertaken with David Sadler in East Slovakia and I am very grateful for his insights. The normal disclaimers apply.

## Notes

1. Much of the work in ECE on flexibility and on SMEs has drawn on the Hungarian experience in which reform attempts during the 1980s led

to a burgeoning small-scale, "second economy" (Neumann 1992). This process was not apparent to the same extent in most other parts of ECE, where more centralized forms of state control prevailed. Neumann however is skeptical about replicating the types of locally integrated cooperation derived from "strong" forms of civil society (which have been seen as so important to the "success" of industrial districts in Europe, particularly in the Third Italy) in ECE given the apparent weakness of civil society in the post-Communist period.

2. See Amin (1989), Amin and Robins (1990) and Dunford et al. (1993). See Bateman (1999) and A. Smith (2003) for critiques in relation to regional clusters in ECE.

3. See, however, Herrigel (1996) for an analysis of the limits of this German model.

4. See, however, Massey and Allen (1995) and Crang and Martin (1991) for a critique of the contradictions of the "Cambridge phenomena" and Saxenian (1983) for a critique of the U.S. high-tech growth poles. See Martin and Sunley (2003) for a more general critique of clusters.

5. See Hudson et al (1997) for a critique of the possibility for transfer of such phenomena to other, different, sociocultural and political-economic environments. Staber, in a study of the knitwear industry in Baden-Württemberg, has also suggested that "clustering may simply heighten competitive intensity and displace otherwise viable firms" (2001; 339).

6. See A. Smith (1998), though, for a critique of the claim that ECE economies were simply forms of "Soviet Fordism."

7. See also work on flexibility, production decentralization, the emergence of the second economy, and the transition to capitalism in Hungary (Schmitz and Musyck 1993; Fóti 1993), and other writers on the Hungarian experience (Neumann 1992, 1993). See also Newbery and Kattuman (1992) for an argument concerning the need to decentralize production in ECE.

8. See Hardy and Smith (2004) for a more in-depth discussion of Phare and other EU assistance programs in ECE.

9. Three RPICs were established in 1991 in localities where dynamic local state personnel had already begun to establish institutional frameworks to support SME development. The original three were located in Nitra (West Slovakia), Martin (Central Slovakia), and Poprad (East Slovakia). The Ministry of the Economy established four more centers in 1992. In 1994 two more centres were established through tenders. All had Phare program funding involving approximately 70% of running costs. The other 30% was financed by the local state or by the ministry. The network

was later expanded to include a series of "satellite" advisory centers' under the jurisdiction of a main RPIC office and the funding regime was changed so that RPIC activities became more commercialized as Phare money was withdrawn. At present there are twelve RPICs and four BICs in operation, although their role will no doubt change with the development of a country-wide network of regional development agencies (see A. Smith 1997; Hardy and Smith 2002).

10. Light industry includes the textiles, clothing, leather and shoes, and printing and glass sectors.

# 6

## Global Market and Local Concerns: Petty Capitalists in the Brianza

### *Simone Ghezzi*

One of the most important consequences of post-Fordist global restructuring has been the "deterritorialization" of capital and its increasing geographic expansion. It is becoming more apparent that capitalist enterprises are able to move effortlessly across national borders and to relocate their manufacturing processes in areas that may offer more promising profit opportunities. In a famous and oft-quoted passage of David Harvey's *Condition of Postmodernity* it is argued that the transition from Fordism to flexible accumulation has been accelerated by an unprecedented trend of time-space compression in capitalist political economy, allowing a faster absorption of overaccumulation of capital, commodities, and labor both through geographic relocation of production and through the acceleration of turnover time: "the speed with which money outlays return profit to the investor" (1989:182). There is, of course, another and quite different view that comes from the literature on industrial districts and regional economies. This view emphasizes the fact that capitalist activity can be organized by means of localized or territorially based systems of specialized production (Storper 1995). These systems are characterized by the presence of clusters of interconnected small-scale factories and artisanal firms supported by active local governments. They provide an institutional framework that creates and fosters the conditions for retaining this kind of economic configuration. It is such "territorialization" (or regionalization) of economic development

that has successfully turned specific areas—for example, those situated in the so-called Third Italy, in Germany (Baden-
Württemberg), in France and in Spain—into regions of specialized
economic activities organized on the basis of subcontracting relations among small units of production. More importantly, the
seeming economic achievement of these areas has become a blue-
print for economic development, a model to reproduce across
Europe. In fact, this newly "discovered" economic regionalism
among scholars has in turn been incorporated into the political
economic discourse of European Union (EU) officials and politicians who see in this model a potential solution to the problem of
developing lagging areas, through mobilization of, and reliance on,
local resources (Amin 1999). Incidentally, this framework inevitably influences how European-funding procedures are designed
and how policy-making strategies are implemented in less developed regions of Europe (see the chapters by A. Smith and G. Smith
and Narotzky, in this volume).

In this chapter I demonstrate how these two discourses are not
mutually exclusive. Industrial districts are not immune from deterritorialization, nor should their economic achievement gloss over
emerging local level problems produced by stiffer global competition. These two aspects become apparent as I examine the local discourse among petty capitalists within an industrial district of the
Brianza in Lombardy, northern Italy. After a discussion of the
origin and characteristics of this regional economy—hit by periodic
economic crises and industrial restructuring—I will use ethnographic examples to illustrate how innovation and competitiveness
within and outside this industrial district masks forms of exploitation and contradictions among petty capitalists. In discursive terms
exploitation is articulated in various sublimated ways, but two in
particular are recurrent in the narratives of petty capitalists. One
is the ideology of "hard work" and the other, more recent, is the ideology of "high-quality product." In the concluding section I stress
that these two discourses should be viewed as responses to concerns regarding the possible deterritorialization of some factories
and increasing competition in cross-boundary markets.

## Setting

Situated in Lombardy, the Brianza extends over three
provinces: Como, Lecco, and Milan. It is a relatively small, hilly,

and densely populated area, enclosed to the north by mountains just south of the two branches of Lake Como, to the east and west by two rivers (Adda, tributary of Po River, and Seveso), and to the south by the city of Monza, situated about 15 kilometers from Milan. It does not constitute a political-administrative entity, but since the 1990s a few economic and political groups have been lobbying for the constitution of the Provincia della Brianza, with Monza as district capital. The Brianza is now widely recognized as a highly industrialized region. Its economic success is often touted by the media, which consider the region a "model to copy" (*Corriere della Sera*, November 11, 2000), and it is backed up by its own people, who proudly speak of their region as the only "locomotive" or "backbone" of the nation. It is characterized by the presence of numerous small industrial and artisanal firms, most of which are family-run businesses, in the sense that the co-owners (and sometimes even some of the employees) are closely related by blood and marriage. These firms are concentrated in small towns where a flourishing entrepreneurial activity in various sectors, especially in those of woodworking (furniture), metalworking (mould making and nuts and bolts), and plastic (compression/injection moulding), have made it one of the most prosperous regional economies in Italy and Europe. The Brianza Milanese is the most populous of the three provinces, with a population of about 816,056 in 1996.[1] A total of 60,074 firms employed about 250,000 people, with an impressive rate of one business every 13.58 inhabitants. As of 1994 over 93% of firms had less than 10 employees, 6.6% between 10 and 99, and less than a fraction (0.33) over 100 employees. While the bulk of small factories are in the industrial sector, these businesses also include companies working in the tertiary sector (service and commerce), and a tiny minority in agriculture.

## The Rise of the Workshops

The first small enterprises came into being partly from a pre-existing rural artisanry, and partly from the textile crisis that this region experienced in the 1950s, with a consequent shift from textiles to light industries, in particular metalworking and furniture. However, a few metal-working factories were already established before the 1920s. In the town where I did most of my fieldwork, Arcate,[2] just before World War II two large manufactories (Sorrenti and Crutz) together employed about 1,500 workers.

Ancillary to the textile sector, they specialized in the production of looms, knitting machines, and various textile accessories. These large and vertically integrated manufactories provided employment opportunities especially for the local male population. In general, sons followed fathers into employment in the same plants until the crisis of cotton industry forced these factories to heavily downsize their workforce and eventually to close down. Interestingly, downsizing was partly responsible for the creation of a few small firms and for paving the way for the further development of the metal-working industry. Being vertically integrated, these two large factories "raised" skilled workers of all sorts: toolmakers, mould-makers, designers, welders, milling-machine operators, lathe operators, and so on. When hundreds of these highly specialized workers and foremen were made redundant during the restructuring period of the fifties, many of them were able to go into self-employment and set up their own workshops, often in partnership with former coworkers.[3]

The reed-weaving firm of Vincenzo Colciago (b.1939), one of the first petty capitalists I came to know in my fieldwork, was created in this fashion. His father was a Sorrenti foreman in the department producing reeds for weaving. When it closed down in 1955, he bought some machinery from the firm at a low cost and brought it home. Originally his three young sons worked in his new business as well. But soon after the eldest son decided to withdraw his partnership, apparently due to conflict with his other brothers, and went to work in a metal-working factory in a town close by. The other two brothers and their father continued to manufacture reeds for weaving, first in the family house and then in an adjacent building erected to accommodate more machines and four newly hired employees. Eventually each son married and for lack of space and environmental restrictions they had to build a factory floor located within walking distance from their family house. With the help of two nephews, Vincenzo, who has outlived his brothers, still continues the family business that his father had begun in the 1950s. The life history of Vincenzo's eldest brother represents an interesting "spin-off," for after working a few years in a metal-working factory, he and a coworker set up a mould-making workshop in 1960, now run by his son Cecilio (b.1964).

An indication of how the model of industrialization in the area of Arcate was taking on features diverging from mass production can be drawn from the oral account of the life of Nello Arpini, now a ball-bearings maker. The recollection of his father's first steps into entrepreneurship is of special interest here, for even if he himself was not an "indigenous" entrepreneur (he was born in a small rural town south of Milan), chance had it that he would build up his fortunes in Arcate. In the early fifties, two lathe operators from Arcate found a job in a sewing machine factory in Milan where Nello's father happened to be a foreman. They personally knew a small industrialist in Arcate who, originally a sales agent for sewing machines, had set up a ten-worker firm producing accessories for sewing machines and was looking for someone who could help him make the mechanical parts of a sewing machine cabinet. These two workers convinced Nello's father, another skilled worker, and a clerk from the same factory to become joint-partners in this enterprise. In 1953 they all quit their jobs in the Milanese factory and began to work in Arcate for this small industrialist who also provided them with a vacant floor located beside his firm. The business partners—toolmakers, lathe and milling machine operators—had the technical knowledge to manufacture the rotation system, including flywheels and treadles, while the clerk took care of the accounting. They quickly became more autonomous as they began to work for other firms as well. In 1960 two partners (including Nello's father) left the company due to some disagreements and set up a new firm each with their own children, while the other three, being childless and already well on in years, gradually retired. In 1966 the firm was closed down.

It is important to notice that these early entrepreneurial experiences in the town of Arcate and its surrounding area coincided with the general restructuring process of the large-scale factories. Hundreds of jobs were lost, but many others were created, thanks to the rise of small-scale firms, as illustrated in these case studies. It is also important to stress that this economic restructuring mainly benefited the male population. As I have shown, the formation of these firms through the industriousness and inventiveness of skilled workers was possible thanks to the expansion of the metal and wood-working sectors, sectors in which men were likely to find a job. While new employment opportunities were created in the two sectors, conversely, the local textile industry, once a leading economy in this area, suffered a terminal crisis. As a result, the female labor force—which constituted the majority of the textile factory workers—was badly affected. Working class women found it difficult to convert their skills in the new labor market, as in the case of Teresa (b.1910), who worked for several decades in a local garment factory that closed down in the early 1960s.

Production in this factory, which employed up to five hundred women, was originally organized in small units of female workers, each under the supervision of a male tailor. The product was manufactured entirely in this unit, from the model to the finished item, and the workers were trained for several tasks. Subsequently, major changes in the organization of the labor process resulted in the breaking up of these units, giving way to a rigid division of labor, modeled on the assembly line system. Women began to do only one specific task, either cutting, sewing, pressing, finishing, or ironing. Teresa was assigned to the sewing department and her job was to stitch collars onto shirts. The factory was heavily downsized in the crisis of the 1950s, but Teresa was allowed to keep her job because of her family situation (widowed with two children). However, with the closure of the factory a decade later, unable to find other jobs, she decided to work as a needlewoman in her son's upholstery business. Teresa notes that many of her younger coworkers were hired as unskilled workers in metal-working factories, while other women left the workforce "to raise their children."

By contrast, the layoffs from the large factories mobilized the energies of male workers toward the creation of workshops. Some began to produce metal parts for the furniture industry, while others made simpler parts of a more complex product for larger factories. The small enterprises founded in the immediate postwar period were mostly established by the initiative of skilled workers and artisans, and only rarely by the instigation of the firms they were employed in. These firms, rather, played a more important role in the 1970s through the 1990s, as the imperative of decentralization and deverticalization, especially in the metal-working sector, stimulated the practice of outsourcing and the creation of subcontracting networks of firms. However, not all of the local small workshops were created as a result of decentralizing strategies via the process of subcontracting. Some in fact began to produce directly for the market—by now no longer limited to regional or national borders—in competition with larger factories and became in turn the initiators of more subcontracting strategies.

Although the current morphology of production organization in the Brianza is remarkably different from the one that allowed the creation of small firms in the 1950s, there are still persistent similarities. Each time the restructuring and/or the closure of a leading local factory took place, a redundant but highly specialized labor force would find its own way into entrepreneurship. Indeed, the firms created by these enterprising second-generation workers

were, in general, more specialized and therefore more interconnected with one another than those created in the past.
Nonetheless, it seems that, as in the 1950's, the remarkable
resilience of the industrial sector in the last twenty years appears
to originate from the continuing reproduction of skills and family
labor rooted in a social milieu where the local institutions (municipality, banks, and artisan associations) also play an important role
(Sabel 1989).

A most remarkable example comes from Arcate. A compres-
sion-moulding factory, Nispelli, created by two brothers-in-law
became one of the leading industrial factories in the area in the
late 1960s, as a result of its connection to important Italian car
makers. When in 1967 the younger business partner left the company due to disagreements regarding his share of ownership the
factory had about a hundred employees. They worked on two adjacent shop floors, one manufacturing moulds, the other compressing
moulded components in various metals. In the mid-1970s the firm
invested considerable capital in a new plant in central Italy, but
this venture never took off. The fall of the company began in this
period. Heavily indebted and strikebound, it managed to survive,
but eventually went bankrupt in the early 1980s. In the meantime
many workers had left the factory. Some found employment in
other manufactories, mostly in the newly established firm created
by partners who left Nispelli, specialized in mould making and
compression moulding of plastic materials; others set up artisan
workshops and small industrial factories specialized in specific
phases of the production of metal components. In the recession of
the early 1980s, several local factories followed Nispelli's fate and
rapidly disappeared from the local industrial map. The workers in
these mid-sized firms followed a course of action similar to
Nispelli's. Some found jobs in local enterprises run by former
workers, whereas others became petty capitalists by creating very
small metal-working or compression moulding workshops in the
same area, often in the basement of the family house. The result
was a multiplication of firms operating in a thick network of subcontracting relations. Most clients and subcontractors operating in
this area knew each other quite well on a personal basis before initiating economic relations. The embeddedness of these relations
has thus contributed to a high level of trust in the district. Even
when there are no direct social ties between factory owners, petty
capitalists may rely on well-informed sales agents to identify and
assess the reliability of potential transaction partners.

The advantage of this system is apparent: by contracting out a few parts of the production process to specialized workshops, entrepreneurs keep their workforce within certain limits and avoid making large investments in up-to-date machinery. At the same time, since the stock of machinery and the number of employees are kept to a bare minimum, factories, as well as workshops, cannot meet market demand by relying exclusively on their own means of production. Virtually no enterprise is vertically integrated to the point that it is able to contract out work only when its own capacities and productive limits are overcome—hence the importance of relying on suppliers. It should be noted that they have to be trustworthy. If one of them is running behind on the completion of a certain phase in the production process, all of the following phases will inevitably be affected. Therefore, it is in the entrepreneurs' interest to be on good terms with their suppliers and to make sure that they are reliable in machining the parts in the time that both parties have agreed upon. In the event of delays—by no means a rare occurrence—factory owners have to rely on their reputation and power to exert pressure on the workshop—such as the threat to give the job to someone else next time—in order to have the work done on time. Stiff penalties for late deliveries are possible, but never apply to long-term subcontractors: where personal relationships are involved, formal rules such as this cannot be enforced. By the same token, detailed written agreements about work orders are virtually nonexistent.

Production in the workshops is carried out for a wide range of factories in and outside the region: the automobile industry, the suppliers of accessories for furniture, household appliance makers, nuts and bolts producers, to name but a few. The fact that the Brianza is increasingly more integrated into a wider (namely global) market makes it more interdependent and therefore highly subject to the uncertainties of worldwide competition. In order for petty capitalists to participate and, more importantly, to succeed in the global market, "innovation" and "competitiveness," are not per se sufficient: family exploitation becomes a necessary condition. As component suppliers, they are more likely to be positioned at the bottom of the production linkages, and for this reason they are more vulnerable to various pressures from their client firms. This fact in turn contributes to exploitative relations within the household, particularly in periods when market demand is strong.

## Family's Hard Work

In the Brianza, family-run enterprises are mainly located near the household residence, if not in part of the dwelling itself. While walking around in residential areas during the day, one can hear the whistling noise of lathes and saws coming from two-story houses; and see loaded trucks and vans coming and going from house backyards or from adjacent buildings. In this way many firms are camouflaged in the residential areas, but a growing number are being conveniently concentrated in industrial parks at the outskirts of the towns, where traffic is less congested and connections with major roads are easier.

In my fieldwork I visited several of these family-run firms during a period of extremely intense work. One of these encounters is illustrated in the following passage taken from my fieldnotes. It concerns a small workshop made up of a husband (Antonio) and a wife (Caterina), situated in a century-old compound, once a brick factory, and now occupied by artisan workshops. Before setting up the workshop with his wife, Antonio was a skilled worker, a milling machine operator in a factory that went bankrupt a few years earlier. His wife worked in another factory, but quit her job to join her husband's enterprise.

It's 3 o'clock and I am in the workshop of Antonio Tracco. He and his wife are working inside their metalworking workshop. Their thirteen-year-old son is here, too. Later they will tell me that they would rather see their child hanging around in the workshop than at home, all alone. The radio is on, but it's hard to hear the tune as the grinding sound of metalworking machines reverberates in the hangar and pierces my ears. As Antonio sees me through the big clear plastic curtain dividing the production area from the rest, he stops working at the milling machine. I follow him through the production area filled with machines, boxes, drums, and the soon to be delivered metal components. We get to the office, a tiny and sooty room where the only amenity is a fax machine covered by a towel. A few rolls of drawing paper stand on the desk. As he will show me later, they contain projects of metal components, new work orders for Antonio and his wife. In fact, his wife who is madly working away is upset that her husband is giving me his much needed time. At one point in our conversation she arrives and screams at him to stop talking and to get back to work. A deadline is approaching. She then calls him a Neapolitan, saying that he is all talk, and no work. I feel very uncomfortable. Antonio twice tells his wife that he will join her, yet he continues to talk with me. As I later learn he will have to continue working on this order right through Sunday. "Author's Fieldnotes."

Antonio and his wife's workshop is positioned at the bottom of the system of production. They have to face the classic dilemmas of all petty commodity producers (Friedmann 1978). They cannot hire workers, because they cannot guarantee work beyond their cash flow (which is three months). Apart from their personal income—a predetermined amount they withdraw from the firm's income—there is very little surplus that they can put back into the enterprise. For this reason they are not willing to apply for loans because this would increase their indebtedness. As a result, they cannot invest in expensive and more productive numerically controlled machines; and even if they could, neither of them knows how to operate one. In the end, labor rests solely on their own forces.

Drudgery is common. There are months in which they toil to meet work order deadlines, and weeks in which the workload is more manageable. Antonio works ten hours per day, and four hours on Saturdays. If he runs behind when a deadline approaches, after dinner he goes back to work until 2:00 A.M. Sometimes he even works Sunday mornings. At times a former female worker, now a housewife, comes to help. Their son sometimes gives a helping hand, too. Antonio wants to enroll him in a private technical high school in Sesto San Giovanni (near Milan), where he will learn the basics of mechanics and the programming of computerized metal-working machines. In the past even Antonio's daughter (b.1977) often helped her parents in the workshop. According to Antonio: "had she been a boy, I wouldn't have had any problem in employing her in the enterprise. But, you know, you can't keep a girl in a place like this." She is employed as a unskilled worker in another local factory. It is interesting to notice how his daughter has been "expelled" from the enterprise on the grounds that "she is a girl," and as such, she is not expected to be a significant participant in the enterprise. By contrast, Antonio's son will become an active business partner. In addition he will be enrolled in a private technical high school that his father has carefully selected, in order to acquire skills in programming numerically controlled machines, which is expected to increase the workshop's productivity.

Antonio's wife takes part in the machining of metal components and is responsible for packaging the product when ready for delivery. But she does other things, as well. At home she does the accounting and also keeps the books of another small workshop. She learned the trade while working as a secretary in a workshop before becoming Antonio's business partner. Moreover, she also is in charge of domestic chores and meal preparation; her daughter helps out. On weekends she does not work in the firm because, as Antonio states, "she has to tidy up the house."

In a family workshop, work may be much more labor intensive for family members than for non-kin employees. That family members must cooperate for the well-being of their own household is almost an axiom, a moral obligation, regardless of the commodification of the social relations involved. In other words, while employees' involvement in the workshop is regulated by wage relations, family members' participation transcends any contractual formality; it is imposed by moral commitments. Would-be (male) petty capitalists are well aware of the fact that they can build their business out of family loyalty expressed in various forms of help and cooperation, from the leasing of money to the supply of flexible labor. Mothers and wives may have some reservations about the choices made by their sons or husbands; but eventually, they are drawn into the frantic activities of the enterprise. Their support is related to the ideological elements surrounding the notion of the family; yet, material considerations are equally important. Once the decision to become a petty capitalist is made and a worker resigns from his job and begins to invest, it makes no sense for women to withdraw their support when this action may jeopardize the enterprise. The risk is real, because the new entrepreneur now needs to work longer hours in order to repay loans. He must also spend part of his working day running errands, such as finding clients, purchasing raw materials, and doing the accountants. These "unproductive" activities—unproductive from a male point of view, as I will argue in the next section—take time away from production, but must be carried out. The pattern is that women respond to these new work pressures through their involvement. Their labor is most often applied to bookkeeping and administrative tasks, yet they may also work on the shop floor in times of intense production. Such labor represents the cheapest and most immediate source of help. In some cases, this means that, in order to meet the labor demand in the workshop, they may have to quit their previous job, if they have one; for others, it means taking on additional demanding tasks.

Active gender support takes place at three levels: directly in production; indirectly in the process of production (compiling invoices, paying bills, cleaning the workplace, and doing the accounts); and directly in the process of reproduction (domestic chores, meal preparation, and family care). Familistic relations make such support seem a "moral" choice; however, there is a great deal of family exploitation inherent in it. In Marxist terms, exploitation is technically a social relationship that comes into being when surplus labor is appropriated through the domination of labor and the appropriation of surplus products that are then alienated as commodities (Wright 1981:150). In simple commodity production the thorny question refers to who appropriates what. According to Karl Marx a petty producer is both a capitalist and a laborer: "As owner of the means of production he is capitalist; as laborer he is his own wage-laborer. As capitalist he therefore pays himself his wages and draws his profit on his capital: that is to say, he exploits himself as wage laborer, and pays himself, in the surplus-value, the tribute that labor owes to capital" (1963:407–408). There seems to be a circular argument in this passage. According to this definition, exploitation cannot occur because the household appropriates surplus through "self-labor" that is carried out using its own means of production. By following this logic, we may infer a notion of self-exploitation, which is not what I am looking for. The accumulation of capital takes place not only through a collective and balanced form of mutual exploitation between family members. Family is an arena where domination is present and is reflected in social relations of production in which the petty capitalist exerts control over labor power. Besides, we cannot assume that accumulation is being redistributed equally, especially when in most of the cases male petty capitalists are either the only owners or, in case of a partnership with family members, occupy dominant positions. In the event that company shares are split in equal parts among spouses, usually the move is recommended by professional accountants who suggest nominally splitting the profits in order to lower taxable income.

When the family labor present in a workshop is disaggregated into its three dimensions—productive, unproductive, and reproductive—exploitation assumes specific attributions of gender and age. The reproductive dimension enters fully in the process of capital accumulation, insofar as domestic labor allows the reproduction of the household as well as of the family business. Yet, it is either dismissed or regarded as "natural" by those who do not contribute to it but benefit from its advantages. It remains uncommodified, but it also remains unreciprocated due to the rigid division of labor that continues to be perpetuated within family workshops.

The "unproductive" dimension requires some elaboration.[4] For a male artisan dealing with labor intensive work on a regular basis, skill and dexterity are highly praised, much less so are the tasks that take time away from production. Typing receipts and bills, keeping track of work hours, and doing the accounts, are considered unproductive activities—albeit necessary—in the workshop. To a certain extent, this view evokes the Marxian assumption that only productive labor creates surplus value, whereas unproductive labor does not, and it may actually be supported out of surplus value (Gough 1972:47). For Marx what determines the designation of labor as unproductive has nothing to do with the specific content of that labor and its use-value: "A singer who sings like a bird is an unproductive worker. If she sells her songs for money, she is to that extent a wage laborer or merchant. But if the same singer is engaged by an entrepreneur who makes her sing to make money, then she becomes [a] productive worker, since she produces capital directly" (Marx 1976:1044). In other words, labor is productive insofar as it is a factor in the self-valorization process of capital (1976:1045), a distinction that is seldom perceived in the androcentric pragmatism of petty capitalists. Here, I wish to stress the derogatory overtones (which are absent in Marx) that are subsumed in the terms used by my informants. Wives, mothers, and daughters fulfill their role in the workshop by taking on tasks which, according to male workshop owners, do not create value. This view can obviously be contested and roles can be renegotiated accordingly, as in the following case, describing an ongoing conflict in a welding workshop run by Carlo (b.1938), a former worker, and his two children (Laura, b.1966; and Davide, b.1964):

> My father is used to working as he did thirty years ago. He is a very good worker, the only thing is, he is a bit unrealistic when it comes to establishing contract prices. When

we're discussing them he always sets a lower price than that suggested by my brother and I. We are more exacting, more calculating. He just wants to get on with the work, but he doesn't realize that what is most important for the firm unfolds in the office. He sets low prices because he's afraid of losing work orders and clients. Afterward, when he realizes that his price is too low he asks the client to renegotiate and of course arguments arise. Now, to avoid problems with clients, my father and my brother set prices together.

Family support in the sphere of production is subject to the same kind of subordination. Again, this is the sphere where women (and children for that matter) may work on a part-time basis, given that they are already fully involved in the unproductive and reproductive activities, or more intensively in times of increased production. In the welding workshop just mentioned, Laura helps her father and brother weld metal components when needed. She did so even while breast-feeding her baby one year before I met her. While she was at work, the baby was cared for by her mother. That was a period in which they were taking in more work orders than usual, in order to pay back the loans for the shop they had bought in a cooperative compound. At work she welded because help was needed and she worked in the office because that was her usual job. All the while she had to go home every now and again to breast-feed her baby. The stress was so great that she soon stopped producing milk: "This made me feel very bad. But, after all, I couldn't have done anything differently because we all needed to work in here."

The expression "to work hard," a common adage I so often heard during my fieldwork, does not simply express an obvious truism: that workshop activity is labor intensive. It is also a powerful discourse and proliferates along with the emergence of the political-economic process I have described here, that is, the path that contemporary capitalism has taken in the Brianza. The discourse of hard work, though, constitutes the basis for building a reputation within this system of subcontracting relations, a necessary "business card" in order for workshops to take work orders from client-firms and thus to establish a steady collaboration with them.

## The Quest for Quality Upgrading and Its Consequences

The fear of losing ground due to competition with other regional economies, and the fluctuation of work orders from client firms are always matters of apprehension for petty capitalists. Furniture makers, for example, although still the most representative producers in this region, are facing increasing competition not only with other regional economies in Italy and Europe, but also with lower-wage developing countries. As far as the metalworking sector is concerned, much of the manufacturing is ultimately stimulated by large firms operating outside the region and even outside the country. To what extent they will continue to rely on artisan workshops in the Brianza rather than looking for subcontractors elsewhere is a question that cannot be easily answered. Tight and trustworthy interfirm relationships do not per se guarantee their stability in the future. For example, a growing number of German and Italian firms, which in the past outsourced production in the Brianza, have already built industrial plants in Eastern Europe, especially in the area of Timisoara, in Romania—also thanks to EU-funded projects (cf. the chapter by Adrian Smith, this volume)—for standardized and low-cost production. A petty capitalist confided to me that one of his most important client-firms, situated outside the Brianza, had plans to move there and he was asked to follow: "I am too old to start from scratch elsewhere. But how many will close here to open there, we don't know." There are no figures regarding this; but it is difficult to imagine that small family workshops would pack up and move elsewhere. The experience of industrial districts shows that "petty capital" is not only kin-based, but also locally rooted and for this reason it does not move so easily. Yet, the concerns of my informant should not be overlooked. While small workshops may not move, some leading manufactories of the Brianza are investing abroad and expanding the number of suppliers in other emerging industrial districts (e.g., in the areas of Brescia and Bergamo in Lombardy). Petty capitalists know that the decentralization of production to other areas will eventually cause a contraction of work orders for workshops and a possible decline of the "Brianza system."

Responses to these apprehensions are manifold. One is political, for various artisan and small entrepreneurial associations operate by lobbying at all of the political levels: from the local bank and municipality to EU agencies. They lobby for measures— such as low-interest loans and other incentives to lower labor cost, the constitution of more industrial parks, better transports, and so forth—that help them remain competitive. The results are not always welcomed, though, as in the cases of EU regulations that have introduced new and more restrictive norms regarding the safety of working conditions. Law n. 626 of 1996, for example, raised complaints as it imposed a series of costly changes relating to electric wiring, air circulation systems, mandatory washroom facilities, first aid and safety measures and so forth.

Another response is discursive, but it is having some political-economic implications in the material conditions and social relations of petty capitalists. At present it seems that most of the large and mid-sized client-firms are seeking higher quality of production, and are therefore pressuring entrepreneurs to modernize their machines, and persuading others to get ISO 9001 certification, a standardized process for quality control. On the whole, by virtue of an incongruous confluence of interests, everyone seems to talk about quality, each in their own terms. Although quality upgrading is widely recognized as an ineluctable strategy against competition, some subcontractors, such as Antonio, are unable to invest in new technology. They have to rely mainly on their manual skills in operating traditional metal-working machines and on the labor of family members. Antonio states that the quality of his work is ensured by his skill, and that there is no substitute for it. By contrast, others are investing in state-of-the-art numerically controlled machines (CNC) to improve both quality and productivity. The main drawback in investing in innovative machinery is that its cost may drive petty capitalists to intensify drudgery, rather than to escape it. To amortize investments in CNC equipment and to achieve a satisfactory return, a workshop owner needs to continuously operate the equipment for many hours a day; with periodical supervision even during the night. Moreover, the fast pace of technological innovation causes machinery to become outdated quite rapidly. Some petty capitalists, therefore, to keep up with technology and the flexibility of demand from their client-firms, are persuaded to buy the more expensive machining centers with automatic tool changers. These latest developments in computer numerical control offer sophisticated tools that are able to machine diverse components simultaneously with consistent accuracy, providing high quality in a short processing time. The problem is that with the high cost of these computer-ized machines, petty capitalists may become more vulnerable even as they work hard to pay their debts. Such fear is evident in the stories that circulated in the time of my fieldwork about small firms being swallowed up by large manufactories. An example is the story of "Mama Fiat."

> This is Mama Fiat's school. Mama Fiat was the first, but now other large firms are doing the same. Managers I have never seen get in touch with me, who owns a metalworking workshop. The machine I have is able to process no more than 500 pieces per week. Mama Fiat offers me steady col-laboration and asks me to machine 1,000 pieces per week. If I accept, I will have to buy one more machine. As I do not have enough capital I will get a loan from a bank. After six months Mama Fiat calls me and says that oooh, I am work-ing very well, she is very satisfied, so satisfied that she asks me to machine 2,000 pieces per week. So I have to buy one more machine and hire more workers. Once again I accept because I see that it is a bargain; in fact I can become very rich, in spite of running into debt when I buy the machines. But, after awhile Mama Fiat came to me and says: I'm sorry, but I have found a workshop that can make your 2,000 metal pieces at a cheaper price. She knows that I am very indebted, and because of this critical situation, I cannot set a lower price for each piece. Without Fiat's work orders I am doomed to bankruptcy. So she offers a solution: "what about if you sell me your business. You get some money and do not have to cope with bankruptcy."

This story and other similar ones always end with the moralis-tic warning that workshop owners should be less greedy and more wary, especially toward strangers.

I was never able to verify stories of this kind; nonetheless I find them interesting. Their relevance lies not in their striking similarities but in their content; to me they illustrate the tensions generated within this regime of flexible accumulation, and the dialectics between what is locally familiar and what is destabiliz-ing because it is without historical roots in the territory. This is precisely the issue: whether it is a large factory trying to cannibal-ize small firms or a manufactory looking elsewhere for suppliers, the point is that territorial specialization is called into question and continuously challenged both from the outside, as these stories show, and from within, as some local client firms are looking for suppliers elsewhere.

The issue of quality is, then, a response—along with the issue of "hard work"—that serves the purpose of coping with such tensions and contradictions, albeit not always successfully, as indicated in the following case. Donato Cedretti—a former worker and now owner of a tool-grinding and sharpening workshop—specialize in processing expensive metal parts requiring complex operations of grinding (e.g., electric spindles) and sharpening (e.g., special metal blades for shearing machines). He notes that

> [The choice of] quantity over quality is risky. When in 1993 the crisis in my sector [*metal-working machinery*] arrived, those who worked to produce high volume went bankrupt or ran into financial troubles. As the demand plunged, they could not increase the price of each piece enough to compensate for the loss of volume. As for me, I didn't have many problems; I continued to do small quantity work at a high price.

During the crisis in the early 1990s he lost most of his casual customers, but managed to keep subcontracting relations with his twenty steady client firms. He is always in search of new clients to keep up a constant workload over the year so that no machine lies idle for long. But there is a caveat. Forced to seek new client-firms outside the local context of the district, he is often unable to verify the reputation (and trustworthiness) of prospective clients or suppliers. When I first met Donato in 1996, he had just started a new business relation with an electric spindle maker located in another region. He was excited by the prospect of a steady supply of work in this new subcontracting relation, and planned to purchase another computerized machine. He consulted his bank for a loan and his artisan association for exploring the possibility of getting a grant from Artigiancassa (a public national program of loans for artisan workshops). Yet, the deal with his client firm fell apart. When I met him again two years later, he expressed his feelings of disillusionment about the failure of this business relation, and his disenchantment toward the whole system, a system by now full of scroungers and deceitful individuals. He had placed trust in that firm and had begun to grind several hundred electric spindles; however, the firm was not able to pay for his work due to financial problems that he was not aware of. As a result, he could not place the order for the purchase of the computerized machine. Donato became even more upset when he found out that this firm had actually gone bankrupt twice in the past and reformed under a different company name.

## Conclusion

With these cases I have not claimed to exemplify entirely what is actually a far richer and complex reality. I could have described a more flattering side of small-scale industrialization, presenting life histories of "self-made men" who have managed to sell their own product in the market breaking out of their subcontracting relationship with client-firms. However, only a minor fraction of firms have the capability to do so. The reality of this industrial district is less glossy than what appears at first glance. Subcontractors seek client-firms because these provide constant work orders; nonetheless, they fear them because they might become exploitative, and exert control over their work process. Subcontracting networks are three-dimensional systems: they constitute a stratified, hierarchical group of companies and production units in which competition and interdependence mask strong tensions and contradictions, which can only partially be reduced through the notorious adage: "hard work."

Even though we are not very cultured, we are real workers. "Aunque no somos muy cultos, somos muy trabajadores" is an expression that Gavin Smith heard repeatedly from Valencianos informants (see his chapter with Narotzky in this volume). "Work is part of our nature" is what the shoemaker Capoccia said to Michael Blim (1990:157) in the Italian region of Marche; and another entrepreneur spoke to him in the same terms: "We were meant for work, and we do not know what to do without it" (1992:266). Should my informants listen to these words, translated in their local dialect, they would think that they had been uttered by anybody from the Brianza. A typical expression they would certainly add goes: "The Brianzoli will stop working only when they die." The similarity of these expressions should not be surprising. Industrial capitalism has its own logic: once embraced, it is hard to escape.

Regional economies may be variably integrated into a wider economic system. Their integration depends on the level of territorial specialization of production that these regions have developed over time (Storper 1995): the more integrated these regions are, the more the local patterns of labor mobilization are highly influenced by the demands stemming from cross-boundary markets. As I have already argued, the major implication of this point is that to participate and, more importantly, to succeed in these global markets, exploitation becomes necessary. Argued in these terms, such an issue was already known at least since Marx's time; but the forms in which extraction of labor, alienation, and appropriation—the three necessary components of exploitation—are carried out, are neither self-evident nor self-explanatory. As I have tried to illustrate in this chapter, in discursive terms exploitation may be articulated in various sublimated ways: one of the most recurrent seems to be the ideology of "hard work," as pointed out in various research. In the Brianza, though, it is not the only local ideology expressed within the social boundaries of the region. As the competition—both in the metal-working and wood-working sector—with other regions becomes deeply felt, "hard work" is no longer enough to characterize the leading economic role of this region. Small entrepreneurs in these sectors increasingly combine the former with the discourse of "high-quality product," as a new marker of the competitiveness of the region.

Yet exploitation encompasses both discourses, and can be viewed as a response to the exigencies of the world economy. As argued, the exploitative character of the social relations of production within and among workshops is intertwined with the artisans' increasing concern for the potential loss of competitiveness in the region. These two aspects cannot be understood as separate entities. Client-firms are well aware of the fact that in order to retain their competitiveness subcontracting has to remain lucrative. The great number of specialized local workshops that contend for long-term clients, make such competition effective. But for petty capitalists this situation is less than ideal. Some subcontractors are compelled to invest permanently in innovative machinery; others remain committed to intensive labor; but even by investing in cutting edge technology, drudgery is just around the corner. The rapid innovation of machinery forces them to continuously invest more money into their business, and therefore to work harder to repay their loans.

A recurrent complaint among artisanal subcontractors is that their economic situation is deteriorating precisely because they are becoming too numerous. In their narrative discourse there is a romantic longing for something that was supposed to be in place in the past, and that has now gone. Frequently I hear nostalgic expressions such as, "in the past we were few and therefore there was room for everybody. There was more trust and there were more honest people around. Credit was easy; loan payments could be delayed; taxes were low..." and so on. How long ago this past was, is always subjective. I understand that there is often a tendency to look back at one's own life in a nostalgic way, but it seems to me that they tend to "exoticize" their past, by viewing it as an harmonic epoch in which principles and people were "authentic," and in which tradition, enduring relationships, and solidarity ruled their lives. To what extent my informants mythologized their past is difficult to tell. I make sense of my informants' words by understanding them in relation to the present context. They tell me more about present tensions and future concerns rather than the reality of the past.

## Notes

1. The following data, provided by the Chamber of Commerce, Industry, Artisan, and Agriculture, regards the Brianza Milanese.

2. The name of this fieldsite, of my informants, and of the firms in which I did fieldwork are all pseudonyms.

3. Of the thirty firms surveyed in my research, eight were founded in the fifties, five of which were mechanic workshops whose owners were former skilled workers of the two aforementioned plants.

4. I will not undertake an exposition of Marx's theory of productive and unproductive labor. It is problematic as well as fragmentary, given that it was meant to be dealt with in the never-fulfilled fourth volume of *Capital*. A classic summary of Marx's view on this topic is in Gough (1972); important implications of this debate on the concept of class are found in Poulantzas (1975).

# 7

## They *Were* Promised a Rosegarden: Reunification and Globalization in Small- and Medium-size Firms in Eastern Germany

*Hans Buechler*
*and*
*Judith-Maria Buechler*

This chapter explores the impact of global competition on enterprise structure, technological development, and marketing strategies in small and medium-sized manufacturing and service firms in Sachsen-Anhalt, eastern Germany. Our focus on the trajectories of specific firms reflects our belief that in order to predict the future success of firms under capitalism, it is a mistake to focus too narrowly on the general contrasts between economic systems such as capitalism and communism, and more productive to examine variations in the position of persons and productive units over time within these systems. We will examine the ownership patterns, background of the firms and the managers, workforce and firm structure, as well as product and market development of firms of different size and elucidate how they have been influenced by globalization and their differential insertion into the western German-dominated economy.

Here, we will concentrate on formally constituted firms ranging from a handful of employees to firms and parts of firms with a few hundred workers but whose parent companies employ well over a thousand workers. By focusing on this segment of the continuum of

121

firms of different size, we do not mean to imply that they constitute a homogeneous category. The largest firms in our sample, but to an extent even some of the smaller ones, share some characteristics with large-scale multinationals. The smaller ones also share some characteristics with informal productive units and some of the firms in this segment of the continuum have emerged out of informal moonlighting operations or are reverting to such practices. However, as we will seek to demonstrate, all the firms included in our analysis have much in common. The commonalities and differences will become apparent through an internal comparison of the larger and the smaller firms in our sample followed by a comparison between the two subsegments.

## The Historical Context

### *The Communist System of Production*

The pre- and post-Wende trajectories of these firms can only be understood in the context of the general economic climate in the GDR (German Democratic Republic) and its dissolution after 1989. The GDR economy was characterized by a hierarchical system of conglomerates composed of related industries tied to a centralized redistributive system wherein shortages and compensatory hoarding of all inputs including labor further aggravated scarcities (see Kornai 1992). Firms were not subject to hard budget constraints. Rather, the state allocated resources and bailed out inefficient units depending on their perceived importance to the economy. Specifically, this meant that the state fostered export-orientation to offset large credits and imports from the west, mainly the Federal Republic of Germany. Each conglomerate, and within it each industry and each factory, engaged in constant maneuvering to gain access to scarce resources. This involved long-term planning at the local level to request inputs. Since access to these inputs was uncertain, each economic unit: collective, conglomerate, and factory attempted to be as independent as possible through vertical integration of the productive process, for instance, by having elaborate repair facilities. It was important to be able to do everything including, if necessary, manufacturing machine parts or even equipment yourself. To offset the perennial shortages a vast secondary economy was brought into play that entailed the exchange of inputs, goods, and services among productive units and among individuals. These transactions included a large black market for untaxed services by moonlighting artisans that was fully tolerated by the state.

In addition to the state conglomerates and the highly dependent agricultural collectives,[1] the GDR tolerated a dwindling private sector composed mainly of artisans and retail trade firms. In 1976, there were still 85,000 artisan firms and 40,000 retail trade firms, but their number sharply declined thereafter (Pickel 1992:11).[2]

In contrast to other Eastern European economies where small-scale firms were often indistinguishable from activities in the shadow economy, small firms in the GDR were highly regulated. The legal framework included guild-like skill requirements: apprenticeships, master classes, and the completion of a master piece at the end of the training period. They were under constant price and income surveillance and were disadvantaged in terms of access to all but basic commodities such as flour.

In spite of the fact that small-scale private businesses could not develop beyond well-established limits, the artisans were still regarded as forming a privileged elite, since their numbers were also controlled and hence they had little competition and demand was never an issue.

## Eastern German Liberal Capitalism

The reunification of the two Germanies in 1990 led to a crash program of privatization through the breakup of firms by the Treuhand, an agency set up already in the last months of the GDR to initiate privatization, find Western investors, and liquidate and close units considered nonviable. The opening of the economy to the West resulted in catastrophic deindustrialization. The immediate monetary union led to the loss of the former Eastern European market because prices became prohibitive, while wage differentials between East and West (combined with obsolete technology) were not significant enough to give the former a major advantage for exporting to the West. East Germans lacked the private capital for starting their own businesses. An inflexible, cumbersome, provincial, and alternately conservative and trendy banking system is, and has not been supportive of, entrepreneurial efforts. At the same time overcapacity in the West led to only very selective acquisition of Eastern by Western firms. In spite of supposed safeguards set up by the Treuhand to guarantee jobs and future productivity, the latter often acquired firms for the secret purpose of closing them to eliminate competition. Nonetheless many, mostly ultramodern, large-scale, capital intensive plants (often larger than their Western counterparts) such as flour mills, sugar factories, and cement factories were built from scratch or by modernizing existing facilities. The privatization process also resulted in a completely Western-dominated distribution system: shopping malls and chain stores, often by taking over parts of the GDR state distribution system.

As far as small-scale firms are concerned, the lifting of restrictions led to the establishment of new firms and the enlargement and modernization of old private artisan shops. But competition from the West, the streamlining of services, as well as property issues and difficulties of financing led to reduction in some areas, and ultimately to an alarming bankruptcy rate.

Eastern German capitalism emerged as a curious mix of an elaborate welfare system (a pension plan providing benefits far surpassing those in the GDR, early retirement at age fifty-five, state-sponsored retraining programs providing training for nonexistent jobs, and work programs), and U.S.-style competition without the protection provided (at least until recently) in the West by long-established networks among firms and between firms and government agencies. In Western Germany too, there has been an accelerating trend toward the introduction of neoliberal economic measures including the weakening of labor unions and other corporate efforts to decrease costs and increase profit. It is within this context of the progression of neoliberal global trends and the continued dominance of western Germany over the economy and politics of the eastern states that we must place the development and mutual interaction of larger and smaller firms we studied in the eastern German state of Sachsen-Anhalt.

## Case Studies of Privatized Factories

Our examples of medium-sized productive units all constitute local production sites of large multisited GDR conglomerates. The first is considered a model of success in the region and beyond; the second was dragged into bankruptcy when the western German parent firm collapsed and was reabsorbed by an Austrian firm; and the third has managed to survive the massive shift of manufacturing to the Third World and to the East, becoming the largest factory in its specialty in Germany. We have followed these and many other firms from 1993 to 1994, shortly after their privatization, a period of general optimism tempered by the general stagnation of manufacturing in Germany and against a backdrop of massive de-industrialization in eastern Germany to 2001, a time of pervasive pessimism because of recessionary trends and continued high unemployment.

The pharmaceutical firm is the successor to a relatively separate part of a large GDR conglomerate that enjoyed a special position in the wider economy because it satisfied 80-90 percent of the veterinarian needs of the GDR in addition to exporting to other East bloc countries. Its autonomy was based on the fact that it added more value to the product than it received from the center. This position enabled it to assemble a team of highly motivated and broadly trained individuals.

After reunification the market for veterinary medicine collapsed but there continued to be a market for human medicine, enabling the firm to survive. The managers were also able to resist transformation into a mere subsidiary of, or distributor for, a western German firm. Instead, a share-holding company was established with substantial involvement of western German capital, but in which the managers, all former members of the former executive board, held a substantial (though not controlling) share.

In contrast, the factory for agricultural machinery specialized in planters and sowers was formerly dependent on a parent company centered in Leipzig which, in turn, was part of a huge conglomerate. Resource allocations followed a hierarchy where Leipzig retained the lion's share of the inputs and controlled production decisions. Ninety percent of the production was destined for the national market and 10 percent was exported to the West, where it could compete largely because of low prices.

After reunification the conglomerate was broken up. The pre-Communist owners came to have a look at the enterprise but did not have the knowledge to take the firm back. The solution chosen by the Treuhandgesellschaft (the agency that privatized former East German state enterprises) was to accept the firm's acquisition by a western German manufacturer who wanted the facility to complement their production of soil preparation equipment. The proposal promised to ensure continued employment for a maximum number of workers in what is one of the last heavy industries in Bernburg. Unlike many similar takeovers by Western firms, it also entailed the local continuation of product development and hence a degree of autonomy. As in the previous example, local management continued in the hands of the man who managed the firm during GDR times.

The third firm, which produces flanges (i.e., junctures for large pipes) has a similar background as the agricultural equipment firm except that its share amounted to 50 percent of its total production. The firm had a relatively diversified output because in addition to mass-producing flanges for export it also had to satisfy the more specialized national needs. It was more integrated into the parent plant that built power plants, a privileged sector in the GDR, which gave it the advantage of being able to show a positive balance sheet even though profits were siphoned off and the factory was forced to take on debt to expand.

Flanges are a less distinctive product than pharmaceuticals. They can be produced fairly easily and faced major competition in the free market after 1989. However, the market for flanges is relatively reliable. They are not entirely subject to economic cycles, since factories, the major customers for flanges, take advantage of times of reduced production to make repairs. After the Wende, (turning point, reunification) the firm followed the model of the western German flange industry that focuses on medium-sized firms. Also the trend was toward breaking up the conglomerates. The Treuhand-appointed, mainly Western board of directors from various noncompeting industries, mainly Westerners, and the workers strongly supported a management buyout with the participation of a German-American and an American who promised to retain a larger workforce. The choice was also designed to thwart absorption and subsequent closure by a multinational intent on eliminating a competitor.

### Reduction of the Workforce and Modernization

Like most former GDR firms, these three had to reduce their workforce through state-subsidized early retirement, reducing the percentage of women, and improving the worker/management ratio. All modernized their operations.

The pharmaceutical company reduced its workforce from 800 in 1989 to 226 in 1994 remaining essentially stable since then, which is rare in eastern Germany. Wage differentials have increased dramatically approximating western German conditions. Since privatization, the firm has invested 67 million DM ($38.6 million) and almost doubled its turnover to 80 million DM ($46.1 million).

In the agricultural machinery factory, the workforce was reduced from 600 to 75 after privatization, and to 50 after the second takeover; half would become seasonal. After annual increases of 2 to 3% until 2000, wages were cut by 15 to 20% or more, but are still high by local standards. With relatively modest investments, turnover increased from 3.5 million in 1992 to 12 million in 2000, only to decrease to 5 to 7 million a year later.

The flange manufacturer initially reduced its workforce from close to 1,000 workers to 240. The new owners promised to retain 160 workers, but since then the number of workers has risen to 250. They have made substantial investments to modernize the plant enabling them to manufacture even the largest flanges. They have rented parts of the large factory complex to outside firms.

*Production Strategies, Competitive Pressures, and Marketing*

In terms of product line and marketing, the pharmaceutical factory built on its former prominence in the eastern German and Comecon market. It generally still produces the same items as before, although modified and packaged differently. To save money, it now subcontracts plastic components of one of its products to a Czech firm that it supports financially instead of buying them from an Italian firm. The manager considers the medium-sized firms to be at the forefront of innovation because of their flexibility, but they frequently sell off their patents to wealthier, larger firms with wider marketing networks. The firm prides itself on its autonomy. It accepts subcontracts amounting to only 10% of the turnover and engages in reciprocal production with a Dutch company for another 10%. Formerly not export oriented, the factory has developed a network of local distributors and also acquired two distributors in western Germany. It sought legal accreditation of its products in other European countries in order to bypass the lengthier German process that in the future will also permit future sales in Latin America.

In contrast, the factory for agricultural equipment had gained some autonomy after the first takeover only to lose it again with the second by a middle-sized Austrian firm that closely monitors its activities and has taken over the accounting and will soon fully integrate computing. From a vertically integrated system, where product development, production and, in part, marketing were all carried out by the Bernburg subsidiary, the factory has become a mere assemblage site that will subcontract much of the production to eastern European firms. This type of development is still regarded with some suspicion in Germany, although it is clearly on the rise. While the former owner had stressed autonomous product development and hence local autonomy, the personnel involved in product design has now been halved. All this sounds like an impersonal system, but the parent company is actually a family firm and places considerable value on solidarity that it fosters by means of celebrations consciously modeled after the Japanese system.

The flange factory made the fewest changes in product lines and the most significant changes in production techniques and marketing. Standard parts are used wherever pipes are employed, leaving little room for design innovation or in materials that are mandated by law. This fact means, however, that the product can be produced anywhere leading to competitive pressure. In particular, producers and middlemen farther east, who often had large inventories left over from Communist times, when producers who had hoarded materials began unloading inventories at dumping prices on the world market during the meltdown of industry. While cheap products from Eastern European markets had always entered the West in Communist times, contracts were often controlled by the Western producers. With the liberalization of trade, their privileged position evaporated and they now sold directly to large-scale distributors. Interestingly this strategy was foreshadowed by the suggestion of one of the members of the board of trustees supervising the privatization of the firm who recommended the sell-off of the factory's inventory as a means of extending the firm's life. In both Western Europe and the United States this competition has led to plant closures, bankruptcies (and consequent dumping of inventories by the liquidators), mergers, and protectionist measures (e.g., the controversial increases in import tariffs on steel products instituted by the Bush administration).

The situation may finally be stabilizing. Some of the Eastern European inventories are now exhausted. Also, factories in the more rapidly industrializing former East bloc states such as Poland and the Czech Republic are buying the special large and low-temperature flanges produced by the firm.

The firm's product strategy is a combination of the old and the new, resulting in a wide panoply of flange sizes and materials. The modernization of the plant enabled it to produce large flanges that only the best-equipped producers could manufacture. When it could no longer compete with producers farther east with smaller flanges, it set up a distributorship (where the son of one of the eastern German partners works) and began selling cheap flanges produced in the east. At least until the recent import tariffs, the firm was able to remain afloat because one-third of its sales were to the United States. Because of the distance, a major problem is the need to finance production in advance. In the absence of its own capital, the firm makes use of German rather than U.S. banks. In Germany, financing was particularly good after the Wende if you were considered creditworthy because of government subsidies including outright grants and subsidized interest rates. In the past two years the firm has been experimenting with the use of German venture capital, formerly not customary in that country.

*Analysis*

In conclusion, the reunification of the two Germanys in 1990 led to a complex maneuvering of middle-sized firms both in the West and in the East in the face of a major economic downturn in the German economy and global competition. The firms we investigated are survivors of the takeover by the West and represent different forms of privatization. The most pernicious approach had been to eliminate competition by acquiring Eastern firms cheaply and then either closing them or making them into mere appendages of the parent firm. In the case of the pharmaceutical firm, that attempt was shrewdly thwarted.

The agricultural equipment factory represents a strategy whereby Western medium-scale manufacturing firms sought to improve their market position by finding Eastern ones to complement their product line. This expansion is taking place in the face of a shrinking market for agricultural equipment because of the narrowing profit margins in agriculture due to GATT (General Agreement on Tariffs and Trade) agreements that reduce subsidies and open the European Union to agricultural products from abroad.

Finally, the flange factory represents a fairly successful combination of management buyout by the former executives of a part of a large state conglomerate and the involvement of foreign partners. Inherent in this form of privatization is the temptation for Western managers to undermine their Eastern partners and workers by blaming their Communist background for poor results.

After reunification the general supposition was that in eastern Germany, there was going to be a tremendous lag in the development of management skills, capital accumulation, product development, and know-how on the one hand and marketing and distribution on the other hand. The comparison of these three firms only partially confirms this notion. Counterintuitively, the pharmaceutical company based on management-buyout is our most successful example of privatization. The key to success may have been its autonomy in GDR times and the fact that the managers brought along considerable cultural capital in the form of education, organizational skills, and flexibility to maneuver in systems where improvisation was a daily necessity. While successful in obtaining Western capital, they had enough of their own to thwart external takeover. They have chosen a path similar to that of their Western counterparts: joint ventures to reduce costs and outsourcing, as well as the purchase of Western distributors in order to decrease the dependency on stifling Western marketing networks. Far from confirming the prediction that Eastern goods would never be able to compete on the world market without the artificial GDR subsidies, their products have gained acceptance in Europe and beyond. In fact, the pharmaceutical firm's only regret was that it had not carried over *more* products from its GDR past. This firm, then, was able to survive and even prosper under capitalism because of its special position in the GDR as well as more general assets drawn from that past, combined with Western capital, neoliberal strategies (outsourcing), and product innovation. In turn, its success has permitted it to attract young local as well as one or two Western scientists, countervailing the brain drain in the region.

In contrast, the agricultural equipment manufacturer suffered a more mixed fate. Unlike most manufacturing firms in eastern Germany it has survived, but in some ways it has replicated its GDR dependence on stronger firms. In spite of the fact that the major investments made by the parent company had resulted in a dramatic increase in productivity and it was beginning to be profitable, mismanagement at the top combined with a 20 percent reduction in demand for agricultural equipment in recent years led to its failure and reabsorption into a new company, with a much diminished role.

The flange factory was able to parlay the initial enthusiasm for firms with Western participation into an ambitious program of modernization and its American connections into the establishment of a major new market made at a considerable sacrifice: the willingness of the German/American partner to commute between the United States and Germany. Like the pharmaceutical firm, this firm could adapt flexibly to new opportunities and constraints because it could count on a reservoir of skills and experience acquired through the firm's position in the GDR economy as a mass producer of exportable standard as well as of specialty products for domestic needs in an economy that attempted to be as self-sufficient as possible. Of particular interest is the firm's experimentation with venture capital, which is not usual in Germany, in order to supplement credit from a banking system, which due to the slower than expected recovery, has turned away from industry and back to more traditional forms of investment.

## Case Studies of Small-scale and Artisanal Firms

An engineering firm, a carpenter, a baker, and a tile layer-cum-retail tile shop, all family-managed firms which, at different times, employed between one and forty workers, will illustrate the problems of even smaller-scale enterprises in the continuum of firms we studied in Bernburg. As we shall attempt to demonstrate, they share many of the attributes and problems of the medium-scale firms. In fact, the traditional distinction between artisanry-cum-petty commerce and industrial production is actually quite blurred. It is not their inherent characteristics, but the origin of small-scale firms that is the major differentiating factor. Some of these firms emerged out of the breakup of GDR productive units into smaller ones (in this case, on the factory, rather than on the conglomerate-level); others represent the continuation of artisan family firms that persisted throughout the GDR; while yet others originated in the shadow-economy in the GDR.

The engineering firm emerged out of a section of a chemical factory, itself a part of a larger conglomerate. It was in charge of installation and maintenance of switching units, a specialty in the GDR. Founded by the former section head, Mr. R., an engineer, and a much younger partner, who was slated to succeed him since he did not have any children, the firm worked as a subcontractor for the parent firm that was taken over by a Scandinavian enterprise and also sought other contracts both in the East and West.

The carpentry shop is a third-generation family firm that pre-dated the GDR and had continued throughout the communist period. Its owners, the N.'s, are presently in the process of transferring the firm to their son. It is one of the most respected artisan firms in Bernburg.

The baker (whose early history has been analyzed elsewhere [Buechler and Buechler 1999]) has a similar background to that of the N.'s. From a baker family, but unable to inherit his father's bakery, he managed to succeed a retiring baker in Bernburg. While most of the bread was baked in large state bakeries, some private bakers, like the carpenters, were allowed to continue throughout the GDR. Just before the Wende, the government had already become somewhat more liberal in allowing new firms to establish themselves. The Wende led to the demise of many of the old bakeries whose owners had reached the early retirement age of fifty-five and did not have any successors. The younger ones and those who had sons (more rarely daughters) to succeed them took the challenge to modernize and adapt to the new market conditions by diversifying their offerings.

Finally, the tile layer had been an employee in a GDR state conglomerate who engaged in the practice, common among artisans working for the state, to moonlight. Such unregulated and untaxed activities, openly tolerated by a state that was unable to provide the services for the individual consumer, could bring in as much as half of an artisan's total cash income. While such artisans had no direct access to state-allocated materials, customers were often able to gain access to what they needed through connections, graft, or even outright theft. The tile layer had already made several unsuccessful attempts to open a private business before the Wende but was always rejected ostensibly because the state did not have enough supplies to allocate to new private firms, so, when the Wende came, he was among the first to take the step into independence. He was granted his petition rapidly with the proviso that he complete the formal training required of master craftsmen.

*Modernization, Employment, and Competition*

All four firms had to make major investments to update their equipment and facilities and either had to reduce the workforce inherited from their past incarnation as parts of GDR conglomerates or, in the case of formerly private firms, build a new workforce when the restrictions on employment by private firms were lifted.

For Mr. R.'s firm working capital is more important than investment that was limited largely to the purchase of the office building from the parent firm and its improvement. The workforce of 40 workers in the original section of the chemical factory was reduced to 14 in 1994, increasing slightly since then. At present, the firm is struggling to survive, and finding work for everyone is often difficult.

The N.'s owners of the carpenter shop, were able to modernize and expand their operation thanks to network connections and assistance of Mrs. N.'s brother in western Germany who guaranteed a 100,000 deutsche mark loan before the couple could obtain the government-subsidized credit. Given the deterioration of the eastern Germany's physical plant and the massive inflow of Western capital for reconstruction, the building trades constituted a privileged sector of the economy of the new Länder (federal states), a situation that was deemed likely to continue for some time, as property relations became clarified and as owners acquired the means to invest. The expansion led to an increase in the workforce from 5 to 6 workers in the GDR to 19 by 1993. But the construction boom turned out to be short-lived. By 1999, the building trades in the entire country were hit by a severe recession. Faced with a decrease in demand of some 30 percent, a large number of construction firms in Bernburg had collapsed by 2001. In the case at hand, the workforce had to be cut back to 14 again.

Mr. L.'s attitude toward technology is in diametric opposition to GDR practices and even to those of many modern Eastern entrepreneurs who keep old technology as long as it is serviceable. When he moved to new larger facilities he sold his 2-3-year-old baking oven and replaced it with an even more efficient model, thereby obviating any need to interrupt production even for a few days. The dealer sold the used oven to a client in Poland. His bun-manufacturing equipment produces the buns he needs, a task that used to require the labor of 4-5 persons working 4-5 hours per night with a single person. As a result of his constant upgrades in technology, he has been able to double production without increasing the number of workers in the bakery proper. He has computerized a large part of the accounting and order-processing and is holding off on further modernization and networking only because he expects the bugs in a newly available program to be ironed out in a year or so.

Unlike the N.'s, the baker immediately took a much more aggressive strategy of expanding the workforce. From 3 workers including his wife and himself he expanded his workforce to 20 in 1993 and 40 by 2001.

The tile layer made more modest investments. After the rapid approval of his business plans, it took four or five months to obtain a 30,000 Deutschmark bank loan at the high rate of 12 percent to pay for a transporter and materials, since obtaining one at the government-subsidized low rates available to new businesses would have taken too long to secure. Since this was his first business loan, he kept it as low as possible. He employed up to 10 workers whom he supervised while also running the tile store, but the slump in the construction industry forced him to reduce this number to 6.

The three firms differ considerably in terms of production strategies. Mr. R.'s firm continues to specialize in the field of the manufacture and maintenance of switching units for industries. Although Mr. R. would have the capacity to engage in all forms of electrical work, he decided to shun the extremely crowded field of electrical contracting for private homes.

Major changes in the carpenter's product line resulted from the transition to capitalism. Although the production of windows had always been one of the workshop's specialties, they had switched to the manufacture of furniture because earnings were better in the GDR and quotas were less stringent. The firm switched back to making windows, but introduced the production of plastic frames as a new specialty. Mrs. N.'s brother arranged for the son to spend a month in a firm that manufactured plastic windows whose owner taught him the trade as his contribution to reunification. In addition, the firm also produces wooden doors. Since regulations concerning historic preservation require old buildings to employ wood rather than plastic, they continue to produce them. In recent years the share of such windows in their total production has even increased.

As far as Mr. L.'s line of baked goods is concerned, he believes that he can outcompete his larger competitors by catering to the specific tastes of the clientele of each of his neighborhood stores. He bakes bread with darker or lighter crust depending on the tastes that predominate in a particular store or provides rolls that are larger and lighter or smaller and more dense depending on local demand. After considerable experimentation and research on techniques employed in other European countries, he has succeeded in emulating the denser rolls prevalent in the GDR, even though he has had to replace the old GDR oven that was particularly suited for the purpose with a modern one, for new sanitation regulations required a complete overhaul of the shop where it was located. He has overcome his earlier resistance and has added ovens to all his stores, emulating his fellow bakers who operate on a much larger scale. In addition, taking advantage of the increasing popularity of fast foods in Germany, he now runs a full-scale snack bar in a mall in the center of the city to the standing snack corners he runs in all of his bakery outlets. Even in this seemingly more extraneous venture, he tries to build on the traditional strengths of his métier. He eschews fried and broiled foods, concentrating, instead on dishes he can prepare in the oven such as pasta and potato soufflés and even some meat dishes. His attempts at introducing exotic new items such as brownies have not met with much success. Mr. L.'s entrepreneurial daring has come at a considerable cost. In an earlier article we reported on his initial miscalculations based on blind faith in the advice given to him by Western experts. Later the forced closure of a store in a mall where, unbeknownst to him, the city fathers had prohibited the establishment of small retail stores, to prevent a wholesale exodus from the city center, cost him some 160,000 Deutschmarks ($92,235) in losses and legal expenses. (Since then, possibly thanks to some deal that benefited a particular politician personally, the city has reversed its policy and allowed such retail outlets in suburban malls.) Burned once, he has categorically rejected offers of Walmart to set up a franchise in one of their stores.

Finally, the tile layer has largely resisted the growing trend in the industry to offer a full panoply of services even those in which the firm does not have much expertise, although he too has added some construction services to his offerings. As a result, he has lost a number of contracts, but is proud of the first-rate quality of his work. Like Mr. L., he has suffered severe losses, in this case in the form of bad debts arising from the nonpayment of contracts amounting to 180,000 Deutschmarks ($103,764) in a single year. With the establishment of giant building supply outlets by Western firms, sales have also decreased in his store. Fortunately he can rely on his wife's secure government job to tide the family over the lean years, permitting him to take regular two-week vacations as far away as Tunisia and Mexico.

The nature of the competitive pressures faced by the firms analyzed here, vary markedly. A major factor is certainly the origin of the firms. The engineering firm was the result of attempts to foster employment by furthering new small-scale entrepreneurship. It suffers from the stagnation in industrial construction in the East and from the domino effect that accompanies the system of subcontracting. And, like other small-scale entrepreneurs whose enterprises were spun off from larger GDR firms, particularly those based on expertise rather than on capital, it must now compete with the countless unemployed specialists who lost their jobs after reunification in the breakup of conglomerates with their bloated labor force,[3] so the owners' considerable knowledge and flexibility is undermined by the sheer number of similarly educated competitors competing in an environment of industrial decline.[4]

With the first flurry of building new factories and the remodeling of old ones completed, and the construction industry in a deep depression, Mr. R. of the electronic firm is searching for markets in western Germany. Particularly near the former border, Eastern firms receive preference due to the lower labor costs there. However, the competition is severe, and sometimes contracts barely cover costs. The farther into western Germany he extends his search the better the conditions, both in terms of earnings and in terms of collaboration. Through contacts established by the parent firm of his erstwhile employer and principal client, he has worked as far away as Turkey and Pakistan. However, his expansion beyond the former GDR is still somewhat limited by a paucity of privileged connections. He describes his anxious wait for orders at the phone and hoping for contacts on the job rather than initiating new ones through extensive travel. Clearly, the former isolation of eastern Germany has left its mark on this entrepreneur. A major problem is the lack of working capital and the risks involved in financing larger projects. He has been burned several times by firms who have gone bankrupt, with major outstanding bills, so he prefers to take on labor-intensive projects where he does not have to finance raw materials and is paid as the work progresses.

In contrast, for the artisan firms derived from private and shadow economy GDR firms, competition comes from both local businesses—which were nevertheless limited in number—and from Western firms. In order to attract a local clientele, they were able to rely on existing social networks. They find it crucial to keep their workshop in the city where clients can drop in and even bring things to repair. Unlike Mr. R., they never sought a clientele much beyond the region. While Mr. R.'s initial clientele was restricted to the successor to the erstwhile parent firm, the N.'s in our carpenter example had served a wide local clientele before. On occasion, they continue to work as far away as Berlin, two hours away. Interestingly, though, the old border between the now defunct GDR provinces of Halle and Magdeburg continues to hold and they have never worked in the city of Stassfurt, a mere 15 kilometers (9.3 miles) away. Similarly, L. was able to base his business on his established bakery and had a built-in customer base in the additional outlets he took over from retiring colleagues. Unlike GDR times, continued survival of both artisan firms was nevertheless predicated upon the assiduous courting of old and new clients. As Mrs. N. put it, "We lived more calmly in GDR times. We always had work. We didn't have to worry about that. At the beginning of the year I received a list of jobs to complete during the year, was allocated the material for them and at 3:30 P.M. we could stop working. Well we never ended our workday at 3:30, but we didn't have to curtail our free time the way we have to today. I could go to the sports' arena, something I no longer have time to do." Finally, the tile layer worked with a large builder of new houses and the semipublic organization that manages erstwhile public housing, in addition to individual customers. The fact that his wife has a city job related to housing may have helped in securing some of these contracts.[5]

However, strong local connections insulate well-established firms neither from external competitors, nor from local upstarts. In the case of the carpenter shop, Western competition takes the form of contractors who hire local people or subcontract to individuals without proper credentials who in turn hire unskilled workers, undercutting prices and undermining the former guild system. This process has accelerated with the drop in construction in the past three to four years, leading to bankruptcies and to the attempt of the workers who lost their jobs to eke out a living by working without paying benefits, which amount to up to 30 percent of wages. Construction has moved increasingly from artisanry to mass production. The N.'s believe that the state has made the error of subsidizing the building of standardized houses on cheap land located in the outskirts of cities, rather than the renovation of urban housing stock. Even the local community savings-and-loan association advertises and supports Western contractors of cheap housing who bring everything from the West or build the skeleton that is then finished by the owners themselves. The inevitable repairs of the flimsy buildings are still some ten years away. While the tile layer has benefited from the cheap housing construction programs, he too has suffered from the competition from workers laid off from large construction companies who have struck out on their own hiring workers subsidized by the unemployment office and using old connections to secure a clientele. At least initially, government start-up assistance permits such microfirms to underbid more established ones. The fact that the government presently has become less insistent in upholding laws that require each artisan shop to include the owner or at least one worker to hold a master craftsman certificate has further undercut the already established artisans. In the future, artisans may become subject to even greater competitive pressures, since member countries may be forced to adopt the liberal policies of the EU regarding requirements to establish a trade. This process of fragmentation of firms is reminiscent of processes of informalization all over the world but particularly prevalent in Third World countries, especially during economic recessions (see e.g., Buechler and Buechler 1992a).

In the case of the baker, Western competition is of a more complex nature. The most direct competition comes from an elderly western German baker who expanded his small-scale artisanal bakery into a large empire now including at least four large bakeries in both western and eastern Germany. With eight hundred employees working for the Bernburg plant alone, he is the largest employer in the city. The principle behind this and another similar operation is to adopt economies of scale at the production level but to maintain variety and freshness impossible to achieve through packaged bread. Freshness is assured by delivery in heated trucks to company-owned outlets taken over from the state, from private bakers that went out of business and franchises in malls and supermarkets. This company initiated a trend to deliver frozen half-baked buns to retail stores where they are baked as needed. Most recently the firm also bakes bread loaves in the stores when the outlets run out of supplies of centrally baked breads in the late afternoon. The second type of competition comes from western German firms who have assumed the functions of state bakeries that were taken over by delivering to supermarket chains that control the centralized distribution system in the east. Recently, some of these have established large bread factories along the major throughways in the east. Interestingly, some Eastern firms have also entered this niche including a firm in Leipzig whose majority shareholder is the city itself, thereby replicating the GDR public ownership pattern, albeit at a lower governmental level. Anxious to maintain employment, the city has decided to subsidize this firm, permitting it to undercut prices in spite of the fact that it is losing money. The frozen bread market is expanding rapidly in an otherwise stagnant market. Most recently, the new trend of delivering half-baked buns to retail subsidiaries has accelerated, in some instances extending to other types of bread as well. At least one supermarket chain imports such bread from the Czech Republic, where flour costs one-fourth of the price in Germany, as well as from Poland and Hungary. This type of bread constitutes a more direct threat than the packaged mass-produced bread, since it is baked locally in the stores, thereby assuring freshness. One informant estimated that such supermarket bakeries account for 10 percent of the market and are continuing to gain market share. The bakers face a new major threat from a global actor, Walmart, a company that appears to be expanding at a rapid rate throughout Germany. Walmart has adopted a policy toward franchise outlets that is far less favorable to the baker subcontractors than those of traditional supermarket chains and mall owners. The policy also reduces the franchises' autonomy, for Walmart gathers and handles all receipts. Although bakers have tried to boycott the company, they cannot afford to ignore Walmart's projected dominance of the German retail market. Another looming threat is the move toward self-service bakeries that question the deep-seated notion of bakeries as based on personalized service.[6] One such company intends to set up one hundred outlets in fifty of Germany's largest cities. The company figures a daily clientele of two thousand to make an outlet profitable.

## Conclusion

In conclusion, the identity of these firms derives from their trajectories from their socialist past to the neoliberal social market economy. As indicated earlier, all the larger firms had their origins in the breakup of GDR conglomerates. Two of the firms had pre-Communist roots as family firms or as share-holding companies, a fact that may have contributed to their distinctiveness within their respective conglomerates. One, however, was instituted in GDR times, but had a unique role that contributed to its identity in the past and continues to bolster its self-image. The nature of the firms' relationship to Western partners or parent- companies was both influenced by this past but their present status is also shaped by the relationship. All three were able to strengthen their former autonomy initially, but one has lost it since, when the western German parent firm went bankrupt. Interestingly the electronics firm, although ostensibly autonomous, has not been able to shed its dependence on the successor of the erstwhile factory of which it was a part. In contrast, the three artisans, both the two who were independent before the Wende and the one who based his new business on a combination of expertise learned in state firms and moonlighting operations, have increased their already considerable autonomy during the GDR.

For better or for worse, Westerners were a major influence on all of these firms. The larger firms sought partners or dominant firms to take them over. The smaller businesses used contacts with western German relatives to obtain loans and to gain access to technical skills, worked for newly Western-dominated firms, sought suppliers and customers in the West, and were influenced by Western advisers who alternately mislead and assisted them. All faced western German and international competition, but it affected them in different ways and they sought different solutions. The larger firms and the small electronics firm sought customers in western Germany and beyond, extending as far as Latin America even in the case of a firm whose management was dominated by eastern Germans. Two of the larger firms created dependent subcontractors in Eastern Europe. In a rare instance of role reversal the pharmaceutical firm with eastern management acquired a Western firm to distribute their products in the West. The third became an increasingly dependent unit of a Austrian family enterprise. Firm integration is still largely by telephone, fax, and face-to-face contact but all proudly or somewhat anxiously pointed to incipient computer networking. Electronic networking is also in the process of being adopted by one of the smaller firms in our sample, the baker.

The recession in Germany and the concomitant high unemployment that continues to be much higher in the East than the West and that affects Sachsen-Anhalt disproportionately, weighs on all these firms. All expand and contract and adjust the intensity of work to fit the circumstances. When layoffs become necessary, all follow union directives to lay off workers according to the degree of vulnerability of their families (defined by marital status, number of workers in the household, number and age of dependents, etc). Only the smallest firms are exempted from these directives. The breakup or shrinking of the latter firms has reintroduced the importance of informal firms constituted of individuals working alone or with undocumented workers who work without social security benefits.

All the firms discussed in this chapter share a combination of Schumpeterian and Kirznerian entrepreneurial strategies (see introduction, this volume) but in different aspects of the productive and distributive process and differentially over time. They all had to be smart and creative from their reincarnation after the Wende. In the case of the factories, it was frequently local managers who initiated the search for solutions for their units including management buyout, the search for Western partners, or Western industries that would take them over with some assurance of continuity rather than strategic acquisition for subsequent closure. In this process workers, who were represented in advisory councils and polled when major decisions were made, sometimes were able to prevail over the schizophrenic policies of the Treuhand that ostensibly sought to protect jobs but that was also interested in selling productive units to the highest bidder. Continued survival entailed keeping abreast with new developments and threats. They sought new market niches and acquired new technology to permit them to take advantage of them. But they also employed tried-and-true models from their socialist and presocialist past as well as from standard western German models that their Western advisors suggested. Sadly, none of them engaged extensively in research and development that had formed a major part of GDR government economic strategies (although often for prestige purposes rather than for actual implementation). The flange company does not engage in much research because flanges are very simple devices where innovation can only take place in the productive process and in marketing; the agricultural equipment factory because its erstwhile R&D department that continued to operate until the most recent takeover, was eliminated by the parent firm; and the pharmaceutical factory because it has chosen to develop its patents carried over from the GDR rather than branching into new fields.

Survival of the smaller firms is predicated upon modest lifestyles and extraordinarily long hours, vacations limited to two- or three-day absences, and hard work. The N.'s have no debt, not even a current account. Assisted by an electrician brother, they do all repairs of buildings and of their vacation home themselves. According to one of his colleagues and our own observations, Mr. L.'s survival was predicated on massive self-exploitation. Indeed he and his wife are involved in all aspects of the business, replacing absent workers, distributing wares, and even engaging in intricate repairs of complex machinery. Mr. L. claims that his extraordinary versatility, born of the need for self-sufficiency in GDR times when new equipment was scarce and repairmen hard to come by, is no longer reproduced among the younger workers who are incapable of making even the simplest calculations, even though he only hires workers who achieved good grades in school, and who are not afraid to be electrocuted when asked to unplug a piece of equipment.

Small-scale firms had to show initiative because they had to convince lending agencies of their creditworthiness to start up or modernize their firms. All employed computers in one way or another. They all still engaged in the kind of tinkering they had relied on as a survival strategy in the GDR and lamented the lack of versatility in this respect of younger workers. They also felt that their school education had been more rigorous and deplore the lack of mathematical skills even of apprentices who had earned good grades.

The issue of being actively involved in the labor process may not be as significant a factor at either the level of small- or of medium-scale firms (as it appears to be in other ethnographic examples dealt with in this volume), unless one defines "active" as being knowledgeable about all aspects of a firm's operation. While being able to substitute for any worker in the firm as well as to manage it and to have the capability of providing services that are usually farmed out to outside specialists was clearly one of the secrets of the baker's success, other managers, particularly women, also of very small firms did not engage in physical labor directly (although women *were* involved in many aspects of physical labor in the GDR). We would argue that it is this comprehensive overview of the whole process of production and commercialization that distinguishes managers of medium- and small-scale operations from their larger counterparts.

Achieving that kind of comprehensive overview of the entire business takes time that is one of the reasons why issues of succession including the grooming of successors are a major concern in both small- and medium-scale firms. A retiring head manager of the pharmaceutical firm was replaced by one of the younger partners. The manager of the electronics firm, who has no children, is grooming a younger partner to succeed him as well. The eastern German partner/local manager of the flange company has a son working in one of the firm's subsidiaries, a likely candidate to succeed him. Like elsewhere in Europe, the bakers are having a difficult time finding successors. Children and their spouses often refuse to assume the heavy burden of taking over a business in an occupation with an uncertain future and where the work is particularly hard. The baker couple is young enough not to have to worry about succession yet. Their daughter is studying graphic design for advertising and has no intention of taking over the bakery. Even in these uncertain times, German firms think about the long term and do not concentrate on present-day profitability alone.[7]

In sum, the firms represent combinations of continuity from the pre-Communist and communist past. The past is indeed an indicator of future success, but not in the manner that has often been portrayed. Success under capitalism is not a matter of overcoming the generic mind-set attributed to individuals who grew up under communism. Rather, the specific nature of positions within the two systems and the dynamics of the contacts between them has allowed some groups to prosper and has doomed others to failure or to a prolonged struggle for survival. It is the diversity within even the seemingly most monolithic systems that requires our attention, for it is that diversity that enables both adaptation in the confrontation with new hegemonic systems and to innovation leading to their transformation. In the case of eastern Germany, this diversity has a variety of pre-Communist, Communist, and post-Communist origins. Firm size is but one of many factors and even when it is highly significant, it cannot readily be disassociated from the historical, social, and economic context.

In conclusion, we do not want to underestimate the traumatic aspects of the transformation from communism to capitalism and the pain and stress of reunification of two economies with vastly different strengths. We also recognize the extraordinary recent changes brought about by globalization, not only in eastern Germany but in the entire new nation and in Europe as a whole. But our informants are of two minds about these processes. They are certainly disillusioned by the gap between reality and the glowing promises of Chancellor Helmut Kohl at the time of reunification of a blooming economy within the next ten years. They still fear the unknown but they also recognize the similarities between the past and the present. They often end a conversation with the cliché, "In the West they also only cook with water."

## Notes

1. For a discussion of collectives, see Buechler and Buechler (2002).

2. See Adreas Pickel, *Radical Transitions: The Survival of Entrepreneurship in the GDR.* Boulder: Westview.

3. Some occupations are far more crowded. In the GDR firms frequently trained apprentices that did not cost the firm much to educate. The result was a proliferation of occupations such as electricians.

4. An exception to the predominance of local competition for firms originating from the breakup of conglomerates is the building industry where Western firms with personal connections to Western customers and frequently working with workers hired cheaply from eastern European countries often receive preference over local firms.

5. The firms also relied on personalized connections with suppliers and collaborating firms. Mr. R. worked with a firm established by some of his former coworkers, a relationship that ultimately resulted in a disastrous bad debt. In the case of the N.'s, Mrs. N. had established what she thought was a loyal relationship with a Western lumberyard with an outlet in a nearby city. She was shocked when the supplier closed the outlet without explanation or prior notification other than a note stating that they would supply her from their main office in Bavaria. Her subsequent search for another supplier made her realize that she had been overcharged all along, a rude awakening to the impersonal and self-interested nature of Western business practices.

(6. Personalized service is also predicated on health regulations that require bread to be placed behind plexiglass doors and prohibit their return once removed from the case.

7. See also our discussions of these issues in Buechler and Buechler (1999, 2002).

# 8

# New Firm Formation and Technical Upgrading in the Taiwanese Semiconductor Industry: Is Petty Commodity Production Still Relevant to High-Technology Development?

## *Jinn-yuh Hsu*

## Introduction

Over the past decade, many political scientists, economists, sociologists, anthropologists, and economic geographers have proposed that there has been a resurgence of regional economies (Piore and Sabel 1984; Sabel 1989; Best 1990; Blim 1990; Scott and Storper 1992). They argue that the concentration of interconnected specialist firms in a region constitutes collective strength for global competition. Most of these researchers focus on agglomerations of small- and medium-sized enterprises (SMEs) that specialize in different but related phases of production in an industry. The vertically disintegrated industrial system prevails in Taiwan's IC (Integrated Circuit) sector, one of the most prominent high-technology industries. Taiwan's IC industry is not dominated by a small number of vertically integrated large corporations, but by a great number of small firms that target certain market niches and collaborate under different roofs (Mody and Wheeler 1990; Mathews 1997). One of the advantages accompanying this industrial system is the easy formation of new firms. The system allows new firms to focus on development of new product ideas, without disturbing other phases of the production process. Furthermore, economies of scope, rather than economies of scale, reduce production costs for participating firms. In addition to the static advantage of cost-saving, the integration of interconnected independent firms creates the possibility of mutual adjustment within the system. This allows firms to handle abrupt crises flexibly.

The process of new firm formation and the method of technological learning in Hsinchu are critical for the rethinking of Petty Commodity Production (PCP) in the globalizing knowledge economy, which is characterized by flexible specialization and industrial clustering (Cooke 2002). Firms' competitive advantage in the new competition era comes not from ruthless cost reduction, but from competence in nimble adjustment of production chains. In the new competition, firms' technological capability for innovation is the key weapon (Best 1990). This is particularly the case for high-technology industries. As PCP is usually connected with preindustrial, domestic, and outdated technology, will it still be relevant to the new economy? If it still works, then in what sense and aspects? Is it just a survival strategy for peripheral sectors, such as Taiwanese SMEs, or part of the ingredients of core competence in the high-technology battlefield? How will Taiwan's small high-technology firms survive and prosper in the global competition, which is controlled by key advanced giants? This research will demonstrate that the decentralized industrial system of SMEs in the Hsinchu region builds up complementary connections with Silicon Valley in technology and industry. Through these connections, an overseas Chinese technical community plays the key role in technology transfer. In a sense, the interpersonal relationships and incarnate trust characteristic of the PCP world could serve as channels of ideas, particularly for tacit knowledge, which could not be transferred in printed formats. Moreover, this chapter will demonstrate that the PCP networks can be institutionalized to render technology transfer and starting up easy and constitute the backbone of the formal cross-border technology agreements and licensing.

In the next section, we will elaborate on the industrial structure and its governance mechanisms to flesh out the social dimensions of Taiwanese IC industrial system. Then we will illustrate the strategies Taiwan's IC SMEs adopt to upgrade their technical levels. Among them, the connection with the high-technology hub, Silicon Valley, is particularly critical. We will argue that thick social ties and industry associations are key mechanisms in the cross-border connections. Finally, we will reflect on the role of PCP in the globalizing knowledge economy, and argue for the growth potential of PCP in the modern capitalist world, as the cross-border technical communities between Hsinchu and Silicon Valley demonstrate.

## The Sources of New Firm Formation

Taiwan's IC industry consists overwhelmingly of specialized small- to medium-sized firms. Unlike huge vertically integrated conglomerates, IC firms in Taiwan operate around a finely detailed division of labor. By 1999, Taiwan hosted more than 230 IC firms, including 100 design houses, 5 in mask making, 21 fabrication firms, 42 in packaging, and 33 in testing. Almost all of the important firms, including the top ten design houses, and all of the fabrication and mask-making firms, are located in the Hsinchu-Taipei Corridor (ITRI 2000). The largest one is the Taiwan Semiconductor Manufacturing Corporation (TSMC) whose initial funding, partly from government initiative, was $145M. Its sales revenues reached $1.6 billion in 1998 and $2.4 billion in 1999. By 2000, TSMC employed 14,000 people (including overseas operations).

New IC firm formation has been phenomenal since the HSIP (Hsinchu Science-based Industrial Park) was established in 1980. As just shown, the sources of new firm formation basically came from the local public lab spin-offs and from Silicon Valley returnee start-ups.

### Spin-offs from Public Lab

Recent researches (Liu 1993; Chang, Shih, and Hsu 1994) attribute the success of Taiwan's semiconductor industry to the spin-offs during the different stages of the public lab, ERSO development. Each phase represented the government's successive efforts to upgrade Taiwan's IC manufacturing technological capability. United Microelectronics Corporation (established in 1980) was seen as a successful example of government initiative in international technology transfer. From technology selection to capital formation, plant buildup, and personnel training, ERSO fostered teamwork to incubate the new company. Among these, personnel transfer was the most critical factor in the spin-off process. To enhance UMC's technology absorption capabilities, ERSO directly transferred experienced staff engineers to the new company.

Transferred personnel included the manufacturing supervisor, testing manager, sales manager, quality control manager, and circuit design manager. Almost the entire ERSO pilot plant was transformed into a new venture. The flow of experienced manpower from ERSO to UMC, as well as from other private companies, became a main feature of the local labor market in Taiwan's IC industry. Through the process of job hopping, people and embodied technology traveled and diffused around the industrial circle, and ERSO was often chosen as the starting point. During the second stage of personnel movement from UMC, new IC companies began to proliferate in the HSIP (Figure 8.1). UMC also provided a model of a successful start-up, encouraging ventures in the burgeoning IC business.

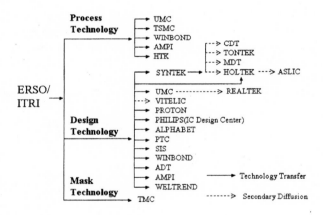

Figure 8.1. The Genealogy of ERSO Spin-offs

In the area of IC design, ERSO also contributed to the establishment of some new design houses. Syntek Design Technology was initiated in 1982 by a former manager of ERSO's IC design department. Based on design technology transferred from RCA, through ERSO channels, Syntek was able to design consumer specific ICs to meet market demand. Other IC design houses in the HSIP such as Holtek Microelectronics, Silicon Integrated Systems, and Weltrend Semiconductor were all founded by people trained in ERSO.

In the process of spin-off, it is the connections between the engineers that lower the barrier to entry of the high-technology business, and different combinations of talented people create the divergent IC specialist firms, and constitute a sound industrial system. The key to the social connections lies in the colleague and classmate relations among high-caliber engineers. In other words, despite recognition that the state leads in the birth of the Taiwanese IC industry, it is the dense networks among the group of engineers that constitute the backbone of the flexible labor market and facilitate new firms capable of racing in high-technology frontiers.

*Silicon Valley Returnees*

Another group of industrial initiatives in the HSIP came from overseas Taiwanese returnees. Most of them came back with plenty of experience and training at midcareer from such companies as IBM, Intel, AT&T, and Hewlett Packard. Once they assembled the required funds, they were capable of recombining their ideas and capital to create their own fortunes.

Miin Wu of MXIC (Macronix International Corporation) and Mr. Alex Au of Mosel-Vitelic exemplified this trend in the semiconductor industry. Wu was a Stanford graduate who had worked in Intel and VLSI (Very Large Scale Integration) Technology for several years before returning to Taiwan. He recruited thirty-eight people from Silicon Valley to join the new company and stressed new product development, rather than simply importing technology. The thirty-eight engineers and their families moved back to Taiwan to start MXIC in 1989. Work experience in Silicon Valley enabled Wu to understand market trends for flash memories, which has proven to be MXIC's major product line. The story of Au is similar. He worked at Fairchild before establishing a design company in Silicon Valley. Afterward he moved the company back to Taiwan to exploit the production capacity there. Mosel-Vitelic was the first local venture in Taiwan that was able to design its own DRAM (Dynamic Random Access Memory).

Nicky Lu of Etron Technology is another example of the returnee entrepreneur. Lu was one of the key designers of IBM's 4- and 16-Mbit DRAMs before he founded Etron in the HSIP, bringing the IBM design team intact from Silicon Valley. Etron then landed a plum contract to design part of the state-funded Submicron project. As well, a number of small independent design houses were established or managed by Silicon Valley returnees, such as the key chipset maker, VIA Technologies, and SRAM

(Static Random Access Memory) maker, ISSI (Integrated Silicon Solution Incorporated). These small firms specialized in market niches that were closely connected to the working experience of the founders. For example, VIA Technologies was transformed from the Symphony Company, a small design house in Silicon Valley previously acquired by Winbond. VIA's president, Wen-chi Chen, worked at Intel before he joined Symphony and then transferred a team back to Taiwan to enter the chipset business. The Formosa Plastics Group was VIA's main financial supporter and the group was also the major founder of FIC (First International Corporation). Thus, it was easy for VIA and FIC to cooperate. Chen's working experience allowed VIA to take advantage of early access to the new CPU (central processing unit) specifications defined by Intel. This helped VIA to design chipsets quickly and accurately matching the demands of the new CPU specs.

As Steve Hsieh, the former director-general of the HSIP, observes, "without these engineers and scientists returning from the United States, the HSIP would be half empty. These are experienced people with advanced knowledge in their fields, and they are very good vehicles for technology transfer. I don't think we could find this caliber of engineers and managers from local companies, at least not yet" (Zhuang, 1996: 201–202).

The waves of new firm formation in Taiwan's IC industry provide the metabolism for the emergent industrial system, and maintain the system's competitiveness on technology frontiers. However, the key to the competitiveness of Taiwan's IC industry comes not from the individual innovative firm itself, but from the collective capabilities of the industrial system of SMEs. In other words, the social division of labor between the IC SMEs, rather than the scale economies of certain firms, constitutes the competitive edge and renders the decentralized system flexible in meeting global challenges. In the next section, we will demonstrate that the social ties that integrate the social division of labor among Taiwanese IC firms basically lie in the interpersonal relations and in the engendered transnational technical communities (Saxenian and Hsu 2001).

## Industrial Organization of Taiwan's IC Sector

*Social Division of Labor*

A finely detailed division of labor exists among Taiwanese IC firms. In addition to a few full-service companies who design as well as fabricate their own brand products,[1] there exist more than two hundred thirty small- to medium-sized independent IC firms specialized in different stages, such as design, mask production, testing, and packaging, in the production process.

Specialization is critical to the growth of Taiwan's decentralized industrial system of high-technology SMEs. Take IC manufacturing as example. Taiwan Semiconductor Manufacturing Corporation (TSMC), the well-performing IC foundry, provides state-of-the-art processing services for domestic as well as foreign IC firms. The establishment of TSMC was an innovative achievement. TSMC was set up to concentrate on manufacturing for other companies, not to compete with them in selling chips. TSMC was conceived as a pure foundry firm, and this idea has proven to be a lucrative one.

According to Morris Chang, the chair of TSMC,

> the concept of a specialized foundry was feasible because of two considerations. First, in comparison with other IC manufacturing companies who own wafer fabrication capacity, we are the preferred partners of many IC firms since we manufacture no product under our own brand name, and thus have no conflict of interest with them. Put simply, the environment for competition with our customers does not exist.[2]

Second, Chang points that "the feasibility of a pure foundry is based on the consideration that the expenditures required to build a new state-of-the-art wafer fab easily exceed one billion dollars. Thus, for small- to medium-sized design houses, the service TSMC provides can eliminate their need to invest in money-consuming facilities, allowing them to focus on quickly getting their product to market."

TSMC provide versatile technologies to satisfy the demands of its different customers. To do this, TSMC modularizes the receipt of each new technology so that it can quickly integrate in different ways, in accord with the requirements of each customer. TSMC also employs a mini-environment manufacturing system (a kind of wafer isolation technology), that allows it to add capacity by setting up a machine next to one that is already in operation. In fact, TSMC was the first major semiconductor company to commit to 100 percent mini-environments in its fabs. Besides the flexible technologies and modular system employed by TSMC, effective integration with patron IC firms requires close communications in the IC manufacturing process. To enhance integrated operations,

TSMC seeks many ways to cooperate with its customers, in addition to standard foundry agreements. For example, TSMC will choose some potentially prosperous IC design houses and provide them with guaranteed foundry capacity and sales. According to Tseng, the CEO of TSMC,

> to help new start-up design companies shorten their product time to market, TSMC is glad to cooperate with them by reserving some foundry capacity for their use. We believe the strength of TSMC does not reside in TSMC itself, but in the growth of the design companies and TSMC together. If a design company possesses growth potential, no matter how small they are now, we'll definitely arrange our capacity for them.[3]

Basically, TSMC's customers can enter the IC production chain at any one of three points in the IC fabrication process. Customers can provide TSMC with masks, database tape, or a netlist, (description of the connectivity of an electronic design) and will receive untested wafers, probed die, or finished, tested and packaged ICs. In other words, customers play the role of both designer and buyer. This leads to a quite intimate relation between TSMC and its customers. To ensure design compatibility and better yields, TSMC and its customers need a seamless transfer of data between them. Frequent meetings and on-site technical support can help to quickly overcome unexpected delays and barriers in the transfer process. "To satisfy our customers, cooperative communication becomes pretty important. More often than not, our R&D staff engineers have to work directly with the designers from our customer companies, maybe in our place, maybe in theirs. Anyway, we have to maintain intimate relations, otherwise, we'll never get things done," Tseng of TSMC added.

Collaborative ties exist not only between the design houses and their fabrication partners, but also between them and their customers. In contrast to big vertically integrated firms, which use their own R&D divisions, high-technology SMEs rely more on their contacts with customers as sources for innovation. Many companies report that they have kept some "critical" customers with whom they frequently meet and exchange information. The concept of "critical" is based primarily on the quick dissemination of new product ideas from the customers to the designers. Sam Lin, the president of Weltrend Semiconductor, a specialized monitor IC design house, illustrated this concept as follows.

> When a new idea emerges, our critical customers discuss it with us first. They are experienced people in the marketing of electronic products, thus they have accumulated a lot of experience and a "market sense" about new product trends. Once they find a profitable product idea, we are the first to be informed, and after intensive communication, we decide together whether to enter the new product line or simply give it up.

### Integration: The Building of a Collective Industrial System

As just illustrated, Taiwan's IC industry takes advantage of flexible specialization by the social division of labor among the small independent firms. However, to depict Taiwan's IC industry as a detailed division of labor is only one side of the full story. Integration of the various stages of work is another part of the mechanisms that get production systems to operate smoothly (Sayer and Walker 1992). Three mechanisms of integration are identified in Taiwan's IC industry:

*Social Ties of Integration.* First of all, the social ties between the owners, engineers, and employees of local companies facilitate formal agreements and informal information exchange within the IC industrial circle. Past experience working together in ERSO or in Silicon Valley provides a foundation for further cooperation. Gorden Gau of Holtek Microelectronics emphasizes the role of ERSO experience in business operations: "Basically we never cooperate with strangers. We will only consider ex-colleagues from ERSO as partners. The cooperation is based on the principle of reciprocity. We provide our foundry service to some of our friends in the design companies, while they come out with some new product designs. Mutual trust prevents the leakage of product secrets." Though such kinds of foundry agreement involve formal contracts, the social fabric between the transacting partners is usually the element that keeps the agreements operable.

Trust lubricates transactions and renders opportunism ineffective (Williamson 1985). Trustworthiness can represent itself in rapid response and accurate quality. Trust-based transactions also occur in relationships between IC designers and their customers. Many design companies reported that their relationships with critical customers lasted for more than five years.[4] Some of these relationships began and continued from the time the design houses started up their business. Often, the supplier-customer relationships could be both professional and personal as they last for a long time enough, and frequent visits become part of the high-technology people's lives. When asked "will face-to-face communication be replaced by other advanced methods of telecommunication like E-mail?" Ching Hu, the president of E-Cmos Corporation, responded:

> You can use email to clear up the technical part of a product development or the written part of a business contract. Email functions quite well in these things. But you can't do business in this way. Without trust, you cannot get things done. To create trust, you have to meet your business partners or customers in person. Only by doing so, you can enhance and revise the mental image of your customers and incubate the feelings of trustworthiness.[5]

In the process of trust breeding, traditional face-to-face communication is believed to enhance trustworthiness, even in the technologically dynamic IC industrial sector.

More importantly, common working experiences lubricate informal, everyday technical cooperation. This kind of cooperation includes the use of friend's equipment, engineering solutions, and even product ideas. The phenomena were mentioned repeatedly by the CEOs of several companies. For example, Ching Hu reported that when he started business, because of the small size of his own company, he went to MXIC (whose president was Hu's buddy in Silicon Valley) to use their workstations to run programs. Nasa Tsai, vice president of Mosel, reports that suggestions from friends are an important ingredient in finding engineering solutions. Sometimes the social network expedites information exchange. When some firm develops a new product or transfers new technology, the information will soon spread throughout the whole HSIP by way of personal contacts. This benefits the IC companies that are challenged by short product cycles. In fact, the informal exchange of information among engineers helps diffuse technology and upgrade the technology level of the IC industry as a whole.

*Integration by Investment.* In addition to the social fabric of integration, cross-investment is another formal means of integration of the various stages of IC production. Investment can be seen as the expansion of ownership and control between different firms. Through partial or whole ownership, some IC firms, particularly the relatively big ones, participate in or control another firm's business. By doing so, they are able to assure smooth operation of the IC production process without risking the rigidity of vertical integration. For example, most of those new packaging and testing companies received a portion of their investment capital from other IC companies. Just to name a few: UMC invests in Caesar and More Power, Winbond invests in Talent and Chantek, and MXIC in Caesar. The new joint investment projects also include a new packaging firm set up by VISC, (Vanguard International Semiconductor Corporation) Winbond and Mosel, a new foundry company is initiated by Syntek (a design house), and SIS (Silicon Integrated Systems) participating in the establishment of VISC. Though these new subsidiaries sometimes serve as subcontractors to buffer high season demand for their parents, they remain independent and do not exclusively subcontract with their parent companies.

The key to cross-investment is the aim to build up partnership between the different stages of the IC production system. Within the process, the role of venture capital in the initiation of new firms, particularly small design houses with specialized product niches, is of growing importance. Some of the venture capital, such as Dr. Ding-hua Hu of Champion Consulting Group, is managed and controlled by IC experts who watch the industry closely. They are involved in business plans, assessing financial requirements, market analysis, management recruitment, and initial public offerings. Venture capital companies have extensive personal networks of investors, qualified engineers, government officials, universities, and public R&D institutes. They are able to play a catalytic role in the mobilization of resources to help new firms.

*The Local Labor Market.* Industrial agglomeration facilitates the formation of local labor markets (Storper and Scott 1993). Local labor pooling, in turn, reinforces the trend toward industrial localization (Krugman 1991). In the case of the HSIP, the agglomeration of high-technology firms draws a swarm of competent engineers into its orbit. Some come from ERSO, some from Silicon Valley. Entry-level engineers come from the neighboring universities and from other colleges in Taiwan, and the HSIP is reported to be one of the most popular working locations for graduating students. Information matching job opportunities and qualified engineers flows easily within the HSIP. According to the president of a design house, "Sometimes a job vacancy appears in the morning, and is filled by the afternoon. You might meet your buddy and neighbor who work across the street, to convince him to hop seats (change jobs)."[6] He continued by describing the relationships between departing employees and his company.

> Even when employees leave our company, they usually transfer to other firms which specialize in the supply of services we require. These services include computer equipment, design tool imports and design subcontracting. We see these departures as an expansion rather than elimination of the strength of our company. Thus, when these ex-employees come back to use our computers for debugging, they are quite welcome.

Technical cooperation proliferates as personal networks spread. More importantly, a repository of specialized industrial skills and capabilities is formed within the social networks in the HSIP. This further attracts investment, and the recruitment of more talented people.

At the same time, experienced engineers move backward and forward among the IC firms in the HSIP. The mobility of middle-level engineers, like production engineers, design engineers, and equipment engineers is quite fluid in the HSIP. The establishment of new firms, above all the design houses, correlates highly with the fluidity of the local labor market (Hsu 1999). The mobility of experienced labor allows small start-up IC firms to recruit key engineering personnel during early phases of growth.

*The Effect of Decentralized Industrial System*

The vertically disintegrated industrial structure benefits each part of the production system by engendering external economies and by enhancing firm proliferation. Moreover, the pattern of vertical disintegration enhances flexibility, enabling the production system to adapt to abrupt crises. The low overheads of the fabless design houses allows them to respond to outside shocks quickly, and to expedite product changes without being dragged down by considerations of fab (fabrication plant) capacity utilization. The responsiveness of the people, emanating from such factors as hands-on management, efficient information flows, and proximity to customers, can give firms a distinct advantage.

Take the incident of Intel's "expansion into the chipset market" in 1994 as an example to illustrate this point. In August 1994, Intel announced it would expand its chipset and mother-board (primary circuit board of a computer) business.[7] Before then, Intel focused on the heart of the PC, the Central Processing Unit (CPU), and left the supporting chipset business to other specialist companies. Among these chipset makers, Taiwan claims three of the world's top five. Intel's invasive action, based on its capability to define new CPU specs and hence those of supporting chipsets, caused a 25 percent sale drop for Taiwan's chipset makers in 1995. The relationship between Intel and Taiwan's chipset design companies has changed dramatically. In the past, Intel would release chipset spec documents to its strategic partners, mostly Taiwan's chipset makers. But now it is no longer open to other companies.

Intel has forced these chipset makers to change their product and management strategies swiftly. VIA Technologies, for example, has chosen to cooperate closely with its customers, particularly First International Computer, one of the largest motherboard companies in Taiwan, to develop chipsets to match BEDO (Burst Extended Data Output) DRAM, and to upgrade the efficiency of the whole system. By doing so, VIA was able to remain competitive in product development without fighting directly with Intel. The incident also pushed VIA into aggressively searching for breakthroughs in system–on-chip design. Accordingly it collaborated with S3 Graphics in Silicon Valley, whose CEO has a collegial relationship with VIAs, to develop the second-generation graphic chip in 1999. Moreover, VIA purchased the CPU department of National Semiconductor to become the third CPU maker, besides Intel and AMD, in early 2000, and posed a serious challenge to Intel's hegemony in CPU business. As a small IC design specialist, VIA responded to the crisis by promptly adjusting its product development, and cooperated with outside competences to enter new fields. Particularly, it took advantage of the transnational connection between Taiwan and Silicon Valley in high-technology industries. In fact, the collaborative relations between Taiwan and Silicon Valley empowered the firms in the two regions to compete in the highly unstable world market. Through the cross-border partnership buildup, Taiwan's

IC firms kept technically upgrading and fostered small start-ups to exploit economic niches.

## The Transnational Collaboration with Silicon Valley

Mutual adjustment and experience sharing of the decentralized industrial system are critical for Taiwan's IC SMEs in order to increase flexibility, but it is also important to keep the system open to outside resources in order to avoid locking in obsolete technologies and maintains its learning momentum (Grabher 1993). In other words, it has to be a localized industrial system within a global industrial network (Amin and Thrift 1992). An open industrial system will continuously upgrade technical levels and develop new products through the establishment of networks. Taiwan's IC industry benefited from the cross-border connection since the initial stage in the 1970s. Taiwan's government launched the IC technology transfer deal with RCA, and further fostered the first local IC firm, UMC (Mathews 1997). From then on, Taiwan's public laboratory and private firms had continuously recruited high-caliber overseas Taiwanese engineers or set up listening posts in Silicon Valley, the most innovative hub of the informatics sectors, to tap into the newly developed industrial technology and management knowledge.

The growing integration of the technical communities in the two regions has created new patterns of cross-regional collaboration (Saxenian and Hsu 2001; Hsu and Saxenian 2000). In some cases, collaboration occurs between the specialized divisions of a single firm. This includes start-ups like Macronix (a Flash Memory IC Maker based in Hsinchu with design center in Silicon Valley) and ISSI (a SRAM maker based in Silicon Valley with manufacturing division in Hsinchu) as well as larger, more established companies like Acer (the largest PC maker headquartered in Taiwan with a division in Silicon Valley). In these cases, the division managers are well connected in the local labor market and technical community and also have close, trust-based working relationships with their colleagues in the main office. This allows them to avoid many of the problems that corporations have when they seek to acquire technology in foreign locations like Silicon Valley. They need to be able to integrate into local social networks to gain access to technology and market information, while simultaneously being able to communicate quickly and effectively with decision makers in the headquarters.

More frequently the cross-regional collaborations involve partnerships between specialist producers at different stages in the supply chain. The relationship between Taiwan-based semiconductor foundries and their Silicon Valley equipment manufacturers is a classic example. Steve Tso, a senior vice president in charge of Manufacturing Technology and Services at TSMC worked at semiconductor equipment vendor Applied Materials in Silicon Valley for many years before returning to Taiwan. He claims that his close personal ties with senior executives at Applied Materials provide TSMC with an invaluable competitive advantage by improving the quality of communication between the technical teams at the two firms, in spite of the distance separating them.

The interactions between TSMC and Applied engineers are continual, according to Tso, and, for the most part, must be face-to-face because the most advanced processes are not yet standardized and many of the manufacturing problems they are confronted with are not clearly defined. Tso reports that he travels to Silicon Valley several times a year, and that teams of TSMC engineers can always be found in the Applied Materials' Silicon Valley facilities for training on the latest generations of manufacturing equipment. Engineers from Applied, likewise, regularly visit TSMC. He argues that this close collaboration helps TSMC develop new process technologies quickly while avoiding the technical problems that frequently arise when introducing new processes. It also keeps them abreast of the latest trends in equipment design.[8]

While Silicon Valley and Hsinchu remain at different levels of development and are differently specialized, the interactions between the two regions are increasingly complementary and mutually beneficial. As long as the United States remains the largest and most sophisticated market for technology products, which seems likely for the foreseeable future, new product definition and leading edge innovation will remain in Silicon Valley. However, Taiwanese IC SMEs continue to enhance their ability to design, modify, and adapt as well as to rapidly commercialize technologies developed elsewhere. As local design and product development capabilities improve, Taiwanese companies are increasingly well positioned to take new product ideas and technologies from Silicon Valley, and to quickly integrate and produce them in volume at relatively low cost.

However, the transnational connection is not governed by a number of big multinational corporations (MNCs). Neither does it exist in a socially neutral environment of market transactions.

Instead, Taiwan's global links with the Californian technology hub unfold in several ways: Taiwan's companies recruit overseas engineers, they set up listening posts in Silicon Valley to tap into the brain power there, or successful overseas engineers return to Taiwan to start up their own businesses. All of these possible links are established smoothly not just on an individualistic base, but with the mediation of overseas organizations, since the experienced engineers such as Steve Tso need to be able to integrate into local social networks to ensure gaining access to technology and market information and to absorb them effectively (cf. Hsing 1997; Hamilton 1996; Kao 1993).

The Hsinchu-Silicon Valley connection suggests that the growth of social and economic ties between individuals and firms in the two regions enhances the performance of *both* Silicon Valley and Hsinchu. The key actors in this story are a transnational community of U.S.-educated Taiwanese engineers who have the language skills and experience to operate fluently in both regions. Their dense social and professional networks foster two-way flows of technology, capital, know-how, and information between the United States and Taiwan, supporting entrepreneurship in both regions while also providing the foundation for formal interregional business relations like consortia, joint-ventures, and partnerships. Just as the social structures and institutions *within* these regions encourage entrepreneurship and learning at the regional level, so the creation of a transnational technical community facilitates collaborations between individuals and producers, particularly the high-technology SMEs, in the two regions and supports a mutually beneficial process of reciprocal industrial upgrading. These interregional relationships support entrepreneurial success in both regions by supporting joint problem-solving and complementary innovation (Sabel 1989). And like the relationships between specialist SMEs and their suppliers in the industrial districts, these interregional networks cannot be understood purely as market transactions or as "commodity chains" linking independent firms in different locations (Gereffi and Korzeniewicz 1994.) Rather, the economic ties are dependent upon a social structure and culture that foster openness and cooperation between producers in geographically distant regions. Close, trust-based relationships among the transnational community of Taiwanese engineers are thus an essential precondition for the flexible collaboration needed to adapt and survive in today's fast-paced competitive environment.

## Petty Commodity Production and Taiwan's High-Technology Industries

Although the scale of operation of Taiwan's IC industry is relatively small in comparison with its Korean or Japanese counterparts, most of the IC design houses and manufacturers are still ventures of millions or billions of dollars, and employ hundreds or thousands of people. In what sense can Taiwanese IC ventures be considered to be PCP? Despite Hill Gates's (1979) observation that the experience of early industrialization in 1960s was in association with the household-based PCP model, it is still not clear if the PCP model could apply to the high-technology sectors, which seems unsuitable in light of level of scale and technology. It seems ridiculous to parallel the fantasy of the IC fabrication facility with the dilapidation of the furnace of the blacksmith. Also it is unambiguous that the high-technology development does not match the confinement of PCP concept, which is usually referred to a domestic mode, tributary, proto-industrial, self-employed, and informal economies (Gates, this volume). Does it mean that the idea of PCP is just outdated, and doomed to be insufficient in explaining high-technology sectors in the knowledge economy? Not necessarily.

Since today's high-technology industries are characterized by their products, markets, and technology being continually redefined and exceptionally short product cycles, the challenge becomes keener for these firms to be able to locate partners quickly and to manage complex business relationships across cultural and linguistic boundaries (Scott and Storper 1992; Castells 1996). In the new environment, flexibility becomes the catchword of the competitive advantage, and cluster of the specialist firms is better positioned in the battlefield to enhance the collective capabilities of adjustment (Best 1990). The key to success in the rapid-changing market lies in the capabilities to identify the right people (know-who), and to accordingly fix the right technologies and products (know-how), as more innovations are human-embodied and team-working (Amendola and Gaffard 1988). Under the circumstances, social ties, such as the overseas Chinese technical communities, enable the small producers to tap innovative expertise and to gain access to manufacturing capabilities and skills across long distances. Even the large corporations, such as TSMC and Applied Materials, take advantage of interpersonal relationships to render technical cooperation and knowledge transfer smooth. Instead of seeing the PCP model as irrelevant to current high-tech development, this chapter asserts that the personalistic relations of production enhanced the adaptability and innovation of the decentralized industrial system of Taiwanese high-technology SMEs.

Nevertheless, one caution should be made here. In spite of arguing against the grain that the PCP model could play a key role in the development of high-technology industries by boosting new firm formation and by promoting technical upgrading, this chapter argues that the effective social ties sector comes from the technical communities, such as classmate and colleague relationships, whose members share the same professional identities in solving technical problems with information exchange, rather than from kinship and other primary relationships, which most PCP studies focus on (cf. Niehoff 1987; Sheih 1992; Ka 1993; A. Smart 1999). The difference matters as kinship-incubated goodwill can render the coordination and allocation of resources between transacting firms easy and economical, but the capabilities needed for industrial upgrading is less likely to be found within the connection. This research implies that Taiwanese high-technology start-ups can be seen as a variant form of PCP because they are driven by knowledge and technology, and therefore the founders and leaders of each firm need to be actively involved in the hands-on technical aspects of the firm's production. Thus, the division between ownership and production is less apparent in even well-capitalized firms, creating similarities with petty capitalism in other contexts.

## Conclusion

Most international business studies take the large multinationals, which possess tremendous technological capabilities and deep pockets, as the central players in the global battlefield (Dicken 1998). Even research concerning late-industrialization in East Asian NICs (Newly Industrializing Countries) focuses on the emerging business groups, such as Korean Chaebol (Amsden 1989). Against the grain, Taiwan's high-technology SMEs in IC industry demonstrate a story of what permits David to defeat Goliath. The keys to the puzzle of overturning the scale disadvantage and leveling the field lies in the developmental state's midwifery, the decentralized industrial networks, and transnational technical connection in the growth of Taiwan's IC industry. We conclude with the following points.

First, although Taiwan's state did foster the IC industry at the initial stage, as its Korean counterpart did (Mathews and Cho 2000), it took different strategies to get the job done. In Korea, the state targeted the *chaebol*, the big industrial giant, to enter the risky industry, with generous banking loans and market protection. Taiwan's developmental state, as just shown, did not choose specific big firms, but provided infrastructures (the ERSO and the HSIP) and subsidies (tax breaks and cheap land), to encourage the formation of spin-offs. In this sense, the state played the role of demonstrator to show private capital the profitability of the seemingly risky business, and lowered the entry barrier for the IC start-ups by subsidies, rather than by playing the role of omnipotent planner as in the Korean case. The divergent strategies led to differing industrial landscapes: while Korean IC industry was dominated by a few key giants like Samsung, Taiwan's IC industry was composed of hundreds of small to medium enterprises (SMEs) who benefited from the demonstration effect.

Second, Taiwan's late-industrializing firms could not only benefit from the institutional embeddedness of the local developmental state, but also from tapping into the transnational connection with the Overseas Chinese technical community. It is well recognized that social and institutional embeddedness exists on the local level (Granovetter 1985; Scott 1988). The story of Taiwan's high-technology SMEs system explores the possibilities of transnational embeddedness in the evolution of the late-industrialization process. Shared language and cultures do help producers, even those located at great distances, gather information about people, capital, and other resources within the community. In other words, such social ties fulfill the need of "know-who" in the learning economy in which the social dimension is the key and often ignored issue in the constitution of competitiveness (Lundvall 1996). In this case, social solidarity derives from common educational and professional experiences among engineers and scientists who have studied and worked together. These professional networks can facilitate economic transactions and managerial and technological learning for the networked industrial system of high-technology SMEs in Taiwan.

Finally, this research also reflects on the literature of the PCP model. It recognizes that the interpersonal ties become more, rather than less, critical in the governance of the disintegrated industrial system and simultaneously remain flexible and competitive in the high-technology industries. From this viewpoint, this chapter argues that the PCP style still contributes to the growth of high-technology industries in Taiwan, through close and transnational networks of people-embodied technology and information flow, and keeps Taiwanese decentralized high-technology industrial system open to the state-of-art technologies and improving on technological frontiers. Despite economies of scale that operate against the PCP, and raise barriers to entry (Harrison 1994), the vertical disintegration of Taiwanese high-technology industries allows the SMEs to cooperate and learn from each other, based on the interpersonal connections that are nurtured by associational embeddedness. As a result, Taiwanese high-technology industries are praised as "the Silicon Valley of the East" (Mathews 1997), and surpass their major late-industrial rival, South Korea, which is noted for the dominance of a small number of conglomerates, the *chaebols* (Levy 1988; Dedrick and Kraemer 1998; Ernst 1998). All in all, in contrast to the modernist expectations, the PCP model is alive and well in the knowledge-based economy.

## Notes

1. Before the mid-1990s, these full-service companies include UMC, HMC, (Hualon Microelectronic Corporation) Winbond, Holtek, Ti-Acer, MXIC, and Mosel. Basically, all of them have their own design departments and in-house fabrication facilities, though they sometimes subcontract a portion of overcapacity fabrication work to other companies. However, UMC became a foundry specialist by spinning off its design department in 1995. The same strategy was adopted by HMC. Moreover, Holtek merged with UMC and turned out to be its fourth foundry fab, and Ti-Acer merged with TSMC. Therefore, only three full-service firms retained their organization figuration as the industry evolved.

2. Morries Chang, interview, October 23, 1995.

3. Fang-Churng Tseng, interview, November 11, 1995.

4. This data agrees with interviews conducted at several design companies in the HSIP. Bear in mind that most of the design houses did not exist until 1988, the year TSMC began operations.

5. Ching Hu, president of E-Cmos Corporation, interview.

6. Ibid., October 13, 1995.

7. The reason behind Intel's vertical integration strategy is not clear. It is generally believed that Intel's intention to expand the sales quanti-

ties of its Pentium CPU caused this action. Because the Pentium CPU needs matching chipsets to work, and because the performance of current chipsets is not able to meet Intel's expectations, Intel decided to internalize chipset making (ERSO 1995)

   8. Steve Tso interview, in Hsinchu, March 15, 1999.

# 9

## Toward a (Proper) Postwar History of Southeast Asian Petty Capitalism: Predation, the State, and Chinese Small Business Capital in Malaysia

### *Donald M. Nonini*

### Introduction

In this chapter, I discuss the relationship between the dynamics of petty capitalism and state formation and class formation in Malaysia over a period of the last forty years from Independence in 1957 up to the present. Although the vast majority of petty capitalist enterprises in Malaysia over this period have been in fact owned and operated by ethnic Chinese (Crouch 1996: 207), I focus on Chinese small-scale capitalism not because it is convenient and efficient to do so statistically, but because the history of petty capitalism since Independence has been inextricably, even definitionally, connected to the making of the collective identity of Chinese as a subject population within more encompassing processes of state formation and class formation. That is, the cultural politics of petty capitalism in Malaysia has been one in which dominant elites whose ideological productions have been central to both class and state formation—however opposed they have otherwise been to one another in their interests and points of view—have until quite recently agreed on an operational set of cultural metaphors: to be "Chinese" has been to be "urban" and to be in "business" of a petty kind. These metaphors constitute a term within a broader

rationality of governance: they form an "as if" imaginary that
structures the relationship between the Malaysian state and a
"Chinese," subject population a relationship of predation or of
tribute-giving. They represent neither a statistically meaningful
empirical category nor a popular idealization. That is, it is far
from true empirically to claim that over the last two decades all
persons "in business" have been "urban" and "Chinese," far from
it, for an increasing number of persons owning, operating, or
employed in small businesses in the cities and towns of Malaysia
would define themselves as belonging to another ethnic group, as
emphatically *not* Chinese but as "Malays" or *bumiputeras* (indigenes),[1] who have entered "business" under state sponsorship.[2]
Nor is it the case that there is an hegemonic view that people
called "Chinese" *should* be "in business" and live and work in
cities and towns. But what has been the case is that by the early
1970s the elite discourse and policies of the government's New
Economic Policy (NEP) sought to employ state intervention to
transform the political economy of Malaysia toward the objective
of creating a Malay bourgeoisie, and that the NEP assumed the
reality of this set of metaphors—that to be Chinese was to live in
cities or towns and to be "in business," that is, wealthy—all in
comparison to *bumiputeras* who lived in rural villages, *kampong*,
were not "in business" and not wealthy—and that this undesirable state was to be the object of transformation.

What I want to argue is that Chinese petty capitalists became
the unspoken antagonistic "Other" against whom the Malaysian
state defined the target population—"Malays and other indigenous
people" on whose behalf its "development" projects existed. For
instance, the *Midterm Review of the Third Malaysia Plan 1976-
1980*, listed among the populations affected by "rural poverty" the
following—"rubber smallholders," "*padi* (rice) farmers," "fisher-
men," "coconut smallholders," "estate workers," and "residents of
New Villages"(Government of Malaysia 1979:30-35). In the *Mid-
term Review*, the sections on rural poverty dealing with these
groups celebrated the government massive "development" projects
of the state targeting these rural populations that were implicitly
ethnicized as Malay. Unlike other rural residents, New Village
residents, the vast majority of whom were persons of Chinese
descent (Sandhu 1964) made their appearance as an anomalous
group who really were "urban," for "the overall growth and performance of urban industries affect the income position of the [New
Village] residents" (Government of Malaysia 1979:33). What lay

behind this official usage was the violent, unspoken of prehistory of the years of the Malayan "Emergency" (1948-1960) when, as one element of the British colonial government's counterinsurgency campaign against the Malayan Communist Party, almost five hundred thousand persons of Chinese descent were forcibly urbanized (i.e., "resettled") into so-called New Villages settlements (Harper 1999). Most New Villages, particularly those sited near larger towns or cities, had through settlement and population growth in the intervening years in fact become geographically urban. Yet, once made urban in this way, their residents—even the minority in "rural poverty" in New Villages in specific regions (e.g., central Perak state) were treated, as the passage from the *Mid-term Review* suggests, as if they were essentially "urban" in a more essential sense: they belonged to an ethnic group cast as urban, in business, and wealthy, for they served within NEP development discourse as the foil to the envisioned ethnic community of impoverished rural Malays. This was the case despite the empirical existence of a sizable Chinese urban proletariat in late colonial Malaya (Simoniya 1961), and despite the fact that the vast majority of Chinese "in business" owned and operated only small-scale family-based enterprises—hence petty. These enterprises, whose ethnocultural provenance was publicly proclaimed by their "shophouse" architecture, Chinese-language signs, and makeshift altars to Tiangong (God of Heaven) sited by their frontage "five-foot ways," whose owners stood for an unruly and "alien" opposition to the indigenizing state, were a distinctive feature of the central business districts of Malaysian cities and towns in the 1970s and '80s. In these downtown districts, Chinese shophouses and their residents, epitomized by the *towkay* (businessman) dressed in his garb of singlets, shorts, and sandals, presiding over his shop's accumulation of wares, stood near the modernist office buildings of the European-, Japanese-, Chinese-, and increasingly state-owned large-scale corporations and banks with their male managers and clerks dressed in Western coats and ties. Although the scale of economic activity of the latter dwarfed the aggregate output of this multitude of small shophouse enterprises, the sheer visible presence of the latter stood as a symbol to state bureaucrats and to Malays of an alien population that "dominated the economy."

Indeed, the urban petty capitalist sector so conceived became the target of displacement in state policies. Elsewhere in the *Mid-Term Review*, the NEP's second major goal (in addition to the "eradication of poverty") was fully set out as being "to remove the identification of race with economic function." As part of that effort, "the Government has assisted an increasing number of Malays and other indigenous people in their various business ventures and enterprises to promote their full participation in commerce and industry" (Government of Malaysia 1979:50). The movement of "Malays and other indigenous people" into "the modern commercial and industrial sectors" associated with urban economic activities" would moreover be "strengthened by the development of new towns and regional growth centres" (Government of Malaysia 1979:54). In effect, new towns could lead to new, modern, prosperous, people. In retrospect, this can fairly be read as a development effort on behalf of "indigenous people" aimed at displacing and supplanting the commercial position of Chinese who were urban, "in business," and wealthy. Since the inception of the NEP in 1971, these metaphors have become widely accepted by the population, even as they have increasingly come to depart from reality with the rise of a Malay middle class, the "new Malays," or Melayu bharu, into prominence. Thus a prevailing Malaysian urbanism coded petty capitalist enterprises as signifying the presence of Chinese in business, living in cities and towns, as wealthy, politically salient (and some Malays might add as "vulgar," *kasar*) a spatio-cultural coding that Chinese themselves came to believe in, and take advantage of, in their political maneuverings vis-à-vis the state (Nonini 1998). How this prevalent coding came to be closely connected to the processes of state formation by way of a predatory relationship between the Chinese petty capitalist sector and the state is one of the subjects of this chapter.

With this proviso, in this chapter I draw on an ethnographic history based on several years' residence in urban Malaysia, to set out several specific propositions about the close connection between the petty capitalist sector, so imagined, and class and state formation in West Malaysia.[3] My approach is avowedly historical, and seeks to trace the transformations in the petty capitalist sector brought about by its relationship both to the formation of the Malaysian postcolonial state and to formation of classes in postcolonial Malaysia, particularly as these transformations bear on its social reproduction. I take it that "petty capital" is a dynamic concept: it does not refer only to the small amount of capital accumulated by an enterprise's owners vis-à-vis other enterprises, but also, and more broadly to the necessarily limited accumulation of capital as means of social reproduction for an expanding population situated within a certain prevailing set of market and property relations.

In Malaysia, the petty capitalist sector has been organized by legal, political, and economic processes that situate productive and other assets of small enterprises under the day-to-day control of individuals who are members of families, and more specifically under the control of older adults, especially males, in these families. Such an empirical description may belie a more dynamic process of change. Let me give an example of the petty capitalist population I know best from my ethnography, who resided in a market town in Seberang Prai, in Penang state. From a commercial census of all businesses within the city's boundaries that I conducted in 1979, I discovered that Chinese individuals and families owned 1,116 business establishments or 88% of the total 1,268 surveyed.[4] For 1,242 establishments for which I had complete data, the average number of owning family members (*jialiren*) who worked in an establishment was 2.3 while the average number of employees (*wairen*) was 3.5 (but the median number of employees was zero)—indicating the widespread use of family labor and the absence or low use of hired employees in most establishments. At the high end, only about 5% of these businesses employed more than 17 employees, and the most employees hired by any business—a truck transport company—was 150 (Nonini 1983).[5] It was necessary to carefully differentiate the majority of petty capitalist enterprises who depended either more on family labor or on approximately equal proportions of family and employee labor from the relatively small number whose large numbers of employees fit Marx's classic definition of a capitalist enterprise, in terms of being enterprises dependent on the appropriation of surplus value from a class of hired proletarians who possessed no other productive property than their own labor power. As feminist analyses have pointed out, Karl Marx's failure to consider the ways in which the unpaid labor of women within a family of business owners contributed toward capital accumulation on behalf of the males of the family is a serious failing of the classical formulation (Gibson-Graham 1996:206-237).[6] In any event, although I have not been able to engage in a more recent restudy of the business establishments of the same city area, I suspect that the use of a large complement of unpaid family labor by most small enterprises still holds, although the labor of large numbers of foreign female laborers now substitutes for that of many daughters and wives among those working for the small enterprise, as I show in the next section.

I seek to advance the following claims. First, petty capitalist enterprises and more broadly the petty capitalist sector have been shaped by the processes of predation by state officials and their clients upon this sector defined within official discourse as a "Chinese" population, processes that have been fundamental to Malaysian state formation since Independence in 1957. This characterization persisted, as I have noted, from the 1960s onward, despite the fact that government policies have led over time to an increasing number of *bumiputeras* establishing and operating urban businesses through public state and UMNO (United Malays National Organization) (ruling party) patronage. The governing rationalities that have driven these processes are oriented toward Chinese as an urban, wealthy, business population that has strategically been placed in a envisioned *disadvantaged* relationship to capitalist markets vis-à-vis another population, specifically, Malays or *bumiputeras*. The array of state rationalities that apply differentially to different populations taken ensemble has been referred to as "governmentality" (Foucault 1991). Specifically, state governmentality has worked to channel the petty capitalist population to act in ways that tend to proliferate a large number of small-scale, family-based enterprises, which have competed arduously with one another, and have been subordinated through channels for goods traded and for credit to the large-scale corporate sector, which is itself partially directly controlled by state officials and political leaders. Over the same period, governmentality has had the effects of simultaneously ethnicizing and personalizing the state as it has presented itself to members of the petty capitalist sector.

Second, I show that in addition to predation on the petty capitalist sector, state-governing logics have provided *bumiputeras* as a population with the technological innovations associated with the large-scale "modern" corporate sector. At the same time, these logics have channeled the activities of the petty capitalist sector toward the ethnodevelopmentalist goals of the state while impeding or prohibiting outright the adoption of innovations by the sector.

Third, I discuss how state rationalities have limited the social reproduction of the petty capitalist sector, in particular, by constraining the choices represented as the horns of a dilemma that its members face. The dilemma is that the petty capitalist sector through demographic reproduction produces a far greater population than its own resources for capital accumulation can provide for: some must opt out of petty capitalism, or be attrited out. If we leave aside either the infrequent instances of business failure that leaves children without family wealth and cause them to fall into the working class, or the even rarer situations of upward mobility where an entrepreneur successfully establishes large-scale enterprises that can accommodate an expanding family labor force, the most common response to this dilemma is to opt out "laterally." That is, families in the petty capitalist population press excess younger members to engage in a process of intensified bourgeois self-fashioning via professionalization to seek the university degrees and certifications that will allow them to participate in relatively privileged professional labor markets. Yet Malaysian state logics until recently have impeded or denied outright their opportunities to engage in such self-fashioning within Malaysia itself; and have led them and their families to opt out (emigrate) from Malaysia. Chinese emigration abroad to seek education and certification as professionals, and to find professional employment, however, has become a social fact whose recognition must now be dealt with in state policies, as I suggest in the following section.

Fourth, I suggest that the national repositioning of Malaysia vis-à-vis the processes of globalization, particularly through its rationalities toward transnational labor migrants, has allowed transformations toward more "modern" gender and generation relations to take place within the petty capitalist sector. Specifically, the surplus labor extracted from foreign migrant women employed in the petty capitalist sector has increasingly come to substitute for that previously provided by younger women (and men) belonging to owning families who have moved out and away from the ambit of small enterprises and their fathers to acquire university degrees and professional certification.

I conclude by pointing to several ironies that have ensued affected these foregoing processes as Malaysia has encountered globalization. One of these is that over the last three decades, as the Malaysian state has successfully brought about the growth of the domestic large-scale corporate sector that has provided both employment and ownership for the *Melayu bharu*, state-connected predation of petty capitalist enterprises has become increasingly exhausted as a development strategy: small businesses are no longer where the action is at; there is relatively less action to be found there given the increased number of tribute-takers. Another is that the association between Malaysian governmentality and state practices of predation on the petty capitalist sector that over the past two decades drove many Chinese property owners to emigrate abroad with their capital (Crouch 1996:208), now encounters neoliberal globalization, whose ideological premises and institutional mechanisms of power now constrain the Malaysian state to seek to attract back Chinese petty capitalists (with their "scarce global capital") which it had previously alienated by predation. A third, and parallel irony is that the privatization of state-owned corporations, associated not only with the self-aggrandizement of the Malay political elite but also with neoliberal discourses about efficiencies arising from a market-oriented logics of profitability, has led these corporations to seek to attract professionals both domestically and from abroad; including highly educated Malaysian Chinese professionals whose parents belonged to the stigmatized petty capitalist sector.

Moreover, as another manifestation of Malaysia's engagement with neoliberal globalization, the valorization of hi-tech scientific knowledge central to the state's vision of Malaysia as a "knowledge-based society" or (K society) has led to a proliferation of private colleges and academies that now compete with state universities, and that attract large numbers of younger Chinese from the petty capitalist sector who are training precisely to enter the large-scale corporate sector on putatively meritocratic terms; on the basis not of *kulit-fication* (one's skin, *kulit*, as criterion) but of "qualification," as one of my informants punned it. This new apotheosis of the technocrat or professional with "Chinese" characteristics is beginning to lead to a reversal of valorization of Chineseness from negative to positive as this figure has come to be viewed as the quintessential Malaysian, particularly vis-à-vis large numbers of illegal transnational migrants who now work in the "unskilled" sectors of the Malaysian labor force.

## State Governmentality and Alternative Accounts of the Malaysian Petty Capitalist Sector

A fruitful investigation of petty capitalism in Malaysia and elsewhere in Southeast Asia must pay attention to the historical specificities of both class formation and state formation in the region. It is widely understood that the capitalist East and Southeast Asian nation-states, characterized as "Asian Newly Industrialized Economies" ("Asian NICs"), "Asian Tigers," or "Asian Dragons" have since the 1960s shown a rapid growth of large middle classes associated with export-oriented industrialization. Thus, for instance, Richard Robison and David Goodman in the introduction to their edited book, *The New Rich in Asia* write of "the dramatic emergence in East and Southeast Asia of a new middle class and a new bourgeoisie" (1996:1). This process is amply evident in the case of Malaysia (Kahn 1996). Thus any theoretical account of petty capitalism in Malaysia, as elsewhere in capitalist Southeast Asia, must be situated within the larger historical processes that have created large middle-class populations residing in urban centers who have, one way or another, come to identify themselves as "modern." In addition, what is perhaps less well appreciated, given the current hegemony of "market populism" in the West (Frank 2000), is that the formation of the middle classes and changes in petty capitalism have both taken place through the active mediation of, and guidance over, markets by the states of Southeast Asia; not through an autonomous or natural evolution of disembedded "markets."

To adopt the argument that shifts in petty capitalism in Malaysia (and more broadly in the Asia Pacific) must be conceptualized in relationship to both state and class formation is, of course, not theoretically innocent. Within recent theorizations, it can be set against two other positions. One is the claim that "we" now "live in a post-Fordist world," or under conditions of "flexible accumulation." This is put forward as a world-historical shift that has taken place within the history of capitalism (see, e.g., Harvey 1989). Since I have dealt critically with this position elsewhere (Nonini and Ong 1997), I will say little except that it is inappropriately evolutionist and universalizing, limited by its economism, and is simply empirically false for Malaysia and elsewhere in Southeast Asia (see Nonini and Ong 1997). The post-World War II Malaysian political economy shows the coexistence of both Fordist (mass-production) and flexible elements in ensembles organized largely by state practices and family politics—for instance, Japanese- and state- owned factories connected to domestic subcontractors and to family-based "putting out" arrangements. A second theoretical position, which abandons any pretense of theory or history, particularizes petty capitalism in the Asia Pacific *as* "Chinese" in its essential practices—the operation of networking based on *guanxi* "(connection)," or trust between individuals created by a shared culture, the use of *xinyong* or "credit," the role of Chinese entrepreneurs as "middlemen" bridging Western businesses and indigenous Asian consumers, and their status as "pariah capitalists" who can adroitly carry out transactions with indigenes that indigenes themselves cannot engage in. This position has been prominent in functionalist explanations whose major purpose has been to correlate one or more of these cultural attributes with business "success" or "failure," and that can be distilled into dispensable nostrums in business schools and business journalism circles (Nonini and Ong 1997; Thrift 1999). But these "essential" features of Chinese petty capitalism are not explanations of its dynamics, but precisely what need to be explained by a theoretical account: in short, explanations derived from them beg the question. What is needed instead are historical accounts of class and state formation in Southeast Asia that explain how these attributes of an ethnic group came to be associated with the everyday practices of petty capitalism within the region.

Instead of recourse to evolutionist and economistic schemes focused on a supposed universal post-Fordism, on one hand, or to essential cultural particularities that themselves require accounting for, I would argue instead that transformations of petty capital in Malaysia have been intrinsically connected to the projects of liberal "governmentality" of the Malaysian state (Foucault 1991; Ong 1999). By a project of governmentality, following Michael Foucault, I mean the deployment of state "biopower" or rationalities that differentially discipline and regulate variegated populations who make up citizen-subjects in ways that align them with market institutions and forces. Over the last forty years, the governing rationalities toward specific populations on which I focus have been part of the formation of the "repressive developmentalist" state in Malaysia, as elsewhere in Southeast Asia (Feith 1982; Tanter 1982). Aihwa Ong (1999) has identified several different populations in Malaysia subject to varying rationalities of state regulation and control—*bumiputeras* or indigenes, aborigines (*orang asli*), European and Asian foreign investors, and various non-*bumiputera* populations, including urban Chinese and rural Indian plantation workers, and foreign immigrant workers. Invoking Foucault's notion of "pastoral governmentality" Ong (1999) emphasizes those governing rationalities that guide the *bumiputera* population toward economic and political positions associated with rational entrepreneurship, market competencies, and attainment of economic wealth, particularly vis-à-vis non-*bumiputeras*. These rationalities of pastoral "care" have been inscribed in the mandated, massive affirmative-action policies and programs that have provided *bumiputeras* with preferential access to accumulated capital, opportunities for investment, employment, and contracts and university education, among other social valuables (Faaland, Parkinson, and Saniman 1990). In contrast, foreign investors have been a population lured by government inducements associated with a "welcoming business climate"—not only by a variety of tax and infrastructure dispensations, but also by provision of large numbers of young *bumiputera* women to serve as an available and abundant labor force located at or near the factory door. According to Ong (1999), these populations have been guided, lured, and induced, by the "caring" logics of "pastoral governmentality." At the same time, however, other populations have been targeted with the full force of disciplinary and coercive powers—non-*bumiputera* workers, aborigines, and one population Ong says little about, petty capitalists.

Within the context of the last four decades, these governing rationalities have emerged as part of a more inclusive process of Malaysian state formation—one in which the *bumiputera* political elite that inherited the state at the end of the British colonial period (1957) has deployed its political power vis-à-vis non-*bumiputeras* and foreign investors to aggrandize its economic base. In this sense, the deployment by state officials of rationalities toward specific populations to bring them into varying relationships to markets and market forces, the amplification of technologies of surveillance, discipline, and incentives associated with expanding state institutions, and the formation of a new class of Malay capitalists, or *Melayu bharu*, have been intimately interconnected.

Viewed in this light, the history of Chinese petty capitalism has over the last forty years centered on evolving increasingly routinized predatory or tributary relations between a multiplicity of state agents and a subject population of Chinese petty capitalists. The importance of these tributary relations as formative political processes sui generis has been largely neglected in the scholarly literature, which tends to be highly economistic, and to regard the giving of tribute as a deviation, an error, a negative. Both Western observers and Asian victims have converged on a certain representation of these tributary relations as "corruption." On one side, Western (and some Asian) discourses depict these relations between business and Asian governments as discouraging enterprise innovation, increasing the cost of doing business (especially for Westerners), and discouraging foreign investment. The analyses of institutional economists have reframed this failure as one of "rent-seeking" bureaucrats interfering in the natural operation of efficient markets—occasionally with good results for "development," but far more often than not with negative consequences

(Khan and Jomo 2000). International economists and business journalists have dwelled on the low comparative rankings of Southeast Asian nation-states in the global contests these organizations promote regarding the degree of "transparency" of government services provided international investors (see Transparency International 2002). On the other hand, my informants, small-scale businesspeople in urban Malaysia, often spoke of their transactions with government officials and employees in terms of the ethnic discrimination and political coercion directed against one group by another; both of whom were equally citizens.

The convergence, such as it is, is largely superficial, for it arises from quite disparate and even conflicting sources. On one hand, Western neoliberal economists, corporate spokespersons, and business pundits used transnational discourses about "transparency" and which national economy had it and which did not (see, e.g., Transparency International 2002) to smooth the insertion of U.S. and European investment capital into the rapidly growing economies of Southeast Asia. On the other hand, the discourses of Southeast Asian citizens about the "corruption" of the state had more to do with its antidemocratic tendencies than with inefficiencies or the high transaction costs of doing business. While I am deeply sympathetic to the complaints of abuse by my Malaysian informants who sought equality of treatment, honesty, and accountability in their relationships with state officials, it is crucial here to examine the underlying regularities that connected the state to illegal behavior by its officials: tributary relations between government functionaries and Chinese petty capitalists— "corruption" in a word—were not separate from, but rather incorporated into, the disciplining rationalities of state governmentality (Heyman and Smart 1999; A. Smart 1999). These rationalities have constructed within broad limits many of the specific features of Chinese petty capitalist production and exchange, and the social relations in which these are situated. Any history of petty capitalism in Malaysia must incorporate at its core the shifts in these rationalities of governmentality that have made Chinese petty capitalists into governable, nominally pliant, if at times elusive, citizen-subjects. This is the first point I wish to substantiate in this chapter by examining the relationship between state techniques of regulation aimed at petty capitalists that keep them both "petty" and "Chinese" while marginalizing them and extracting surplus capital from them for the economic and cultural aggrandizement of *bumiputera* beneficiaries of "care."

## "Corruption," "Rent-seeking"—or Governmentality?

In August 1985, I interviewed a man then working as a hawker selling fried fish in a nearby public market on the fringes of the town of Bukit Mertajam in Penang state. Ang, as I shall call him, had for several years before owned and driven his own small truck, but in 1984 went bankrupt. In that business he drove sundry goods between Bukit Mertajam and Georgetown, and back, delivering them at multiple stops in the city of Georgetown. The entire trip, as the crow flies, was about thirty miles. In meticulous detail, and with great bitterness, he gave me an accounting of his expenses for a round trip, which—despite its short distance—required a full day's work:

> My highest costs were the police, who always wanted coffee money. Leaving Bukit Mertajam, by the time I arrived at Prai, I would have encountered at least one police roadblock, and the policemen would not be satisfied by less than 4-5 ringgit. (1 ringgit = US $.39.) At the wharf, before entering the ferry, my truck would have to be weighed, and if it was overloaded, I would have to pay money to the scales attendant, which would come to perhaps 6 ringgit. On the ferry, the attendant who directed me to park demanded $.20. Once I got off the ferry in Penang, there would be another roadblock outside the ferry building. This one would have 4 to 6 policemen, each of whom wanted a sum of money. I would pay between 20 and 25 ringgit to them, which they would divide up among themselves. In Georgetown, I often had to double-park and each time I did so other policemen would threaten me with a summons if I didn't pay coffee money, so each one I might pay one ringgit.... And on the way back I might be stopped by a police roadblock between Butterworth and Bukit Mertajam, and would then have to pay yet more coffee money.... I would earn a total of 110 ringgit in transport charges for the day, but might spend up to 40 to 50 ringgit in coffee money per trip.

Such a narrative was in no way remarkable—in fact what marked it was its sheer quotidianness, both in the sense of its repetitive everydayness for this man, and the great frequency with which stories like it were told me by the small businessmen whom

I interviewed in 1985, and earlier during my first stay in Bukit Mertajam from 1978 to 1980. Whether a truck transporter like Ang, or a vegetable wholesaler ("Baba") who provided an illicit rent to a Malay partner ("Ali") for the use of the latter's government permit to operate his business; or a shopkeeper downtown speaking of monthly visits by a police constable seeking "coffee money," or a wealthy supermarket owner providing his "friend" the OCPD (officer in charge of police district) with a fat "red packet," *angpow*, on Chinese New Year Day; or a man attempting to have electricity extended to his cold storage room and having to pay money "under the table" to installers from the government-owned electrical utility, as for innumerable other Chinese petty capitalists, such transactions were the essence of the ordinary. What varied instead was the extent to which these transactions (or better put, exactions) actually affected the viability of a business—Ang claimed with great bitterness that they had driven him out of truck transport— or merely became a source of recurrent, predictable inconvenience for those who, with greater financial resources than Ang, appeared resigned to treating them as one of the inevitable costs of doing business if one were Chinese in Malaysia.

In fact, such exactions and the pervasive tributary relations that underlay them were actually much more. These exactions were called corruption (*tanwu*) by my informants, and whether rich or only middling in income, informants referred to them as harassment—accompanied by implicit or explicit threats of force—something negative that detracted from the processes of their doing business and accumulating capital. My informants made it quite clear that these exactions were intrinsically connected to the fact that they were Chinese, that the exacters were Malay, and that the latter were acting as the instruments of the state, and of the UMNO Party that ruled it. Viewing these exchanges not as arbitrary or capricious events but as the manifestation of tributary relations at the heart of state governmentality, it is worth following up these insights of my informants. If it is taken as evident that examples of corruption such as that described by Ang could be indefinitely multiplied, what then are the net effects of such tributary exchanges taking place between a very large number of persons on either side—that of those persons directly or indirectly connected to the state and that of petty capitalists? And what larger social and political order underlies these exchanges, which makes them positive and culturally formative for the petty capitalist sector rather than constraining and diminishing it, as more often argued? Let me point to the following characteristics connected to tributary or predatory relations between petty capitalists and state officials that have been crucial to creating a distinctive governmentality toward Chinese petty capitalist families as a population.

First, the varieties of everyday predation by direct and indirect agents of the state on small businesses were so prevalent a feature of life "doing business," *zuo shengyi*, in the petty capitalist sector, that it is an illusion not to see the workings of such predation and the market-oriented behavior of the petty capitalist populations of urban Malaysia as intrinsically and even necessarily connected to each other. Indeed, from the point of view of many *bumiputeras*, the practices of extracting "coffee money," demanding fees for the uses of licenses, and so forth, by state agents were not predatory, but rather facilitative, placing the *bumiputera* with state connections and the Chinese *towkay* (business proprietor) in a relationship of "mutual help," or *tolong menolong*, in which one party prospered only if the other did. What was surprising was that, despite extensive complaints by Chinese like Ang, many others conceded that such relationships did, when all is said and done, allow them to "get by," *guo shenghuo*; after all, *bumiputera* clients made business possible, were at times customers themselves, and served as intermediaries who introduced *towkays* to other government officials, who could facilitate new business deals. What was, of course, being traversed in the differential response by Chinese to these exactions was their movement within the shifting class hierarchy of Malaysian society; for instance, in Ang's situation, he was in effect driven back into the working class from which his parents came through predations by police and by others on his small truck transport business; but in other cases other more felicitous outcomes for small businesses proved possible. From the perspective of a class analysis, the cumulative effect of these practices of extracting money through a multitude of such dyadic ties has been a net transfer of surplus capital to the new members of the state-connected *bumiputera* middle class, the *Melayu bharu*, and to petty state officials and police.

The operation of a shadow economy grounded in everyday tributary relations, however, has had a certain underlying logic; namely that the more capital held by the business in question; and by the family owning it, the more eager have been state agents to extract capital from it, and among more powerful *bumiputeras*, more closely connected to higher levels of the state bureaucracies, state police, and the governing UMNO party, the greater the tendency to seek a significant share of the profits of the business through forceful methods. The net effect of the shadow economy has therefore been to constrain the families owning businesses to depress the visible size of petty capitalist enterprises, that is, to appear to be "poor," to "just get by."

Above a certain level of capitalization, in addition to the everyday forms of predation, the differential monitoring by government ministries of large versus small enterprises with respect to their ethnic ownership, as guided by the Industrial Coordination Act (ICA) of 1975, encouraged Chinese proprietors to aspire to form smaller and dispersed enterprises rather than larger and concentrated ones. Chinese businessmen repeatedly mentioned to me that smaller enterprises remained largely beneath the notice of regulatory officials, whereas the owners of larger enterprises found themselves the object of unwelcome attention by the Ministry of Industry in its extended efforts to secure increased *bumiputera* equity in Malaysian businesses. The ICA thus served as the foundational document for tributary relations between the state and the petty capitalist sector. It stipulated that if a private industrial enterprise had a capitalization of more than $100,000 *ringgit*, and employed more than 25 employees, it was required to sell no less than 30 percent of its equity to *bumiputera* partners, and that, moreover, the capital required to purchase this equity was to come out of profits from the firm after its actual acquisition by *bumiputera* shareholders (Crouch 1996: 207).[7] Chinese proprietors repeatedly told me that the ICA and the monitoring that accompanied it discouraged the growth of their enterprises by increasing the probability that the larger they became, the more their businesses would be seen by government ministries as an appropriate target for "takeover." Indeed, some of the most bitter claims about the discriminatory ethnic character of "their government" made to me were those of Chinese *towkays* who themselves felt coerced into finding *bumiputera* partners to whom they had been required to sell equity under the ICA, or who knew others who had experienced such coercion.

But there is another way to look at the tributary relations formalized by the ICA. The constant surveillance by *bumiputeras* working as state agents encouraged business proprietors to remain small, or, putting it more accurately, to continue to appear to remain small by growing through dispersion—by incorporating multiple businesses, in different lines of trade, often in more than one city or town. Such businesses, although they had shareholders in common, were separately registered with the government, and appeared vis-à-vis the state as independent entities. This was quite clear, for example, in the proliferation of limited liability companies held by owning families and duly registered, as separate entities, with the Malaysian Registrar of Companies (see Nonini 1983).

Was it always, however, only a matter of appearance? Dispersion was not by any means always nominal—a means of hiding the actual size and operating scale of an enterprise. It was one means by which proprietors diversified and sought to reduce risk by setting out to accumulate capital in different lines of business subject to varying market conditions. A textile-retailing firm owned by a family might founder, while its small-scale housing project could flourish. Given the prevailing discourse of "filial compliance," or *xiao*, moreover, dispersion provided different family members, especially adult sons, with their own separate spheres of business to specialize in, although the different legal businesses were usually effectively managed by their father—the man who established them. While one son worked selling fertilizers in one family-owned business, another sold vegetables wholesale in another. One son managed one branch of a business, say, that of a truck transport firm; another branch, incorporated in another city, under another name, was managed by a daughter and her husband; while the majority shareholder and effective proprietor of both firms was their father. Such divisions of labor among grown sons (and daughters and their husbands) might be one of the only means for preventing or lessening conflict and quarrels between potential heirs that appeared to be an endemic feature in the succession processes associated with petty capitalist enterprises. For instance, Ng, about seventy years old when I interviewed him, was the proprietor of a truck transport company with twenty trucks that hauled sundry cargo between Bukit Mertajam and Johore Bharu and Singapore to the south. His eldest son managed the Johore Bharu branch of the company, while also acting as a partner in another truck transport company headquartered in Bukit Mertajam. His second son, with whom he had fallen out because of his son's previous mismanagement of the company's money, had left to start his own transport company near the town. His third son worked for him at the Singapore branch of the company, dealing with consigners and freight for the return trips to the north. The strategic significance of such a division of labor between a father, grown brothers (and/or sisters and their husbands) within the operation of a business depended, of course, on bourgeois Chinese male subjectivities grounded in Malaysian (and before it British) common law, that is, on the legally validated practices of Malaysian patriarchy and heteronormativity, a subject I cannot go into here (see Freedman 1950; Hooker 2002).

Second, tributary relations between Chinese business families and the petty government officials, police, and employees of state-owned enterprises had the simultaneous effect of ethnicizing and personalizing the state. As my informants observed, such relations existed as dyadic ties between very large numbers of Malays—the petty officials, state employees, and police officers and very large numbers of owners and operators of Chinese petty enterprises. One might note, for instance, that in this form, when regularized, as many such relationships were (e.g., the police officer who dropped by for his monthly tip), they represented one of the few situations in which individual Malays and Chinese had an opportunity to interact with each other, rather than as members of ethnic-based sodalities (political parties, educational, or religious associations) whose interests were generally predefined as opposed. The Malay Ali who owned a business license rented out by a Chinese might become a problem-solver, a "fixer" with state officials, for the Chinese Baba he paired with. These dyadic personalistic ties often developed as the basis for comity, and in some instances, even friendship. Malay friends were invited to the weddings of Chinese, and vice versa, for instance. At the same time, petty capitalists imaginatively transformed their experiences of repeated exactions of tribute by their state-sponsored Malay patrons (e.g., the Malay Ali with the license) and by their petty Malay clients (this telephone lineman, that police constable) into encounters with the state as such. These exactions were rationalized, Chinese knew, by a hostile indigenist narrative in which Malays were cast into unjust poverty by greedy Chinese. It was, as Chinese petty capitalists put it, "*their* government," *tamen de zhengfu*, which so many complained about to me.

Moreover, there were two other effects of a state rationality that exacted tribute all the way down the line, while encouraging Chinese petty enterprises to remain small and dispersed. First, the dispersion of petty capitalist enterprises by virtue of the effects of the shadow economy implied an absolute statistical increase in the number of petty enterprises in the same line of business. I was surprised, for instance, by comments such as the following made by the executive secretary of the North Malaysia Lorry Commercial Association, the regional organization of truck transport company owners, that "in recent years the government has given out many truck permits to any bumiputeras who applied for them. Thus there are now many more trucks in this area than there were previously, since permits are so easy to acquire." The proliferation of Chinese small trucking firms, often each consisting of no more than an individual owner who drove his own truck, was made possible through the mediation of the Ali-Baba relationship , one in which the increased glut of permits granted to *bumiputeras* by the government (often as forms of political patronage) facilitated the establishment of large numbers of new, very small, transport companies owned by Chinese.[8] Similar Ali-Baba arrangements applied in other lines of business than truck transport.

This in turn generated what my informants characterized as intense competition between a large number of marginal small-scale enterprises, each vying with others for the credit and patronage of large-scale enterprises. This depressed the costs of production of commodities for corporate industries, and enhanced the profit margins of the latter. In the case of truck transport, for instance, a large industrial enterprise such as Mitsubishi or Malayan Sugar simply played off one small-scale Chinese-owned truck transport company against another for the lowest transport charges in carrying its freight. Irrespective of the actual instrumentalities involved, since these large-scale enterprises were themselves in part either directly state-owned, held for Malays by state-controlled trusts (Majlis Amanah Rakyat, or People's Trust Council) or had wealthy Malay shareholders serving as directors along with Chinese *towkays*, this was one mode for transferring surplus capital from the petty capitalist sector to *Melayu bharu*.

A second effect of state-induced dispersion was precisely the process of subcontracting, about which so much has been written in other contexts as one central element of "flexible accumulation" (Harvey 1989). In fact, flexibility has not been a novel discovery in Malaysia arriving with a period of supposed "post-Fordism," but rather one connected closely over three decades to the tributary relationship between the expanding Malaysian state and the small-scale petty enterprise sector. Rather than acquire greater visibility to state agents by extending the scale of operation of their enterprises as they grew beyond their core activities, many petty capitalists instead subcontracted out value-added operations in the production chain to other enterprises legally distinct from them. For instance, long-distance truck transport proprietors, who owned fleets of large trucks, rather than also buy small trucks for local delivery, instead contracted out with owner-drivers of such smaller vehicles to deliver their long-distance freight for them, and in return gave the latter a cut of their transport charges received from a faraway consigner (Nonini 2003). The proliferation of new small-scale operators made possible as just noted by the increase in the number of permits and licenses provided to *bumiputeras* also meant there were many new business owners willing to step into such subcontracting relationships with larger enterprises, ones whose owners were themselves unwilling or unable to expand the scale of their businesses.

I should add that state-sanctioned predation was by no means the only aspect of governmentality that constrained enterprises in the petty capitalist sector to remain small, stimulated fierce competition among them, and promoted subcontracting, but it was by far the most important. To it should also be added the state's commitment to leaving capitalist growth relatively unregulated in certain crucial respects—manifested, for instance, by laws and policies that allowed new small businesses to be easily set up and for debtors to able to escape their creditors and start businesses anew (usually by leaving the area), and by laws from the colonial period that prohibited Chinese from owning land in many rural areas deemed "Malay Reservation lands" and thus pushed them into business rather than into agriculture. There was also an overall state orientation that promoted export-oriented industrialization—there was, after all, a *liberal* governmentality that sought to bring about new relationships between populations and capitalist markets. Thus, for instance, the location of nearby factories in export-processing zones in Butterworth and Penang Island meant that many small businesses in Bukit Mertajam profited by operating as industrial subcontractors, packagers, assemblers, and transporters that served these factories. As UMNO officials and their supporters put it when pressed about state policies and practices that discriminated against Chinese, "if the pie is growing due to overall economic growth, then the fact that the part of it controlled by non-*bumiputeras* is shrinking in relative terms won't matter that much."

## Limits to Accumulation: Governing Rationalities of Displacement and Prohibition

A broad set of governing rationalities with respect to different populations of citizen-subjects implied that to offer "care"—economic sustenance and opportunity—to a population of *bumiputeras* implied its denial to another population, the petty capitalist sector defined simultaneously as "urban," "wealthy," and "Chinese." If "caring" was defined as seeking to bring the *bumiputera* population into a rational entrepreneurial relationship with expanding labor, land, and capital markets associated with export-oriented industrialization, obversely it required placing prohibitions on the petty capitalist sector in precisely those areas associated with the "modern." Let me give an example.

From the late 1970s onward, with government assistance, *bumiputera* elites sought to successfully enter the truck transport industry, which had previously been a "Chinese" one, and sought in particular to compete with Chinese carriers along major routes that connected the urban industrial zones to the major cities and towns of the peninsula. The new trucking businesses were capital-intensive joint corporate ventures between prominent *bumiputera* individuals with state connections (with, e.g., family ties to federal cabinet members or UMNO leaders) and semistatutory state agencies such as MARA. Lori Malaysia Transport was one such venture. Purchasing a large fleet of more than one hundred large-capacity trucks, from the mid-1970s through the 1980s Lori Malaysia sought to win over large consigners, such as foreign-owned factories, away from Chinese-owned small- and medium-scale transport companies such as those located in the town of Bukit Mertajam. With managers who had little, if any, business experience in the transport industry, with high fixed costs and a prevailing situation of overcapacity in the industry, Lori Malaysia was unable to successfully dislodge these smaller carriers whose owners in contrast had extensive experience in the industry, long-standing ties with factory managers, wholesale distributors, and shopkeepers, and ran with lower operating costs. After operating for several years with state subsidies while incurring very extensive losses, Lori Malaysia went out of business.

By the mid-1980s, the state's failure to guide *bumiputeras* toward successful competitive status vis-à-vis the small-scale truck transport sector led state officials to initiate new state practices and policies that effectively changed the rules of the market under which the truck transport industry operated. These focused on "modernizing" transport technologies for the large-scale corporate sector, but either kept these away from, or prohibited them altogether from, the petty capitalist sector. For instance, in the late 1970s the Malaysian government allowed a Thai corporation to carry fish in refrigerated, locked, and bonded trailers directly from southern Thailand to Singapore. Such trucks were allowed to pass without inspection through Malaysian Customs; a great time-saver. This had an adverse impact on Bukit Mertajam transport companies that carried fresh fish packed in crates on ice from southern Thailand to Singapore, yet it proved impossible for the owners of these companies to obtain similar cooperation from Malaysian Customs. Ironically, and yet a fact lending support to my argument that state officials had come to define the petty capitalist sector in Malaysia as "Chinese" and by extension as "urban" and "wealthy," was that the Thai corporation operating the refrigerated and bonded trucks was a joint venture between the Thai government and a large conglomerate owned by a prominent Chinese family; however, being Thai, *their* Chinese status had little relevance.

In addition to impeding the petty capitalist transport sector as in the example just given, the Malaysian state also simply prohibited it from adopting modern innovations. This was the situation in the case of the standard-sized "containers" that could be moved directly and interchangeably from ships to rails to trucks, an innovation that appeared in Malaysia in the early 1980s. In August 1991, I interviewed Lim, whose trucks operated out of Bukit Mertajam on routes to Kuantan and to other cities and towns in the eastern state of Pahang.

> DMN: On Kulim Road and elsewhere I've seen trucks carrying "containers." Do any of these belong to the local transport industry?

> Lim: In the case of these detachable containers, only Malay companies are allowed to do this kind of transport. The large company in Butterworth that has the right to do this is called Bumiputera. Throughout the country, there are only five companies with an exclusive right to carry containerized cargo—two in Penang, two in Klang, and one in Johore Bharu. Thus large-scale factories now pack containers with their goods, call on the trucks of these companies to carry them to ships at port such as at the Butterworth wharves, where the containers are then transferred to ships. There is indeed discrimination against the Chinese because we are not allowed to carry such containers. Indeed, aren't I, who was born in Malaysia, as much a bumiputera as any Malay? The government has allowed racial ideas to influence its policies.

What is crucial to note from this bitter statement by Lim and similar exchanges is that the small-scale transport industry did not stand outside the legal and political relations stipulated by Malaysian pastoral governmentality, but instead was, as in the effects of the shadow economy and tribute-taking, the *product* of the state and class formation process shaped by this governmentality. Its enterprises remained small, dispersed in power, and "backward" in relationship to the rapidly expanding state-supported large corporate sector increasingly organized of, by, and for *Melayu bharu*.

## Intensified Bourgeois Self-fashioning versus State Logics of Exclusion: Going Global

It is ironic that the social reproduction of the middle-class position among the members of those families forming the petty capitalist sector takes place only when a very large proportion of persons who initially belonged to it, have left it. While the possibilities for increased capital accumulation and business expansion have been limited by the state rationalities of predation just described, it is also true that the number of male and female grown children who have been potential heirs to the family businesses founded by their parents has far exceeded the capacity of these businesses to support them.[9] Economic and thus social reproduction within the petty capitalist sector has therefore been precarious and insecure. As a result, most of the heirs to family enterprises—grown children—have left them for other means of livelihood; while in each family one or two of a sibling set (most frequently the eldest son) have remained to continue the family enterprise. By far the most common strategy for successful class reproduction has been the provision of subsidies by family enterprises to the grown children of the family to pursue the university degrees and certificates required to enter professional work. The biographies of their sons and daughters have repeatedly shown that these experiences of intensified bourgeois self-fashioning—the making of professional selves and identities, in which they have sought the educational capital (embodied in advanced degrees and certificates) that connote the source for new economic capital accumulation; as computer engineers, biochemists, corporate managers, accountants, physicians, architects, and the like. Moreover, as they have pursued higher degrees and certification in Malaysia and abroad intensified bourgeois self-fashioning over the last three decades has become a process oriented toward professional labor markets whose scale is not national, within Malaysia, but increasingly pan-Asian or even global.

Malaysian governmentality, as should now be clear, has encompassed not only the petty capitalist sector as such, but also the "urban" Chinese population to which this sector stands in a metaphoric relationship. Thus the technologies of state governmentality center on generating specific social and economic conditions for the cultural reproduction of both *bumiputeras* and Chinese.[10] Since 1970 the Malaysian state has adopted various practices that limit and channel access by young Chinese adults from the petty capitalist sector precisely to the universities within Malaysia that provide degrees and certification. Crucial state regulation of Chinese as a population has taken place through the disciplining associated with control over education and access to it. To those familiar with political controversy in Malaysia, it is no surprise that for three decades after Independence in 1957 a recurring flashpoint in conflicts between Chinese political parties and organizations and the Malaysian state has been issues centered on control of primary, secondary, and university educational institutions for the Chinese population (Tan 1992). From the early 1970s onward through the 1980s, ethnic quotas for entry to Malaysian universities that favored *bumiputeras* over non-*bumiputeras* were set by the Ministry of Education: no more than about 30 percent of all positions for incoming first-year university students were reserved for non-*bumiputeras*. This had the effect of disqualifying a large number of academically highly qualified Chinese applicants (most of them from urban areas well endowed with educational resources) from entry, who were passed over in favor of less well-prepared *bumiputeras*. One mechanism that was widely resented among Chinese by which Chinese applicants were excluded was the comprehensive national battery of examinations administered at the end of the Form 5 year of secondary school that included in addition to exams in math, biology, physics, and other academic subjects, exams in Bahasa Malaysia; the national language.[11] During the late 1970s and through the 1980s, very large numbers of Chinese youths failed or barely passed the Bahasa Malaysia tests, often despite extraordinarily high scores in other subjects, and on this ground were excluded from admission to Malaysian universities.

Outrage among Chinese was universal. This was understandable. Whereas the wealth generated by petty capitalist enterprise provided the economic means crucial to pay the expenses of a university education, and an extensive set of factors among Chinese secondary school students pushed them toward high academic achievement in terms of examination scores, particularly in mathematics and the physical sciences, such strategies were only viable for a large proportion of families in the petty capitalist sector if positions of entry to Malaysian universities were available to qualified applicants. But this was precisely what Malaysian government policy sought to frustrate through its ethnic quotas, which Chinese almost universally deemed to be completely unbalanced, and thus "unfair." It is not surprising therefore that my informants perceived a close connection between these quotas and what they deemed to be a biased grading of Form 5 Bahasa Malaysia exam scripts by government examiners, which they claimed led many Chinese students to fail the examination and served as pretext for denying them admission to Malaysian universities.

Despite considerable protest and political organizing among political leaders and community associations. as in the campaign led by the Dongjiaozong[12] in the 1970s to organize a privately operated Chinese-funded university, Merdeka University, these efforts proved ineffective in political and legal confrontations with the unified leadership of UMNO. As a response, Chinese petty capitalist-owning families turned to a strategy of "traversal" in which grown sons and daughters were sent overseas for university education and certificates either to Anglophone countries (Australia, Canada, the U.S., Singapore, and to a lesser extent Great Britain and India), where they enrolled in second-tier institutions, or to Taiwan, if they were among the "Chinese-educated" products of the independent schools system (Nonini 1997). To give relevant figures: whereas in 1970 Chinese students formed 52% of total enrollments in Malaysian universities and *bumiputeras* only 41% by 1985 Chinese made up only 26% of enrollments while *bumiputeras* constituted 67%. Connected to this, reflecting the trend since 1970, in 1985 the proportion of Chinese university students being educated overseas was almost 60% whereas only 20% of *bumiputera* students were enrolled in universities outside of Malaysia (calculated from Munro-Kua 1996: table A6). Many educational migrants after graduating overseas sought successfully during the deep recession of the mid- to late-1980s, to remain overseas by finding professional employment and seeking permanent resident visas abroad, while, for many, by serving as conduits for family capital expatriated to their new countries of residence as part of a broader effort at family relocation. The interviews with middle-aged *towkays* in Bukit Mertajam I recorded from the mid-1980s through the mid-1990s were replete with descriptions of their grown sons and daughters seeking university degrees in science, business, and the professions in the United States, Australia, New Zealand, Britain, Singapore, India, and Taiwan, and of the professional employment overseas they sought subsequently. In its strategies of reproduction, the petty capitalist sector had already begun to "go global" by the mid-1980s.

## The "Modernization" of Gender Relations and New Sources of Surplus Value

In 1979, I interviewed an attorney in Bukit Mertajam whose clientele were the small business families in the town, and asked him about the status of women when it came to inheriting the property owned by the families. "Women," he said,

> are still not given equal shares with men in inheritance, but the situation varies from family to family depending on the desires of the older man holding property. But the female children are usually given something, a smaller share, or money. If a family has many daughters and only one son, then the daughters will undoubtedly get something. If there are only daughters, they will get quite a lot, but if there are many sons then the chances are they will receive little.

Several years later, when I interviewed *towkays* and professionals in Bukit Mertajam from 1985 through the early 1990s about their hopes for their children, they frequently asked me what I thought about "weighing males over females"; *zhongnan-qingnu*—assuming (correctly) that they knew what my response as a "liberal American" would be, and then go on to inform me that although "the older generation" had practiced this, they themselves were determined not to do so. In particular, they said "our generation" were committed to educating their daughters in universities as well as their sons; even though they would go on to qualify their visions for daughters by pressing them to train for gender-typed occupations like nursing, teaching, or accountancy, while they expected their sons to seek degrees in medicine, computer science, engineering, and business management. The intensified bourgeois self-fashioning that I just discussed does in fact appear to apply both to young women as well as to men. Women have left their natal families after graduation from secondary schools to enter universities in Malaysia and, as noted, increasingly overseas; I have many examples of the daughters of small business families being sent to Singapore, Taiwan, Australia, and even to the United States, Canada, and Great Britain for university degrees, rather than allowing themselves to be pressed to work for the family business, to find employment immediately after secondary school graduation, or to immediately begin seeking a husband locally.

This evidence from anecdotes suggests to me that one aspect of class formation in the petty bourgeois sector in Malaysia that deserves further attention is the modernization of women's occupations, as Chinese petty capitalist families have become increasingly exposed to media examples (e.g., from women's magazines, TV sitcoms from Hong Kong, or serials from the U.S.) regarding the appropriate occupations for young, "modern," middle-class women. How this complex process of culture change has taken place in Malaysia and elsewhere in Southeast Asia is beyond the scope of this chapter (see Sen and Stivens 1998). Here I want to point to only one aspect of this process, one that is vital because it is central to the accumulation process within the petty capitalist sector from which so many middle-class Chinese women in Malaysia come; how is it that the unremunerated or undercompensated labor provided previously by unmarried daughters, who have more recently gone on directly from secondary schools to university educations, has been replaced?

I want to propose, not as an established fact, but as an hypothesis subject to further investigation that young women's university educations and the overthrow or at least moderation of *zhongnanqingnu* (weighing males over females) within the petty capitalist sector in the period from the 1970s to the mid-1990s have been made possible by the substitution of the unskilled labor of daughters by that of female immigrants within the labor process present within small businesses in Malaysia. In the course of my field research in the Penang region during the 1990s, I repeatedly noted the presence of young immigrant women, particularly Indonesians, working in the small businesses I visited; as maids, cooks, ven-

dors, cleaners, waitresses, nannies, seamstresses, laundry workers, and in many similar kinds of labor that previously were performed by either unmarried daughters of the owning family, or by
other Chinese women. Although my observations have not been
systematic, they are consistent with evidence given elsewhere for
the very extensive presence of unskilled female immigrant laborers working in homes and businesses in urban Malaysia (see, e.g.,
Chin 1998).

A second and related claim is that state rationalities toward
migrant labor have, in effect, underwritten this cryptic, because
infrequently acknowledged, component of the accumulation
process in the petty capitalist sector. From the mid-1970s through
the 1980s, Malaysian immigration authorities allowed a large
influx of Indonesian and Filipino immigrants to enter West
Malaysia to labor in the highly undesirable work in the rural plantation economy; 100,000 estimated in 1979. By 1983, it was estimated that there were between 300,000 and 600,000 Indonesian
labor migrants in Malaysia; the vast majority there illegally (Chin
1998:65–66). During the late 1980s and into the 1990s, large numbers of illegal migrants—Indonesians, Bangladeshis, and Pakistanis—entered to reside and work in urban Malaysia in the
construction industry, factories, domestic work, and in the petty
capitalist sector. It is from the more recent migration of
Indonesians to urban areas (where very large numbers of migrants
are women, unlike the case of Bangladeshis or Pakistanis), that
the women whose labor now supplants that of daughters and
wives appears to be drawn.

One argument made by non-*bumiputeras* over the past two
decades in the semipublic debates in Malaysia over its immigration "problem" is that the Malaysian government, and its
Immigration Department more specifically, have been complicit in
allowing illegal migration by Indonesians because they would
easily be taken for, and would sooner or later *become, bumiputera*
in a process of swamping non-*bumiputeras*: "non-Malay objections
to the large-scale and uncontrolled presence of Indonesian migrant
workers were based less on economic reasons . . . but more on their
fears that the Indonesians, being Muslims and culturally almost
identical to the Malays, would in fact stay as immigrants and
numerically increase the Malay population number" (Dorall
1989:299–300). This allegation appears valid; state policies with
respect to immigrant laboring populations appeared to favor large
numbers of Indonesians entry into Malaysia and its labor markets,

while in the process guiding such migrants toward a status of sub-*bumiputera*, or one of being *bumiputera*-candidates. In official eyes, on one hand, they were Muslims, spoke languages similar to *bahasa Malaysia*, and shared many features of *adat* (custom) with *bumiputeras*; on the other hand, the divide between citizen and noncitizen positions them within state logics to work in these unskilled labor markets and provide surplus labor to the larger capitalist accumulation process, but in positions implying a dependent lower status vis-à-vis non-*bumiputeras* (as maids, servants, cooks, etc.) which few *bumiputera* citizens would accept today due to alternative economic opportunities made available to them through state-sponsored programs that have come to embody "care." In short, within Malaysian state rationality, Indonesian migrants have come to form an ideal population of "outside" insiders toward whom a provisional and discreet surveillance has been combined with a pastoral care extended to them; a care with an edge to it. This was made manifest during the Asian financial crisis as the Malaysian economy went into free fall in 1997, in a demonstration lesson few Indonesian migrants could ignore when large numbers were imprisoned, harassed, or tortured by police, and then deported back to Indonesia (Far Eastern Economic Review 1998); a signal to Indonesians residing illegally of their ambiguous status.

## Ironies of Globalization

As Malaysia has globalized over the last twenty years, and the irreversible changes associated with the New Economic Policy (1971-1990) and the New Development Policy that followed, have occurred, certain ironies have become apparent. In effect, Malaysian governmentality has represented such a successful project that it now calls its own seamless hegemony among a very large number of Malaysians, both *bumiputera* and non-*bumiputera*, into question. It makes little sense to continue tributary relations between state agents and families in the petty capitalist sector when the latter have become increasingly less relevant to the trajectory of national economic life, and capture an increasingly smaller proportion of the national wealth. Instead, export-oriented industries located in the large-scale, corporate economy, with a very large state-owned sector, are clearly where the action is. Predation by state officials and police on the petty capitalist sector no longer, as it were, suffices to sustain the predators, who must turn to other sources, or expire. When they turn to the new sources of wealth among *bumiputera* small businesses, whose owners, managers, and professionals belong to the *Melayu bharu*, then the Malaysian state is engaged in political self-cannibalization. Under these conditions, the ideological underpinnings of state governmentality—one of pastoral care for *bumiputera*—come under great strain. This might explain in part the deep concerns many middle-class Malays now express about "corruption" and account for why so many have supported the reforms associated with Anwar Ibrihim and become increasingly critical of what they see as the sclerotic Mahathir administration (Loh 2002).

Another irony has to do with the ways in which globalization, particularly the new triumph of neoliberalism in postcrisis Southeast Asia, has rewritten national narratives about Malaysia's place within "global markets" for outside capital and technical expertise. Malaysian government officials, for instance, have recently made concessions to Chinese political parties (especially the Malaysian Chinese Association) over issues of culture and education. In part this is because so little is now at stake, unlike the past, since *bumiputera* cultural hegemony is now assured, unlike thirty years earlier. This is also because of the sense that Malaysia needs to attract back for domestic investment much of the capital and talent that were expatriated by Chinese in Malaysian as they went "global" by relocating abroad from the 1980s onward in response to pressures from state surveillance and predation;[13]after all, the "exit option" (Hirschman 1970) was the only one that state governmentality could not adequately contend with.

A similar irony has occurred with respect to the higher-education process that was central to Chinese bourgeois self-fashioning, as Chinese Malaysians went global (Nonini 1997). By the mid-1980s large corporations in the financial, trading, utilities, and industrial sectors, which previously had been taken over by state-owned statutory enterprises (e.g., MARA) began to be privatized. This reflected the state's dire need for revenue given the region-wide recession that had devastated its export markets; it was in conformance with newly influential neoliberal discourses promoted by the World Bank, the International Monetary Fund (IMF) and other Western think tank and financial institutions, and provided Malay state officials, bureaucrats, and aristocrats—the trustees of *bumiputera* wealth up to that point—with the valuable national corporate equity from which their own fortunes could be made (on the last point see Crouch 1996:208). Privatization exercises involving even the national monopolies such as Telekoms (the national telephone utility) and Tenaga Nasional (the national electricity utility) were fully underway (Crouch 1996). One outcome of privatization was, as elsewhere in the world where it has been instituted, the widespread retrenchment of staff hired during the period of state ownership but now considered redundant in operations viewed as burdened by state-induced "inefficiency." Many of those retrenched were Malays previously hired preferentially through state policies. As Malaysia moved out of the recession of the 1980s and recommenced rapid economic growth, new market-oriented hiring criteria favored highly educated Chinese managers, technocrats, and professionals. This reversal was by no means a smooth one, being bitterly opposed by certain factions of UMNO leaders and their followers, but they were in a minority. The 1990s, therefore, witnessed a paradoxical "reverse brain drain" as the highly educated and certified sons and daughters from families in the petty commodity sector returned from abroad to find corporate employment in Malaysia. By the 1990s, petty capitalist families sought to incorporate the possibility of return after university study and certification abroad into their strategies of reproduction.

By the 1990s, moreover, the frequent strategy of Chinese families sending their grown sons and daughters overseas for university degrees began to be no longer necessary due a second globalizing measure undertaken by the Malaysian state in the face of neoliberal hegemony. This was the partial privatization of tertiary education as part of a broader campaign aimed at creating the new high-tech K society required for Malaysia's ascent to "developed status" by 2020 in the state's "Vision 2020," Wawasan 2020. In contrast to the unsuccessful attempt to establish the private, Chinese-controlled Merdeka University in the 1970s, from 1996 onward, the Private Higher Educational Institutions Act allowed the establishment of privately funded universities and colleges whose curricula were to a much greater extent than previously less strictly monitored by the Education Ministry in terms of cultural and language content. Privately funded colleges and academies, formed as profit-making corporations, began to be established by Chinese entrepreneurs in large numbers throughout urban Malaysia. Many of these became partners in "twinning arrangements" set up with Australian and with other foreign universities, in which Malaysian students spent their first two or

three years of university study in local colleges with curricula certified by these foreign universities, then went overseas for foreign
study only in their final year, but at the end received a degree
from the foreign university (Loh 2002). Malaysian state discourse
emphasized the pressing need of the country to develop its "high-
tech" professional population in the face of "global competition,"
while the new twinning arrangements were justified as preventing
capital in the form of tuition or fees from leaving Malaysia as foreign exchange. While privately funded universities and colleges
became increasingly popular among *bumiputeras*, including segments of the *Melayu bharu*, over this period, the vast majority of
students they have attracted have come from Chinese families of
the petty capitalist sector.

This brings me to the greatest irony. The imposition by
global forces of neoliberal-inflected discourses and practices upon
the Malaysian state—indexed by the increased prevalence of
terms such as privatization, market-orientation, and knowledge
society in state laws and documents—represent new pressures
toward a neoliberal governmentality that sits uneasily with a
prior one of pastoral care. Francis K.-W. Loh writes of this transition as one in which Malaysian politics has shifted from a "discourse of ethnicism" to a "discourse of developmentalism"
associated with economic liberalization, mass consumerism, and
a new emphasis on individual self-fulfillment over obligations to
social groups (2002). At a point of tension between the old and
new forms of governmentality, there is emerging a novel market-
defined conception of Malaysian nationality—one where subject-
citizens, irrespective of their ethnicity, are defined as "true
Malaysians" due to their capacity and willingness to contribute
as entrepreneurs toward Malaysia's progress toward the "developed" status of Vision 2020 vis-à-vis other nation-states within
Southeast Asia and beyond. *Bumiputeras* are now said, as Prime
Minister Mahathir Mohamad has repeatedly pointed out, to have
"much to learn from Chinese" in the conduct of globally competitive businesses. Insofar as Chinese are inscribed as essential
capitalists within state discourses of globalization, their moral
stature within the national narrative has been inverted in a surprising way compared to the three previous decades; they have
shifted from the selfish and overprivileged "urban" and "wealthy"
defined invidiously by the New Economic Policy, toward ideal
Malaysians who, along with the *Melayu bharu*, are now viewed
as the model market-oriented citizen-subjects ready to perform

on behalf of the nation-state under the conditions of universal "global competition."

## Notes

I wish to thank Alan Smart for his comments on a previous version of this chapter. The research on which this chapter is based was supported by a National Science Foundation Dissertation Grant (1978-1980); an American Council of Learned Societies/Social Science Research Council Mellon Fellowship in Chinese Studies (1985); and by the University of North Carolina at Chapel Hill (1991-1993, 1997, 2002). Above all, I would like to acknowledge the assistance and gracious hospitality of residents of Bukit Mertajam in the state of Penang, Malaysia. They have tolerated my eccentric inquiries and irregular visits as a guest and friend for more than twenty years. In particular, I wish to thank Ng Bak Kee, Dr. Tan Chong Keng, and Ang Bak Kaw for their invaluable help and for their deep insights into Malaysian society. The names of informants given in the text are all pseudonyms.

1. In West Malaysia, almost all *bumiputera* or "indigenes" are Malays, with the exception of "aborigines," or *orang asli*. Hence, since I am referring to West Malaysia, in what follows I use the terms *bumiputera* and *Malay* interchangeably. In contrast, in the East Malaysian states of Sarawak and Sabah, indigenous status includes a large number of ethnic groups in addition to Malays, such as Kadazans and Dyaks.

2. In certain lines of trade, such as textiles and grain-milling, those involved have defined themselves as Indians, persons of South Asian descent, but their participation in these lines of business have not increased since the 1980s.

3. In this chapter, I use the past tense to indicate throughout the historical status of my ethnographic observations.

4. The town's total population in 1979 was about 40,000 persons.

5. These figures are based on a commercial census of all permanent business establishments within the town boundaries of Bukit Mertajam in 1979; these figures are analyzed in Nonini (1983: chapter 2).

6. Gibson-Graham's focus on the household as a site of production and distribution as well as consumption seems particularly apposite in the situation of small-scale Chinese enterprises, still far more often than not marked architecturally by two- or three-story houses, in which the upstairs and inside domestic work of women blends, particularly for unmarried young women, into labor done downstairs and outside in the shop, open for public business, on behalf of the family enterprise.

7. During the recession in 1985, the ICA was amended such that the minima required for 30 percent *bumiputera* equity were raised to $1,000,000 *ringgit* in capital and 50 employees (Crouch 1996:208).

8. This was an open public secret. A reporter in an article in the Penang newspaper *The Star* cited Puan Zainab, president of the Pan-Malaysia Lorry Owner's Association, who said, "anyone [any *bumiputera*] can apply to the Licensing Board for lorry permits and even non-operators can and apply and receive a permit." "The Government should stop issuing these permits as the market is already saturated" (H. C. Ong 1985:6).

9. Meillasoux pointed out a very similar contradiction long ago in the case of the lineage mode of production (1975).

10. As far as Chinese were concerned these governing logics have increasingly operated in ways that supplant the influence of local Chinese elites, as I indicate in Nonini (1998).

11. Even into the 1970s, the use of *bahasa Malaysia* as a language of instruction was hotly contested among Chinese, even after public debate was prohibited by an amendment to the Sedition Act statute passed in 1971 (*New Straits Times* 1985). Chinese people I talked to claimed that the required use of *bahasa Malaysia*, in first, primary, and then in secondary schools for Chinese was a means by which Chinese children were being forcibly parochialized, so that instead of mastering English and Mandarin, languages that could be used throughout Asia and elsewhere in trade and in the professions, Chinese children's class time was given over instead to learning to speak and write *bahasa Malaysia*, which only few Asians in only two (Malaysia and Indonesia) spoke. "They themselves [i.e., *bumiputeras*], don't move forward, but they instead pull us back," was the way one informant in 1979 referred to what he perceived as a deliberately invidious policy.

12. This was a coalition of the merchant-led and -funded United Chinese Schools Committees Association, *dongzong*, and the United Chinese School Teachers Association, or *jiaozong*, which had both local chapters and a national federation (Tan 1992:180ff.).

13. "The NEP and the Industrial Coordination Act had a generally negative impact on Chinese investment, as indicated by signs of significant capital flight. Between 1976 and 1985 more than $3 billion per year appears to have been sent out of Malaysia while the finance minister announced that some $10 billion had been transferred overseas between 1983 and 1985" (Crouch 1996:208).

# 10

## Labor Standard Regulation and the Modernization of Small-Scale Carpet Production in Kathmandu Nepal

### Tom O'Neill

## Introduction

Production of Nepalese carpets for a predominantly Western European market received a major setback in 1994, when NDR, [Nord Deutschler Rundfunk] a German television network, ran a documentary entitled "Nepalese Carpets: German Merchants Profit from Child Labor." The documentary, which revealed that thousands of Nepalese children had been put to work in the carpet factories in the Kathmandu Valley, had a devastating effect on carpet sales to Europe, where consumers rolled up their carpets and "hid them with shame" (USAID 1994). The industry has been in decline ever since, for a complex of reasons such as overproduction, declining quality, and a saturated consumer market as well as the controversy over child labor. In this chapter, I will examine the impact that decline has had for the large petty capitalist sector that grew around carpet exports in the late 1980s and early 1990s. The need to regulate the industry to enforce labor standards, standardize product quality, and discourage supply side overproduction placed new restrictions on small scale capitalism: as one producer told me in 1995, "within two years there won't be any small carpet factories anymore."

This was a common sentiment in Nepal at the time, and reflects an assumption that as industrial capital progresses small-scale production will eventually disappear. Many Nepalese petty capitalists expected this, and people in government and non-government-regulating bodies shared this view. There was a consensus that modernization would eventually transform the conditions that made petty capitalist production possible, even though the small-scale carpet production sector, consistent with theories of petty commodity production, emerged in response to the extension of Western markets into the production of a "traditional" Tibetan craft. In what follows, I argue that this is not a function of a priori evolutionary development. Recently we have recognized that flexible specialization provides a context for the expansion of petty capitalism as investment and labor costs are reduced by decentralized microproduction (Lash and Urry 1987; Harvey 1989). Jinn-yuh Hsu, in this volume, shows, for example, that the decentralization of Taiwan's high-technology industry into small, flexible firms is an adaptation to rapid shifts in technology that privileges "economies of scope, rather than economies of scale." But even though vertical disintegration may characterize regional economies in many newly industrialized countries, in the Nepalese carpet industry petty capitalism is an impediment to a desired modern, vertically integrated industrial sector. Small scale producers are thought to produce too many low quality carpets and jeopardize the international market by employing child labor, thus regulations are formulated that limit their ability to accumulate capital. Since 1994, new industrial standards and international child labor monitoring schemes such as "Rugmark" contribute to negatively transformed conditions for small-scale production, and many petty capitalists and their investments have been sacrificed in the interests of modernization.

There is an irony to this. The industry proudly represents its product to the world as a handicraft, and the state categorizes it as a "cottage industry," yet production is being concentrated in large export companies where Tibetan carpets are mass-produced by a waged proletariat. Meanwhile, the small-scale weaving units that might more properly fit the description of a "cottage industry" are losing ground, and those that remain are becoming increasingly subordinated to exporter capital. I will describe this process in relation to the informality of the petty capitalist sector; however, I will not speak of an *informal sector* in an effort to avoid both a dichotomization of types of production and the association of that term with poverty alleviation and grassroots entrepreneurialism (see e.g., Ypeij 2000; De Soto 1989). Informality, according to Bryan Roberts, is "income earning activities unregulated by the state in contexts where similar activities are so regulated" (1994: 6). By informality here I mean the ability of small-scale carpet producers to shift between subcontracting to relatively autonomous but riskier stock production that is viewed as a threat to the sustainability of carpet exports.

In the first section, I examine the position of petty capitalists as self-employed entrepreneurs subordinated to export capital. Modernist theories view petty capitalism as a transitional stage that will be eliminated by the growth of formal wage employment, and this modernist teleology shapes regulatory regimes in Nepal. In the second section I discuss small-scale carpet producer strategies for surviving in an export-dominated industry. Export registration is the state regime that governs the industry hierarchy, and the flexibility petty producers deploy to accommodate that hierarchy inevitably runs foul of that regime. In the third section I analyze the effect of child labor regulation on small-scale carpet producers. Social-labeling schemes aimed at eradicating child labor practices, I argue, reinforce existing industry hierarchy and a modernist discourse on petty capitalist production that contributes to its decline.

## Self-employment and Petty Capitalist Autonomy

In the summer of 1995, I surveyed three hundred carpet production facilities in the peri-urban community of Boudha (Kathmandu Ward #6) and the adjacent "village" of Jorpati that had become a major center for carpet production ever since exports of Tibetan carpets from Nepal in the early 1970s began.[1] I have discussed the history of the carpet industry elsewhere (O'Neill 1999), but for present purposes it is important to begin by stating that the Boudha, in particular, is an ethnically Buddhist community in a predominantly Hindu nation that has been historically linked to "Lama" households from Sindhupalchok, located in the hills north of the Kathmandu Valley. In 1995 most carpet exporters in Boudha were the children of Tibetan refugees who fled to Nepal after 1960, while most of the small subcontractors and stock producers with whom this chapter is concerned were their Nepalese coreligionists from the Yolmo, Tamang or Sherpa castes and many were from Sindhupalchok (O'Neill 2001). As the carpet industry expanded rapidly through the 1980s and early 1990s, many other Nepalese moved into carpet production in Boudha, as well.

Despite religious affinities, the complex relationships between exporters and their subcontractors are shaped by the impetus to extract surplus value from production. Small-scale carpet producers in Boudha were dependent on exporters for carpet orders, and thus for access to the world market. Neoliberal informal economy theory and neo-Marxist petty commodity production theory have long dominated our accounts of small-scale enterprise, and so I begin by considering how these perspectives inform my analysis of small-scale carpet producers.

For neoliberal theorists, informal economic activity is an entrepreneurial response to the limitations of the wage labor market—where formal sector employment in established industries is hard to obtain, people make their own employment by beginning microenterprises. Keith Hart (1973) recognized that unregulated, unorganized economic activity in Ghana was highly organized grassroots entrepreneurialism and introduced the term *informal economy* into anthropological, economic, and sociological treatments of "Third World economies." The informal economy has been characterized ever since as an important mechanism for poverty reduction, and as a viable economic strategy for rural migrants to rapidly growing cities (Roberts 1978; De Soto 1989, 2000). Kathmandu, the fastest-growing city in South Asia, is alive with informal economic activity, particularly in peri-urban areas.

Despite this enthusiasm for the entrepreneurial spirit of informal small-scale producers, there still remained the assumption that the informal economy was a transitional phenomenon that would wither away as developing countries modernized their industrial infrastructure. The low wages earned from informal enterprises by both laborers would increase in formal industrial enterprises, as these became established with the benefit of standardized investment and increased productivity. Neoliberal theory thus saw a gradual movement of workers from the informal to the formal sector. As Alejandra Portes and Saskin Sassen-Koob observed at the end of the 1980s, however, the proportion of informal to formal workers has remained static in the case of most modernized Latin American countries, and the notion that laborers would flow into the formal economy from the informal is not borne out in the data they examined. They argue, moreover, that significant income variation within the informal sector has meant that in some cases the movement is in the reverse direction, with many workers leaving formal wage labor voluntarily to risk small-scale production on subcontract to the firms where they used to work, for better remuneration (1987:37).

Neo-Marxist critics of informal sector theory maintain that the celebration of informal entrepreneurialism ignores the subordinated position of most petty producers vis à vis the merchants or market middlemen that they rely on for market access. Petty commodity producers, in this view, are only a form of disguised wage laborer from whom surplus value is extracted, and are maintained in a position of powerlessness with little hope of independence or upward mobility. Rigid and dichotomous classifications of wage labor and self-employment in industries often conceal the degree of subordination of the latter, even if, as Alison MacEwan-Scott (1979) points out, self-employed petty commodity producers believe themselves to be autonomous and in control of their enterprise. Without autonomous access to the markets where their goods are sold, and with limited access to the raw materials of production, it could be argued that small-scale carpet producers are merely earning a wage as middle-level weaving masters, even if they maintain some control over their means of production.

To view petty carpet production as merely a form of disguised wage labor, however, significantly undervalues the risks that producers take in their enterprises. Most of the small-scale carpet producers surveyed owned the looms that their weavers work at, the basic tools of the trade and managed their small enterprises in rented facilities where they provide living quarters for their workers in addition to the piece wages they pay them. They also provided raw material inputs—paper designs, colored wool, and weft string—at their own expense. Many petty capitalist producers in Nepal are thus more autonomous than others who are dependent on merchants and middlemen for their raw materials. They are, however, dependent on carpet exporters for access to the primarily European international carpet market through an export regime that is regulated by the government. The prices that petty producers receive for their work are set by exporters, under a "floor price" set by the government, so that analytically their surplus labor is appropriated by the export company, even though they in turn appropriate the surplus labor of their workers.

Carpet producers in Nepal varied in both size, investment, and in the degree to which they were autonomous from export capital.

Some small factories sold their carpets to a single exporter who invested in their creation and who controled all aspects of factory production. These "satellites," as they are known locally, are often managed by kin or by clients of the exporter, for whom they weave exclusively.[2] Most other small producers, however, made the initial investment for their own enterprise and performed a direct "management function" which, according to Scott Cook (1986) refers to their ability to combine both material and human resources in anticipation of profit. They also had to continually search for carpet orders as these were never guaranteed. When no subcontract could be found, producers often shut down temporarily or wove "stock" carpets (see below) in hopes of selling them later. They alone bore the consequences of any decision they made, thus befitting the classical Schumpeterian definition of the term *entrepreneur* (Greenfield and Strickon 1986).

The numerous case studies of small-scale informal entrepreneurialism, and of small-unit subordination to capital enterprises are a testament to the range of diverse manifestations that petty capitalist production has taken in economic development, rendering a global prediction of informal economy outcomes impossible. Detailed ethnographic accounts of local variants of petty capitalism are critical because they demonstrate the variation of local capitalisms that are out there. One reason why this diversity exists is that informal petty capitalism exists within national legal and regulatory regimes that (1) impose costs that provide incentives for formal enterprises to hire services from, or subcontract to, informal producers and (2) provide significant disincentives for informal producers to bring their activity into the regulated economy (Portes 1994; Roberts 1994). State regulations, along with market hierarchies and the uneven distribution of all forms of productive capital, provide a structure in which informal petty capitalists bear the risks for the choices they make. In the present case, the need to encourage and regulate carpet exports in order to bring in much-needed foreign currency earnings into Nepal has resulted in a regime that renders registration of small enterprises unnecessary and even, from the point of view of some small-scale carpet producers, undesirable.

## Subcontracting, Stock Carpets, and the Export Regime

Tsultim Lama began a small carpet factory in 1991, following the lead of several other men from his village in Sindhuplachok, in the Himalayan foothills north of Kathmandu. When I met him in 1995, he was struggling to maintain his unregistered business, and had to sell some land he had purchased from his earlier successes in order to continue paying his small workforce for the "model" carpets he was weaving. The model carpets they wove were intended to convince an export company that his product was of a high quality, and that he deserved to be given a "program" order. After their use as "models," these carpets ended up being sold to a stock dealer, at a price below their production cost. Tsultim's troubles in 1995 were symptomatic of the contraction in carpet exports to Europe that year, which Tsultim, like most other small-scale carpet producers, described using the English term *off season*. Exports in 1995 were off by almost 20 percent from the previous year, and people in the industry blamed the child labor controversy precipitated by the NDR documentary, overproduction, poor carpet quality and the interference of India in an attempt to defend their own failing industry.

Unregistered factories like Tsultim's were held by many to be largely responsible for this downturn. During the boom years of the industry in the early 1990s, hundreds of carpet factories appeared on the Kathmandu landscape. Large, fortress-like facilities with hundreds of looms were built on prime agricultural land of the Bagmati river valley in Jorpati village, and scores of small brick workshops operated by former weavers or by new entrepreneurs like Tsultim appeared in residential areas, and in the new settlements (*naya basti*) that sprang up in the valley. Longtime Kathmandu residents began to complain about what one newspaper columnist described as "the sudden explosion of amoeba-like, self replicating, carpet related industries," and the Nepali Congress government of the day announced in 1992 a plan to shift all the industries out of the valley, a plan that was never implemented because of unstable governments and the recognition by all parties that the foreign earnings the industry provided were critical to the national economy (*Independent* 1992).

The proliferation of small factories was also a major reason why the carpet market fell off after 1995, according to some local carpet exporters. The government of Nepal monitors exports by mandating that payment for all exported carpets be received by a Nepalese bank prior to customs clearance for carpets to be shipped abroad, and in this way is able to attempt to enforce an official "floor price" of at least $54 per square meter for every exported carpet and to ensure that this money remained in Nepal. By 1995, however, the real price of carpets, determined by predominantly

German buyers, was much less and exporters were forced to sell their carpets for as low as $36. After the official "floor price" was received in the Nepalese bank and the carpets shipped, exporters kicked back the difference between the floor price and the market price tax free to their German buyers. Because of the essentially corrupt practices at the export level, piecerates across the industry fell in 1995, and small-scale carpet producer profits were marginal. One producer from a registered, medium-sized facility put the blame for this on his unregistered competition:

> Eighty percent of factories are registered. No, sorry, only 20% are registered. People put four, five or six looms in their homes and weave carpets. They are the main guys who are putting us at a loss. This is the reason (for the "off season"). I found that they sell at a price even below their production cost. For that reason we cannot demand a good price.

By "registration," what is meant is that a firm has signed on with the Department of Cottage and Small Industries (DCSI), the government agency responsible for all craft industries in Nepal, including carpets. This registration allows a firm to export carpets, for which a fee of 1.5 percent was collected from every square meter of carpet reported. Firms must also have registered with the Department of Revenue for income tax purposes—however, a tax holiday of five years is applied to most export industries. Registration with the DCSI was important not only to access international markets, but it legitimated businesses and allowed for applications for loans from banks, but for small units like Tsultim's, registration appeared to carry few if any benefits. In the past many small companies did register with the DCSI in the hope that they would be able to develop direct commercial links with European buyers and to obtain bank loans to increase their investments in the industry, but small-scale carpet producers soon found that they did not have the production volume to compete at the export level, nor the necessary social or cultural capital to foster international links with foreign buyers. Economies of scale, too, mitigated against their success as autonomous exporters. European and American carpet importers preferred to place large orders, in the order of thousands of square meters, with a single exporter in order to reduce unit shipping costs. Exporters had the capacity to fill those orders, and what exceeded that capacity could be easily and cheaply obtained through subcontracts. Small-scale carpet producers also found it difficult to establish links with foreign buyers. Tibetan and Nepalese exporters are relatively well educated, can communicate to their buyers in English (the lingua franca of carpet transactions), and oversee large, bureaucratic, and efficient businesses (O'Neill 2001).

For small producers like Tsultim, registration was a costly and irritating yearly ritual that seemed to serve no end, as he would still have had no independent access to the export market, and banks were very unlikely to give credit to a small, insecure operation selling carpets at less than cost. Registration by the DCSI was an arbitrary process, as well. One small producer, Narendra Poudel, told me that he attempted to register in order to qualify for credit, but was told that the office was no longer accepting applications until after the government followed through on its plan to relocate the carpet industries out of Kathmandu, even though this scheme never became the official policy of the government. He may well have received the registration document in return for a *ghus* (a bribe), but this would only have increased an already pointless business cost.

Like Tsultim, Narendra is a small-scale carpet producer who came into the industry at the height of the carpet boom in the early 1990s and, again like Tsultim, he had no previous experience with carpet weaving or production. Unlike Tsultim, however, Narendra had managed to purchase a small plot of land and build a house in the *nayabasti* (new settlement) that are growing rapidly along the banks of the Bagmati River and Dhobi River where I found his small carpet factory in 1995. Only a handful of weavers were left at the time, working to pay off advance payments (*peskii*) that Narendra had made to them when business was better. His factory closed soon afterward, and reopened a year later when Narendra managed to get another subcontract with a large exporter.

Narendra and Tsultim, and most small-scale carpet producers in Kathmandu, come into the business for different reasons and with different levels of entrepreneurial prowess. Although some, like Tsultim and Narendra, had little or no experience in the business prior to starting their own carpet factories, many others rise through the weaving ranks, first by becoming carpet masters, or floor supervisors who dress the looms prior to weaving and monitor progress and quality. After working as masters, they moved on to establish their own independent or semi-independent factories, usually by producing on subcontract to their former employers. Relative outsiders like Narendra and Tsultim established trust with export patrons with difficulty, but they were the first to lose subcontracts after production declined after 1995, and were left to weave for the "stock carpets market." Most petty producers shifted between subcontracts and stock production in order to protect their investments in equipment, labor, and land.

Stock carpets are produced for a local spot market of Tibetan carpets for export (Odegaard 1985), and sold either to traveling agents of one of the several carpet buyers located in Jawalakhel across town, or to one of the local carpet shops located along the main road running out of Kathmandu through Jorpati village. Although stock carpets are produced for export, they are not part of a specific order that uses the exporter's designs and wool colors, and are generally held to be of inferior quality and destined for European discount sales. Stock producers often hire freelance designers to produce carpet designs, to create their own designs or, occasionally, to steal or copy designs from inside an export factory. The latter practice is a serious risk for exporters, as European buyers can pick up the same carpet on the stock market for a fraction of cost that would be paid to the exporter. Many exporters told me that designs or colors needed to be strictly protected from this, and for that reason post security guards at the gates of their factories. Independent stock producers are regarded as diminishing the export market by increasing the volume of inferior carpets, and are also seen as a direct threat to cultural capital that exporters see as proprietary.

### Table 10.1
### DCSI registered and non-registered units compared

| | registered (n=105) | non-registered (n=73) |
|---|---|---|
| Subcontract to exporter | 59 units | 29 units |
|     Mean employees | 43 | 24 |
|     Mean piecerate (rupees) | 348 | 347 |
|     Mean month end production (m$^2$) | 124 | 68 |
| Weaving stock | 46 units | 36 units |
|     Mean employees | 25 | 16 |
|     Mean average piecerate (rupees) | 340 | 337 |
|     Mean month end production | 77 | 60 |
| Subcontract to nonexporter | 0 units | 8 units |
|     Mean employees. | – | 11 |
|     Mean average piecerate (rupees) | – | 338 |
|     Mean month end production | – | 33 |

The survey data in Table 10.1, taken in the summer of 1995, is a subset taken from the sample of 300 factories that compares nonexporting enterprises that produce standard grade 60-knot carpets, for which a comparable piecerate is paid to weavers (n = 178).[3] Unregistered factories were significantly smaller in size, indicating both the meager investments those producers were able to muster and the comparatively marginal share they had of overall production. A majority of registered units produced carpets on subcontract to exporters, while most nonregistered units produced either for stock or as a subsubcontract, or equivalent subcontract, with another subcontractor (Ypeij 2000). It should also be noted that the mean weaving piecerates did not vary significantly between either the registered and unregistered sector, or between subcontracting and stock weaving units.

Small-scale carpet producers in both the "regulated" and "unregulated sector" moved between subcontract and stock production as circumstances warrant. When carpets are not being produced, small-scale carpet producers receive no income, and begin to live off cash reserves or other investments until another order is secured. When lucrative subcontracts were not found, most switched to stock production in order to keep income coming in and, just as importantly, to provide an income for their weavers, who would otherwise move on to another factory. Stock carpets were sold to buyers at a cost at or below production cost, and at lower rates than was received by subcontractors. Narendra, for example, sold carpets to a stockist at one time for 1,600 rupees per square meter; when I interviewed him he told me that he sold the same carpet, "same string, same colour, same design" for 1,200 rupees per square meter. At about the same time, subcontractors reported making on average about 1,800 rupees per square meter, but Tsultim told me that he needed 2,000 rupees to make an acceptable margin. The export "floor price" at the time was nearly 2,700 rupees per square meter ($54 in exchange).

Subcontracting between small-scale carpet producers was not common, but nevertheless was a strategy unregulated producers sometimes employed. Equivalent subcontracts are ideally negotiated between equals, and surplus value extraction is not the intention behind such negotiations (Ypeij 2000:70). Equivalent subcontracts occur when a small-scale carpet producer is not able to supply carpets to an exporter because of a short-term labor shortage or because the order exceeds his immediate capacity. Rather than turn down the subcontract, which most producers desperately need, small-scale carpet producers put out what they cannot produce themselves to another small producer.

In the summer of 1995, for example, Tsultim came into some luck when one of his previous export patrons began exporting carpets after a hiatus of several months and passed along an order to him. Tsultim had the necessary capacity in space, looms and equipment, but the five weavers he had on hand at the time were insufficient and finding trained weavers was difficult. He traveled to his village in order to hire some of his former workers who had returned there after he was forced to resort to weaving model and stock carpets, but they had all been recently hired by a *thekadaar* (labor contractor) for an export company. Without the hands to weave, and reluctant to hire unknown workers, he turned over much of the order to another small producer. Because of the arrangement, he had to pay this producer the same rate as was paid him by the export patron. Exporters frown on this practice because proprietary designs and colors pass out of control, and increase the likelihood that they will be woven as stock somewhere else.

Stock producers had a considerable reputation for cutting production costs any way they could. One controversial practice that was on the minds of many in the regulated sector in 1995 was the use of *jhindu* wool in stock carpets. The Tibetan and New Zealand wool used in the production of Nepalese export carpets has long fibers and is valued for its durability; *jhindu* is the wool fiber that results from trimming finished carpets. *Jhindu* collectors, wearing their characteristic lowland *dhoti* cloth (loincloth), go door-to-door cleaning these trimmings from factory floors and reprocess the wool, primarily for use in knitted sweaters and hats sold in local tourist markets. Some of that wool has been used in carpet weaving, however, where the short fibers degrade the quality of export carpets. Raw material costs soared in 1995, making recourse to the use of cheaper *jhindu* a tempting alternative for many small-scale carpet producers.

A second cost-cutting measure ostensibly employed by small-scale carpet producers was the use of unpaid family labor, and in particular child labor. According to representatives I interviewed from the Carpet and Wool Development Board, a semigovernment regulatory body, child labor had been eliminated from the export sector and from most regulated subcontractor factories, but remained in unregulated factories like Tsultim and Narendra's. An industry report in the fall of 1994 made the same claim, but charged that many children were released from their employment with inadequate provision after the airing of the Panorama documentary (NASPEC 1994). In 1995 an employee at a prominent nongovernmental organization (NGO) combating child labor in Nepal informed me that in the small carpet factories "it is 100% child labor, and some are even chained to the looms...."

For unregulated small-scale carpet producers the association of illegal child labor with what they did was almost impossible to dispel, as their factories operated extra-legally and were invisible to state regulators. They produced carpets with little profit margin and frequently at less than production costs, which led credence to the view that they would be tempted to employ under- or unpaid family or child labor. In many other South Asian industries, unpaid family labor is critical for the self-employed, particularly when their enterprises operate on an "irrational" footing (Mayoux 1993; Nieuwenhuys 1994). Carpet producers had to lower production costs in order to maintain profit margins or, more commonly, to mitigate the rate of loss, making reversion to illegal child labor a compelling strategy. Informal stock production was the least viable in the market; not only were small-scale carpet producers making carpets at less than cost, but their product was undermining overall prices and the reputation of the industry. Many in the industry wanted to see this form of production stop, and thus stigmatizing them with the claim that they depended on illegal child labor can be understood as a useful claim that addressed, at one level, the declining international reputation of the industry precipitated by the Panorama documentary and, at another level, the elimination of unregulated petty carpet production in a deflating industry. In the next section, I will discuss labor standard regulation as it pertained to small-scale carpet producers. The international popularity of 'social labeling' schemes (Hilowitz 1997) to target child labor has added a regulatory level that is accelerating a process of modernist industrial rationalisation, further constraining petty carpet production.

## Labor Standard Regulation and Small-scale Carpet Producers

Nepal signed the 1989 U.N. Convention on the Rights of the Child in 1991, but like many developing countries it had few resources with which to implement it. Article 32 of the convention, in particular, stipulates that state parties endeavor to protect children from economic exploitation and hazardous work that is detrimental to a child's health or to optimal physical and social development. A new labor law was thus announced in 1992 that set the minimum age for full-time work at 16, and that prohibited child labor before the age of 14. Teenagers between the age of 14 and 16 were permitted to work only 36 hours a week. This new law was not put into force until later, a victim of Nepal's frequent and chaotic changes in governments. The absence of a formal law at that time added to the confusion about labor standards in the carpet industry, where thousands of children were weaving carpets, often under exploitative *thekadaars*: labor contractors who forced their young charges to work long hours in return for little more than barely adequate food and appropriated most of their wages during excessively long apprenticeship periods.

The presence of children in carpet factories was not unusual in the sense that children have traditionally been important to the household economy in agrarian Nepal (Nag, White and Peet 1978; Fricke 1986). But children at work in the factories of an export industry in contemporary Kathmandu aroused considerable concern because their economic exploitation was for exchange value, and so contradicted the cultural logic of children's place in modern capitalism (Stephens 1995; Nieuwenhuys 1996). As well, the conditions in which those children were found to work were detrimental to their health and well-being. Children were separated from their families, and performed repetitive, physically demanding work in poorly ventilated workshops that were often thick with wool dust. Adverse publicity about these conditions in the carpet markets of Europe and North America were widely perceived to have contributed to plummeting carpet orders from Germany after 1994, and the government was under some pressure to step up factory labor standards.

For some small-scale carpet producers, this meant random spot inspections for child labor and another level of state surveillance of their activities. For many others, no inspections occurred. The apparatus that the government deployed to conduct this surveillance was, however, not sensitive to the widespread diversity of types and sizes of carpet factories, as it focused on the documented export sector that was easier to monitor. The Department of Labor was charged with the task of conducting random factory inspections for child labor in 1994, but had only two inspectors dedicated to the task. The Department of Cottage and Small Industries kept a cumulative list of 1,844 registered carpet enterprises in the

Kathmandu Valley, but many enterprises were registered but never wove a carpet, and many others closed down and were not removed from this list. There was no estimate for the number of unregistered enterprises. The Department of Labor did not use this list to begin inspections, but relied instead on a list of enterprises provided by the Central Carpet Industries Association, an industry lobby group that represented only the export sector. Inspection for compliance to new child labor regulations was thus targeted at the formal export sector, and small carpet manufacturers were only inspected if their factory was located nearby a major exporter.

Department of Labor inspections posed difficulties for both exporters and small-scale carpet producers in 1994, as there was some confusion about what the standards were, and how to apply them. Many large-scale exporters worked at the apex of a corporate hierarchy and had very little face-to-face contact with the carpet weavers who worked for them, so that it was quite common for producers to reasonably claim not to know who was working in their factories. The need to apply new child labor standards thus led to new apparatus for surveillance of the workforce. Most weavers were undocumented, that is, they did not carry any state-issued identity papers with which their age could be verified, so that identification of workers under the age of sixteen was often a matter of appearance. This invariably led to the dismissal of legal workers along with children, and many producers resented having to make these decisions, as one exporter commented:

> Children have been pushed out. Because after the government passed this new rule we pushed them out, sometimes under very sad circumstances because that's the rule and I can't change it. When we were weeding out the children, they've got no birth certificates, its just my judgement, I have to say "OK you can't be 14," because all of them claim to 14 and above. "Oh no, no no, you can't be 14, you are too small." And he says "Well I didn't get to eat like you how do you expect me to get big, you know?"

Small-scale producers experienced similar problems when inspectors came around. One small producer who ran a small subcontracting unit next door to Narendra's factory reported that in the previous months inspectors came to his factory and ordered several weavers to stop work, even though they claimed to be eighteen years of age. Their small stature, not unusual for a population that experiences chronic growth stunting, led the inspectors to conclude that they were underaged and small-scale producers were vulnerable to legal action if they protested their dismissal. Where large-scale exporters had both the material and cultural capital with which to deal with state authorities, small-scale entrepreneurs had few of these resources, so often acquiesced despite their reservations.

Small-scale producers were however sometimes tempted to employ cheap child labor despite the new regulations, and some even went to some length to avoid prosecution. Dawa Lama and his brother Norsang, for example, operated one of the small factories that was visited by Department of Labor inspectors in early 1994. The inspectors found a number of children working at their looms, so they were issued a warning, and their names and the factory location was recorded. The brothers decided, very shortly afterward, to move their factory to a new location nearby, ostensibly because it was cheaper and reduced their overhead expenses. They moved several times during my fieldwork, finally to a large brick factory building that they shared with another carpet-producing tenant. They also continued to use child labor. Although one half of their workers were young (between 14 and 20 years of age) and were hired directly by Dawa and Norsang, others were below the legal age limit, and were under contract with a local *thekadaar*, a woman who ran a grocery shop nearby. According to Dawa, *thekadaars* were used to obtain labor from distant locations, as he said people from his own district were not enough to keep up with a new, lucrative subcontract he obtained from a nearby exporter. The *thekadaars*, we were told, were responsible for training, supervising, feeding, and caring for these child weavers, so that Dawa and Norsang "would have no headache" from them. In return, they received a portion of the weaver's piecerate and sent an additional portion back to their parents as a remittance. Neither Dawa nor Norsang were forthcoming about the amount of these portions.

This was an unusual case for 1995, as knowledge about the child labor controversy (even details from the Panorama documentary that few in Nepal had seen), had diffused to almost everyone working in the industry. *Thekadaars*, moreover, were more common in large factories where they acted as intermediaries between weavers and the exporters who profited from their labor. Small producers turned to *thekadaars* when the caste, ethnic, and regional networks that their enterprises rose out of no longer provided sufficient labor, and they had to look farther afield for workers. This could be a significant risk in an unregulated industry; both Narendra and Tsultim lost considerable money in the past when *thekadaars* they contracted ran off after collecting an advance payment, leaving them both with subcontract orders they could not meet because they did not have the workers to weave them. In addition, many small producers preferred not to employ children as weavers, not because it is morally wrong or contrary to state law, but because very young children do not have the stamina required to weave tight, precise carpets. As Narendra Poudel remarked:

> Making them weave carpets, this is not right. Because for one thing rich children go to school, whereas poor children have to eat after working. Although they are poor the government should manage to make them read. For children's welfare there is no rule about education in Nepal. I have travelled in India also and there is some welfare for laborers there, but here the weavers are dominated. That management should be there. It is good to make them read and write. The second thing is making them work children's future breaks. If we make them read and write they may get a good job in the future. You don't get benefit from production by hiring a lot of workers, and another thing if children weave the quality is not good because they cannot cross [looping the guide rod on the loom] and they cannot hit [hammering the guide rod down when it it is fully crossed] and they don't have the energy for that work. In fact we should not make them weave.

In some ways Narendra's articulation of the child labor dilemma was not representative of the views of most small producers, particularly his emphasis on the importance of education, but the belief that young children did not make good weavers was widespread. While teenagers and young adults are in optimal physical condition for the strenuous task of Tibetan carpet weaving, young children do not have the required stamina to weave tight knots around the metal rod that forms the pile, and then beat that rod down a tight weft to form the carpet (O'Neill 1999; see also Denwood 1974). Both Narendra and Tsultim employed teenagers and young adults in their factories, although some were as young as fourteen years of age and could work, legally, no more than thirty-six hours a week. These employment practices were more the norm by 1995, especially after the clampdown after the "Panorama" documentary was broadcast when factories released underaged children from employment and researchers began to find many of them living on the streets in Kathmandu (Onta-Bhatta 1997).

For some producers the benefits of employing children through a *thekadaar* outweighed the potential risks. Labor contracting, for them, ensured adequate access to cheap labor, and that a comfortable distance between them and their workers was maintained. Labor contracting was organized by weavers themselves as most *thekadaar* were themselves weavers or former weavers. Blame for abuses of the system were often conveniently laid upon them. "The so-called exploitation really doesn't take place," said one exporter, "because I pay by the square metre, regardless of whether that person is 80 years old, or he is 25 years old or he is 12 years old, or he is a boy or is a girl it really doesn't matter as long as the carpet is up to the standard...." That weavers exploited each other was also of little concern to some carpet producers.

Labor contracting as an *occupation* must be distinguished from labor contracting as a *management function* that most producers must perform. Other small-scale carpet producers performed some of the tasks associated with the *thekadaar* by attracting weavers to work, providing housing for them in Kathmandu, and directly supervising their production. They also performed many other tasks in their factories in direct contact with their weavers. Narendra and Tsultim, for example, could often be found in their factories, setting the weft for new carpets, repairing equipment and even, if needed, assisting with the spooling of the raw wool for the weavers. Weavers received their wages directly after work is completed, or salary advances before, with no middleman to extract a portion. Because of the close proximity with which small-scale carpet producers worked with their employees, many stated a preference for hiring workers that were from the same village or district, not only because this was where an abundant supply of labor was located, but also because that labor could be trusted more; the *thekadaar* (labor contractor) and weavers who ran away from Tsultim and Narendra were from the distant lowland *terai* region with which neither was familiar. The relationship between small-scale carpet producers and their workers was not on an equal footing, however, as intergenerational and gender inequities ensured that management dominated labor.

Labor costs were one of the few inputs that small-scale carpet producers could to an extent control, whereas the prices of other resources were beyond their influence. In the year that followed the Panorama documentary, for example, the price of raw wool increased by nearly 60 percent in one five-month period, from 170 to over 270 rupees per kilo (1,000 rupees = 14.17 U.S.). Profit margins for even the most stable subcontract shrank, and the survival of small-scale carpet producers under those conditions was made even more problematic. Resort to *thekadaar*-supplied child labor under those circumstances was one way to maintain control over labor costs, but the benefit of this was limited as the piecerate that the producer ended up paying to the *thekadaar* for each weaver was little different than what they would have to pay a weaver directly. As well, a shrinking labor market with a lot of employee turnover meant that there were plenty of experienced carpet weavers looking for work, so bringing untrained children to Kathmandu to work was not a valued alternative.

Labor turnover was very high in 1995. Throughout several months of structured observations inside factories it was commonly noted that many weavers frequently moved from place to place, often because the carpets they were working on were finished but also sometimes in order to follow friends or relatives who found work elsewhere. This mobility, as Tsultim frequently found, was a serious problem for small-scale carpet producers, who would lose their best weavers to other factories. The often stated preference for working with young weavers who were familiar because of kin, ethnic, or regional proximity was thus a strategy to control weaver mobility, but this preference was little more than a sentimental memory for most small producers who were forced to hire workers from distant sources. Export capitalists had more financial resources at hand to pay weavers higher piecerates and to offer substantial wage advances, but labor turnover was a problem for them as well. A scheme to issue identity cards to all carpet weavers was discussed by the Central Carpet Industries Association, the Carpet and Wool Development Board, and the Trade Union Congress was proposed several times. These identity cards would have associated weavers with specific factories, and allow employers to trace their movements, but the incapacity for cooperation between agencies has so far prevented the implementation of the cards.

The need to regulate labor standards in the industry with the aim of eradicating child labor must be understood in the context of this volatile labor market. The conditions for labor bondage, coercion and exploitation did seem to exist because small-scale carpet producers, in particular, faced material costs that were spiraling out of control and labor resources that also constituted a considerable risk to their ability to accumulate capital. Because this sector of the industry was largely unregulated, poorly understood, and regarded as a threat to the industry, the claim that they employed child labor was convincing in the absence of contrary evidence. Efforts to eradicate child labor through regulation therefore ought to have rested on making this sector more visible and accountable for its practices. It is significant, then, that current schemes to monitor labor regulations begin with the export sector of the industry, which is already more or less regulated and accountable.

It is also significant that these regulation schemes are no longer managed directly by the Nepalese state, which did not have the resources to adequately carry out the task. In December of 1995, the Nepal Rugmark Foundation was formed by an international nongovernmental organization (NGO) already active in the Indian industry, to build a program of voluntary child-labor free labeling of carpets. Rugmark licenses enterprises, submits them to frequent, random inspections for child labor, and issues "child labor free" tags to label their carpets for export to European and American carpets. By 2001, there were 130 licenses issued to enterprises, comprising 412 separate factories and covering about 65 percent of all Nepalese carpet exports (*Rugmark* 2001). Rugmark label fees, collected from European and American importers as well as from Nepalese carpet exporters, are put to use by funding vocational programs to "rehabilitate" children "rescued" from carpet factories. By 2001, 407 children had been rescued by Rugmark since the program's inception.

The benefits of child rehabilitation to those rescued are considerable, but my intention here is not to comment on the overall efficacy of the Rugmark program but rather to comment on how the program reinforces a preexisting industrial hierarchy that subordinates small-scale carpet producers to export capital. All licenses held by Nepalese enterprises in 2001 were held by exporters, including eight of the ten largest companies in Nepal. Under the scheme, a licensee would also identify small carpet companies that are supplying carpets to them on subcontract basis and provide them with a sign or marker so that Rugmark inspectors can find and inspect these factories as well. At least some of the 282 factories covered in addition to the 130 licensees are autonomous small producers who are inspected only when they weave on subcontract for a specific licensed exporter, although inspectors will, on occasion, visit factories that have not been identified as suppliers when they suspect that a supplier has not been reported. Some small-scale carpet producers face inspection by Rugmark representatives even though they are not a part of the scheme. Otherwise, they produce carpets that do not receive the Rugmark tag.

One criticism of the scheme voiced tentatively by some exporters is that it is not really voluntary at all. One exporter told me in 1998 that he was compelled to participate in the program by his European buyers, despite his doubts that the plan really did enough for all children of working age and suspicions that it was prone to corruption. Indeed the 407 children who have been "rescued' and "rehabilitated" since 1995 were only a fraction of the estimated 2.5 million working children in Nepal, most of whom work in sectors of the economy that remain largely beyond international attention. Rugmark inspections, moreover, were limited to verifying the age of weavers; other aspects of working conditions for all weavers were not considered (see also Hilowitz 1997).[4]

The Rugmark label bifurcates all production into two commodity flows; those carpets that are labeled as child labor free, and those that are not labeled are thus placed under suspicion, even when, as were most of the factories I studied in 1995, child labor was not a necessary condition of their production. Small-scale carpet producers weave child labor free carpets only at the pleasure of licensed exporters who provide the identifying signs for inspection. When an order is finished, producers may need to locate another subcontract and/or weave stock carpets to remain in the field, but in an environment of decreasing carpet exports and marked difference between child labor free and other carpets, the utility of that flexibility is reduced. A representative of the Central Carpet Industries Association told me recently that stock production, moreover, was almost completely eliminated by 2001, as export orders began to dominate the entire carpet market. If 412 carpet factories accounts for 65 percent of all carpet production, it is not unreasonable to expect that many of the close to 2,000 carpet factories that existed in 1995 are now closed, and to speculate further that most of those are small-scale carpet producers who were always poorly articulated to the export regime.

There is no need to speculate as far as Tsultim Lama and Narendra Poudel are concerned. Tsultim finally closed his carpet

factory in 1996, having lost several *laakh*[5] rupees in investments
and chose rather to perform the grueling *gupa* meditation in which
he lived as a hermit, speaking to no one for a period of three years,
three months, and three days. When he accomplished this, his
family celebrated it as a great achievement of religious merit, but
for Tsultim the self-sacrifice involved was preferable to his struggle as a carpet producer. Narendra shut his factory down around
the same time, but he started up a year later and began to search
for subcontracts that he found were more difficult to obtain than
before. Stock production, which had allowed him to weather inter-
vals between subcontracts in the past, was still possible but the
unit prices he received were far below production cost. Narendra is
a shrewd and prudent manager and has been able to convert previous surpluses into fungible forms of capital. These trajectories
are not at all unusual, as many of the small-scale carpet producers
from Sindhupalchok I began working with in 1995 were either out
of business by 2000, or were struggling intermittently to keep
their independent enterprises viable.

## Conclusion

International efforts to eradicate dangerous forms of child
labor from developing industries have intensified ever since the
UN Convention on the Rights of the Child was promulgated in
1989, but local configurations of this global movement contribute
to a regulatory apparatus that prejudices a specific form of industrial hierarchy, or what I have termed in this chapter *export
regime*. Petty capitalist small-scale carpet producers in Nepal
occupy a precarious and diminishing position in that regime. Many
small-scale units were directly controlled by export capitalists, and
were assured that subcontracts would come to them, but those
others who I described as independent entrepreneurs, because
they alone bore the risks of the management function, had to rely
on the informality of stock production to remain viable. Poorer-
quality stock carpets posed a direct threat to that export regime,
because they undercut export prices and degraded the quality of
export carpets, so from the point of view of carpet exporters and
the Nepalese state who were anxious to preserve one of Nepal's
largest sources of foreign currency income, the stock trade had to
be eliminated. Rugmark labeling, however well intentioned, reinforced their ability to do so.

The demise of informal petty capitalism in the Nepalese carpet industry is unique for Nepal, where in 1998 informal self-employment accounted for 73 percent of all employment outside of the agricultural sector (HMG 1999:61). Most of that self-employment was in occupations that did not employ other workers, were located in rural areas, and were primarily in service, craft, and elementary (low-skilled) occupations. The focus of the carpet industry in the Kathmandu Valley not only put it in close proximity to migrant labor markets, air transportation, and the tourist hotels where European buyers do business, but also to international, media, and government scrutiny that drew attention to the industry that few other economic sectors in Nepal faced. Because carpets are a commodity-marketed internationally, the morality of their production became the central international concern that Rugmark was designed to address.

Rugmark labeling has likely prevented a return of the widespread exploitation of child carpet weavers that was reported in the early 1990s. The simultaneous fall of real carpet prices and inflation of raw material costs in 1995 could have meant a greater temptation for carpet producers to employ cheap and/or unpaid labor in order to remain in the industry. Small-scale carpet producers were particularly vulnerable to the claim that they did just that, as their activities were largely unregulated and/or unobserved. As I have argued, some small-scale producers did succumb to this temptation, while others did not, but a regulatory regime that labels "child labor free" carpets automatically stigmatized unlabeled carpets as having exploited child labor employed in their production, even if that was not the case. Petty capitalist small-scale carpet producers were ultimately dependent on exporters for access to the more valuable socially labeled carpet market.

It is important to state that social labeling alone did not produce these effects but rather that it joined an already unfolding process of industrial modernization. By locating carpet work in visible factories, this process places modern export sector labor beyond those spaces considered appropriate for modern child development, including the household (James, Jenks, and Prout 1998). Many small-scale carpet producers had organized their enterprises around households, kin groups, and regional affiliations and employed a style of production that this chapter takes as fundamental to petty capitalism, that is, direct involvement with the process of production. It is ironic that a product defined as a handicraft and produced in what is officially defined as a "cottage industry" is undergoing a process of modernization that increasingly marginalizes small-scale producers who best fit that definition. The evolution of capitalism in the Nepalese carpet industry may fit classical neoliberal and neo-Marxist models of development, but this evolution is shaped by the selection of regulatory policies which, taken together, take the demise of small-scale production as a central premise. Small-scale producers like Tsultim Lama and Narendra Poudel are the human victims of that reflexive process.

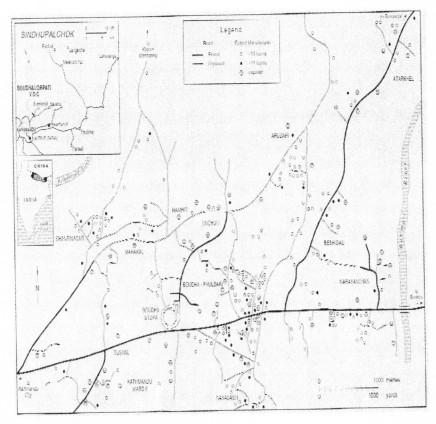

Figure 10.2. Map of Boudha/Jorpat

# Notes

1. Field research was conducted in 1994–1995 and in 1998 in Kathmandu Nepal, supported by the Social Sciences and Humanities Research Council of Canada doctoral and postdoctoral fellowships, as well as by the McMaster University Faculty of Graduate Studies, Hamilton, Canada.

2. The vast majority of export entrepreneurs were male. One exception to this rule was the daughter of a Tibetan refugee who took over her father's factory when he died, but was pushed out of her position by her younger brothers after she had children.

3. This subset excludes those factories in which higher-grade 80- and 100-knot carpets were also produced. Weavers for these "high-end" carpets receive higher piecerates than for 60-knot carpets that compensate for a lengthier weaving time. The 60-knot carpet was, in any case, the industry standard, and comprises most exports abroad.

4. In a meeting in the fall of 2000, Rugmark acknowledged this criticism and has begun to discuss how to expand its inspections to investigate worker conditions more comprehensively. Unhealthy work environments, less than minimum wages, extortionate labor contracting, and the abuse of salary advances are among the problems that occur in factories for workers of all ages. The expansion of Rugmark inspections into these areas would further usurp state responsibilities for labor standard regulation.

5. One laakh equals $100,000.

# 11

## Fair(er) Trade for Global Markets: Capitalizing on Work Alternatives in Crafts in the Rural Philippines

*B. Lynne Milgram*

## Introduction

Anthropologists have investigated the effects of market economies on the lifeways of peoples worldwide for decades. The global theoretical framework now capturing researchers' attention, however, often obscures the embedded activities that take place in and around this wave of global capital. The expanding market model assumes that free individuals compete in a rational system on equal footing and are subject to constraints they themselves accept (Carrier 1997). Absent in this analysis is how people actually interact when they produce, trade, and consume goods and thus an understanding of the critical importance cultural values and practices play in shaping economies. As Carla Freeman suggests, "not only do global processes enact themselves on local ground but local processes and small-scale actors might be seen as the very fabric of globalization" (2001:1008).

Women's work in crafts in the northern Philippines resonates with Freeman's premise. Building on their historic engagement in artisan trades, women are refashioning their work in production and marketing within the context of dramatic social, political, and economic change. They seek autonomy and status that farming may not provide and that transnational factory work often destroys. Many female artisan-traders (or petty capitalists) seize new opportunities to conduct business across greater distances as they seek out wider national and transnational markets for their goods. Independently and in cooperative associations, they expand their roles as producer-traders, nurturing their ongoing relationships with local artisans while fostering connections with national and transnational buyers. In a bold new initiative, some female petty capitalists have entered the global craft market on their own terms by forging linkages with alternative trade organizations (ATOs)—organizations that conduct their buying and selling activities according to a philosophy of "fair" rather than "free" trade. To operationalize these connections, women interweave situated and localized practice with new craft commodities that enable a personal local-to-global reach.

In this chapter I explore the alternative economies of women's petty capitalist work within independent and cooperative craft practice in Banaue, Ifugao, northern Philippines. As a work-alternative to the farm and factory, artisan trades have increased significantly worldwide, and most prominently in those countries that have embraced promarket reforms and global integration such as the Philippines (Colloredo-Mansfeld 2002). Female petty capitalists' ability in this locale to realize opportunities within such profound socioeconomic change thus disputes the earlier steamroller model of global capital. This research argued that with dramatic economic expansion, the differential opportunities for men and women often resulted in women losing the autonomy they had as producers and traders (e.g., Ehlers 1990; Nash 1988). Studies also suggest that this marginalization was more prevalent in household production where women often worked for low returns, in order to combine their productive work with their reproductive tasks (Singh and Kelles-Viitanen 1987). Although some women in the Philippines have been similarly disadvantaged (Miralao 1986), others have overcome obstacles to their participating in development, diversified their market trade, and learned different skills to take advantage of the changing economy.

The opportunities fashioned by some petty capitalists in crafts, however, does not mean that their initiatives can provide sustainable options in work and social change for all women with the advent of global capital. Such a proposition belies the tremendous structural forces at play against them, and the level to which globalization (in the form of transnational, capitalist institutions, and structural adjustment policies) has transformed social and economic relations at so many levels (see Balisacan 1995; Chant 1996; Clark and Manuh 1991; Winslow 1996). I want to suggest, however, that the current acceleration of global systems still leaves space for petty capitalists to maneuver and to claim their share of transnational markets.

Drawing on Whatmore and Thorne's (1997:287)[1] analysis of coffee trade networks, I argue that Ifugao's petty capitalists in crafts similarly negotiate "lines of flow" that mediate between local producers, national buyers, and global trade organizations (e.g., ATOs). The linkages they develop shift attention from the logical hand of the market and the dichotomies it creates to the "interweavings" and "*situatedness*" of people, social institutions, processes and knowledges; and frame these as always "contextual, tentative and incomplete" (Sarah Whatmore and Lorraine Thorne 1997:288–289, emphasis in the original; see also Appadurai 2000:5–6; Freeman 2001:1008–9; Featherstone 1990). As petty capitalists in crafts, women in particular incorporate cultural parameters into an economic arena marginal to state influence. Through their risk-taking ventures, they fashion spaces of agency, innovation, resistance, and compromise to consolidate the intersecting, albeit contradictory and often ambiguous, positions they occupy (Gibson-Graham 1996; Li 1999). I suggest that women's petty capitalist enterprises, in turn, consolidate cultural identities and economic community commitments even as they may produce cleavages in material well-being (Colloredo-Mansfeld 2002:114; see also Smith and Narotzky, this volume).

Working with craftspeople in the northern Philippines, I quickly learned that these petty capitalists, men and women, continue their activities in both skilled labor and trade, individually and within cooperative organizations. In this chapter then, I consider such artisan trades as small-scale, minimally capitalized commodity production and sales (Colloredo-Mansfeld 2002:115). Rather than viewing trade within the separate sphere of distribution, recent scholarship characterizes "as a unified process the production of goods for exchange, their passage from producer to marketer, and the realization of the exchange value of these goods as they pass from marketer to consumer" (Babb 1989:46; see also Cook 1986; Gates, this volume). Most petty capitalists in crafts began their careers in the industry as artisans learning and maintaining their skills through personal involvement in the labor process. They add this knowledge to their trading initiatives and present themselves in the marketplace as capable of fulfilling both roles. To realize their goals, they mobilize whatever resources are at their disposal, including financial resources and social networks that grant access to information or influential individuals. At the same time, they operate according to the constraints and standards prevailing within their groups but fashion personalized paths.

It is more useful then, to regard petty capitalists as petty commodity producers, managers, and sellers rather than solely as petty entrepreneurs, as artisan-traders do not divide work that produces goods and work that circulates them (Babb 1989:44; Cook 1993:67). Women's engagement in Banaue's craft industry, in particular, demonstrates how such petty capitalists "operate a flexible range of productive activities from a varied range of capital, labor and environmental resources that come under their control" (Karim 1995:28).

I begin this chapter by reviewing studies that dismantle lingering dichotomies such as "domestic" and "public," and "informal" and "formal" with regard to women's work and the global economy. To highlight how women move across multiple spheres, I focus on two sites of craft practice: independent household industry and cooperative organizations. This chapter makes a particular contribution to research on women's work by applying a gendered analysis that includes both culture and economic practice to women's current participation in the emerging fair trade movement. I conclude by demonstrating how female petty capitalists shape, not just respond to, the forms global capital takes and the significance it acquires in any location.

## Petty Capitalists, Gender, and Work

The craftwork of female petty capitalists in the rural northern Philippines offers a particularly useful lens for the analysis of gender and economic outcomes with globalizing market forces as women's workforce participation throughout the Philippines is among the highest and most varied in the "developing" world (Broad 1988; Ofreneo and Habana 1987; Pineda 1995). Recent studies examining women's microactivities, whether identified as small-scale or micro-entrepreneurs (Simon 2003; Ypeij 2000), petty commodity producers and sellers (Cook and Binford 1990), or market women (Babb 1989; Clark 1994; Seligmann 2001), treat as an analytic whole both the economic and cultural practices women use to shape the conditions within which they work and live. By considering how the cultural dimensions of a global economy and of state and international agency interventions either constrain or facilitate women's activities, these studies challenge the totalizing market model; they highlight, instead, the complexity of, and contradictions in, women's changing positions and the "cultural calculations women can impose to transform their economies" (Seligmann 2001:2; see also Brenner 1998; Horn 1994; Lockwood 1993).

Current research clearly demonstrates that women work across different spheres including household and market, rural and urban spaces, and local-to-national-to-global economic arenas (e.g., Babb 1989; Brenner 1998; Freeman 2001). Their multifaceted activities dissolve determinist ideas about discrete and bounded socioeconomic categories. Studies of women's work in both rural and urban spheres make visible how household and market interact dialectically; women borrow social and economic relationships and practices from one sphere, adapting and reapplying them to the other. As Wazir J. Karim argues for Southeast Asia, women secure a "continuous chain of productive enterprises" for family and personal well-being by establishing "a repertoire of social units" linked to household, market, and environmental resources; and they "unlink" themselves when situations change. Women thus create an "open-ended" and "multi-focal" system of socioeconomic relations with "undifferentiated boundaries" and "varying connotations of 'space'" (Karim 1995:28).

This bridging of activities is facilitated in areas such as Southeast Asia where an "ideology" of gender parity is couched within the values of community frameworks. As Suzanne Brenner (1998) argues for market women in Java and Jefremovas (2000) demonstrates for female vegetable marketers in the upland Philippines, where custom supports women's engagement in local and regional trade, women accumulate capital and can move into different petty capitalist ventures. Shelly Errington (1990:5) cautions, however, that in this region of Southeast Asia, although women predominate in market trade and household finances, such economic control does not instill the highest status. Rather, skill in public oratory and election to political or religious office—spheres primarily held by men—remain the most prestigious forums. Such customary notions of hierarchy contribute to the contradictions and ambiguity women may experience as they reconfigure their work options in regions such as the upland Philippines.

Studies examining female petty capitalists' "survival strategies" or tactics in business highlight how women develop extensive social networks as potential sources of economic or political capital on which they can draw for work (Horn 1994:147–149; Seligmann 2001:8). Annelou Ypeij (2000:13, 136) points out that women may be more dependent on such neighborhood and kin-based networks than men as they may have less access to formal institutions such as banks. Lynn Stephen (1991), in her work with Zapotec weavers in Mexico, similarly describes how women choose the members for their weaving cooperatives for capital accumulation from those women with whom they participate in activities of social reproduction such as churches and other community groups (see also Narotzky 1997:190 1997a). In the upland Philippines, most craft cooperatives, as well as patron-client arrangements, are also based on pre-existing relationships established through reciprocal labor exchanges (see Milgram 1999). Such networks result from, and continue to depend on, nurturing long-term associations.

Expanding on this premise, Mary Ann Littrell and Marsha Ann Dickson (1999:37; see also Ypeij 2000:138) argue that although profit maximization figures prominently into women's business motivations, female petty capitalists identify other factors as key in launching and sustaining their businesses and sense of personal worth. Along with realizing profits, they talk about building their information and social networks, maintaining autonomy, achieving personal recognition, and securing the needs of their families. On a practical level, good social networks enable female petty capitalists to maximize their often scarce or minimal resources; strong social connections facilitate ready access to informal loans or credit that require little if any paperwork, and encompass negotiable interest rates and repayment terms (Milgram 1999). Such access to credit is particularly relevant to women who do not control household cash and have restricted access to the formal banking sector, as occurs in parts of South Asia and Latin America (Wood and Sharif 1997).

Female petty capitalists also move between so-called formal and informal sectors forging linkages similar to those between household and market. Although past studies tended to treat these two spheres as mutually exclusive, current research demonstrates their interconnectivity; it also argues that such resilient divisions, concomitant with Western ideology and thought, are often fostered by the agenda of government policies (Seligmann 2001:19; Hart 1992; Halperin 1996). Suzanne A. Brenner (1998:15–17) destabilizes this divide by demonstrating how female entrepreneurs in Java's batik industry move from family to marketplace, among wider national economic arenas and then back again. Other studies argue that, in practice, household members engage in occupational multiplicity, juggling and relying on activities from both sectors to make a living (Illo and Polo 1990), while still others suggest that female entrepreneurs may purposefully choose informal over formal sector work (e.g., Browne 1996). Research points out, moreover, that policy makers' political promotion of the potential of the informal economy for women's work actually rationalizes the former's failure to initiate infrastructure change that can facilitate women's access to resources, whether from informal or formal sectors (Seligmann 2001:21).

The imposition of national economic policies along with expanding prescriptive global systems also contributes to the growth in women's informal workforce participation and to the varying degrees of control women have over their labor in this sector (Chant 1996; Clark and Manuh 1991). Deborah Winslow (1996:701–2, 718) demonstrates how in Sri Lanka, exogenous programs (government projects, structural adjustment programs, a cooperative movement, often initiated by international lending agencies) may interact with "fortuitous and idiosyncratic local factors" (certain individuals and location of production) to, in fact, increase female (as well as male) potters' control over the terms of their informal sector activities.[2] Other studies argue that, in many cases, women are disadvantaged by neoliberal policies that have fueled the gap separating rich and poor, segmented labor conditions and often undermined female petty capitalists' local customer base as men and women with less work have less income for consumption (Seligmann 2001:17–18, Ypeij 2000:112). In the upland Philippines, similar contradictions arose in women's positions with the Marcos government's introduction of structural adjustment policies in the 1970s. Programs targeted larger lowland- and urban-based enterprises leaving rural home-based tradespeople to fend for themselves. Some have effectively established links with fair trade collectives while others continue to rely on personal skills to negotiate effective networks that will mitigate the fluctuating market for crafts.

Research on female petty capitalists also explores women's agency to determine their survival tactics. As Ypeij (2000:13–16) points out about microentrepreneurs in Lima, Peru, although women may gain access to resources and challenge particular ideologies, they are still constrained, to some extent, in operationalizing opportunities because of the isomorphic nature of household- or street-based work and because the economic differentials in their positions divide them (see also Seligmann 2001:16). In addition, power structures within households, the gender division of work, as well women's "double" workday may also constrain women's choices (Simon 2003). Social actors, Norman Long (1992:22–23), argues, then, can and do make decisions, but the degree of choice they have is not unlimited and is asymmetrical. Naila Kabeer's (1994:223) processural model of power (power to, power over, power within) similarly roots the extent of women's agency in the strength of their social relationships as well as in their control over broader social and economic state structures. In Ifugao's craft industry, then, female petty capitalists' decisions may certainly be empowered by their command over both economic and cultural resources but, at the same time, their agency or potential to exploit opportunities, including the labor of their employees, is constrained by cultural community expectations, state-imposed parameters, and by the risk to social networks that certain decisions may entail.

Given the embedded circumstances of women's work, the frameworks of "hybrid networks" and multiple "modes of ordering" as suggested by Whatmore and Thorne (1997:289) provide an entry to understanding the opportunities women can realize and the constraints they experience in seeking alternates in crafts. Women strategize to strengthen and extend their producer-buyer connections by simultaneously performing social and market skills at different points in, and at different levels of, their broader-than-local networks. In so doing, they can potentially capture contested spaces (Whatmore and Thorne 1997:302), creating room to maneuver and new opportunities with which to engage. As Tom O'Neill (this volume) points out, such hybrid networks operate alongside corporate and state systems, sometimes overlapping them, and sometimes occupying different sites that can include points of both connection, and contention (see also Whatmore and Thorne 1997: 295). By reconfiguring economic networks through culturally informed practice, many of Ifugao's female petty capitalists negotiate "the uneven and contested terrain" of global market forces (Tsing 2000:330) to craft innovative and often surprising livelihood options.

This chapter focuses on the craft industry in Banaue, Ifugao, the center for handicrafts in the upland northern Philippines. In the town center, at any one time, there are approximately twenty to twenty-five craft stores selling weavings, wood carvings, and baskets; and the majority of these are owned by women. In addition, approximately twenty-five to thirty female traders work from their homes and do not maintain retail outlets. In the mid-1990s, with initial support from the Ramos government's development programs, petty capitalists seeking alternative market outlets for their products founded weaving cooperatives in four Banaue villages and some established links with Alternative Trade Organizations in Manila. The following discussion focuses on the petty capitalist practice of both of these independent and cooperative-based businesses specializing in textile production and trade.[3]

## The Setting for Ifugao's Craft Trade

Ifugao is located in the Gran Cordillera Central Mountain range that extends through much of northern Luzon. The main economic activity in the Cordillera, as throughout the Philippines, is wet-rice cultivation carried out in irrigated pond-fields, and in many areas, such as Banaue, the high elevation (1,500 m.) and cool climate limits cultivation to one rice crop per year. With no mixed agricultural production base and little agricultural surplus for sale, most families combine cultivation with nonagricultural income-generating work such as producing crafts, working in the tourist service industry, or operating dry goods stores. The increase in tourism since the 1970s means that crafts, formerly made for local use and regional trade, are increasingly targeted for commercial sale especially during the busiest part of the tourist season from December to May.

Men and women both work in extrahousehold income-generating activities and the region's socioeconomic systems of bilateral kinship and inheritance, ambilocal residence, and primogeniture means that women own land and inherited wealth and have ready access to economic opportunities. Most women manage and allocate household finances and hold power in this sphere. Men, however, dominate in public positions in politics and in religious office, and although men participate in domestic tasks, women still assume the bulk of childcare and domestic responsibilities (Milgram 1999). Men and women thus continuously renegotiate gendered roles and power relations as they redefine their work and positions in Ifugao's commoditizing economy. Throughout the

Cordillera, moreover, the differences among women, depending upon factors such as social class (landed elite, tenant or landless) and education, mean that some women may have more of an advantage than others to gain social prestige and accumulate capital through their work as petty capitalists in new craft enterprises.

## Organization of Craft Marketing

In Ifugao, although both men and women sell handicrafts, women, either as sole owners or in husband-and-wife-teams, dominate this trade and are the main risk-takers in this business. Because crafts remain low-technology, household enterprises, trade channels throughout the Cordillera are not monopolized by established classes; anyone with enough capital can often exploit the business opportunities that may come his or her way facilitating the shift from producer to petty capitalist. Indeed, the Cordillera ideology of *kanya kanya*, or "independence" (Milgram 2001:137), and the absence of constraints, at least ideologically, on upward economic mobility (Rutten 1993:138) means that female artisans, in particular, can move into trading if suitable opportunities arise. Although women more commonly trade weavings, both men and women buy and sell wood carvings and baskets such that the products marketed are not gender specific. For the most part, the production and trade of handicrafts in Banaue is too small to support an intervening level of intermediaries. Female petty capitalists, to varying degrees, characteristically continue to be involved in some aspect of production such as manufacturing weavings into functional products, weaving prototypes, or finishing (sanding and varnishing) wood carvings or baskets. This tacit knowledge of the labor process enables these women to more easily innovate on and improve their products as well as more knowledgeably supervise their contracted workers (see also Smart and Smart, this volume).

As the linchpin in the handicraft industry, these businesswomen obtain their stock directly from local artisans and, in turn, sell goods directly to urban buyers. They issue cash or in-kind advances to artisans and negotiate the terms of purchase orders, delivery dates, and extensions with Philippine craft store buyers in urban centers and with international buyers from Europe and Asia, all of whom communicate through fax, phone, or personal visits. On the buying side, they respond to specific orders from their urban buyers; they seldom secure advances, except for larger orders, and often obtain pieces from artisans on consignment enabling them to obtain stock when they are short of capital. On the retail end, they sell their products through their shops if they have local retail outlets, independently through their own network of urban buyers, or through craft cooperatives if they are part of collective organizations. As the pivot in the cash flow, these female petty capitalists thus negotiate a network of social and economic contacts that link geographically dispersed urban buyers with rural artisans.

Petty capitalists in crafts must also formulate strategies to cope with the fluctuating seasonal demand for these goods. Sales within the Philippines, generally, are slowest during the wet and nontourist season from mid-May to early December when heavy rains also make it difficult to transport finished products to markets as roads, the only means of transport, are often closed. While the market for baskets is expanding internationally, affording more opportunities in the trade of these goods, recent restrictions on logging threaten the local wood-carving trade. Women dealing in weavings, independently and through the new cooperatives, must continue to innovatively explore marketing options as demand for textile products is more vulnerable to fluctuating trends in fashion.

Positioned between the demands and expectations of urban buyers and those of rural artisans, petty capitalists' businesses are vulnerable to interruptions in their cash flow that may arise from problems with either group. To facilitate the sustainability of their businesses then, petty capitalists negotiate a mutual understanding, however tenuous, through a *suki* relationship. As William Davis notes, only by forming "personal networks of obligatory relationships" (1973:211) can those in business overcome the barriers posed by a lack of trust and by a weakness in institutional credit facilities. Nurturing their *suki* relations, petty capitalists can, in theory, be somewhat more certain of receiving the products they have ordered and the sales they have been promised. Gavin Smith and Susana Narotzky (this volume) identify a similar situation that keeps small-scale entrepreneurs, distributors, and workers in Spain "tightly bound to each other" in "shifting but necessary alliances."

To maintain the loyalty of both suppliers and buyers, Cordillera women, in particular, operationalize the *suki* bond by transforming their skills in reproductive spheres to their business practices. They develop new personal ties, activate existing relations of kinship and neighborhood, and instill a sense of personal obligation on the part of producers by fulfilling the latter's requests such as those for credit. To foster allegiance, traders put no time limit on when artisans must repay these advances, often used for health care and food, and indeed, no interest charges are due. Thus, depending upon the strength of the trader-artisan bond artisans have access to interest-free loans for unlimited periods of time.[4] Although traders gain the loyalty of producers, they bear the financial burden of having their capital tied up for long periods of time in outstanding loans that do not accumulate interest. When artisans betray their allegiances, many petty capitalists feel that reemploying the artisan is the only way to recoup their investment, socially and financially, and they must build this cultural liability into their market model.

Petty capitalists also continually seek out information on current national and international craft prices. Because demand for these goods fluctuates and because bargaining is the usual means of negotiating a deal, prices may vary considerably from transaction to transaction. Many traders hesitate then to entrust their capital to employees whose bargaining skills may not meet the formers' expectations. This often results in petty capitalists maintaining their independence. Petty capitalists thus try not only to maximize their turnover, but also to occupy a strategic position in the marketing system that will optimize their access to price information (see also J. Alexander 1986). To achieve both goals, the most successful craft capitalists need to be skilled in shrewd bargaining as well as in strategically nurturing personal networks— "a mass of currents rather than a single line of force" (Whatmore and Thorne 1997:291).

Further affecting opportunities in crafts, especially for women, are the national macroeconomic policies and structural adjustment initiatives instituted by the Philippine government in the 1970s. Upon the recommendation of the World Bank and the International Monetary Fund (IMF), the Marcos administration instituted a program to aggressively promote foreign investment and an export-oriented and outward-looking pattern of development (Broad 1988; Balisacan 1995; Chant 1996).[5] This national government agenda, however, differentially trickles down to local craft industries through the initiatives of the provincial offices of the Department of Trade and Industry (DTI).

In 1992, for example, the Ramos administration passed a bill to "fast-track the development of the countryside" (DTI 1992:1).

Within this initiative, the National Economic Enterprise Development (NEED) program was founded to "focus on handicraft production for export development" in designated provinces. Under this umbrella, DTI offers different programs, but most target medium- and larger-scale businesses (employing more than ten people). The membership fee of 4,000 pesos ($95),[6] for example, from the outset, limits those who can take advantage of DTI's initiatives. Similarly, it is primarily those already successful in business who can participate in the yearly national and international craft trade fairs that DTI organizes as their main avenue to promote crafts. Those participating in the fairs may also take advantage of DTI's workshops (e.g., product and marketing development and price setting) in preparation for these events. The high costs of the trade booth rental, travel, and living in urban centers during the fair, plus the difficulty in fulfilling the large orders that may result (given the often limited production base) preclude most rural petty capitalists from participating in this DTI program although participants may apply for a subsidy of up to 25 percent to cover the first year's expenses (DTI 1992:2). Such large-scale fairs seem better suited, and indeed have met considerable success with popular and functional crafts such as bamboo and rattan furniture and household products. These goods are manufactured in small workshops (employing more than ten people) in southern Luzon where there is an abundance of raw materials and where a lowland location enables easier market access (Aguilar and Miralao 1985).

Despite the uneven results of their initiatives in the Philippine Cordillera provinces, the Department of Trade and Industry interprets its unfavorable results as evidence of petty capitalists' timid implementation of the neoliberal model. Many rural traders have been left little choice but to eclectically build on historical precedents of production and trade to fashion a new connectivity within the complex spheres of craft practice.

## Crafting Local Networks for Global Connections

*Independent Enterprise*

Cecille Kimmay,[7] a former weaver and thirty-five-year-old mother of four, started sewing weavings into functional products in 1995 and currently operates her own textile business. Her husband works in wage labor in agriculture and in community development projects. Cecille's household-based enterprise is similar to the many other independent operations run by Banaue's female petty capitalists buying and selling textiles. She regularly works with four to six artisans who weave independently in their homes and with as many as ten artisans when demand is high. The seasonal demand for woven products means that she negotiates *suki* arrangements with artisans that will ensure her a supply of weavings during the busy period, but exempt her from having to overstock when demand is low. When Cecille receives rush orders or orders for more "high-end" items, she requests that weavers set up their backstrap looms in her courtyard, facilitating her closer supervision over the quality of their work. Such incipient workshop conditions mean that weavers often feel compelled to work longer hours, for which they do not necessarily receive additional monetary compensation. At the same time, working in such close proximity with traders gives producers some leverage to bargain for benefits as the former ultimately depend upon receiving such specialized craft products in a timely manner. Thus, Cecille, like other petty capitalists, advances, interest-free, cash or food to artisans when requested, promises to pay them the fair market price for their weavings and to buy as much of their work as she can afford when sales are slow. Weavers promise to bring her all of their pieces during the busy season although they may be approached by other buyers.

In the late 1990s, to enhance her competitive edge, Cecille renegotiated her arrangement with producers. In the past when she had given cash advances to weavers she often lost control over the quality of the product as artisans would purchase poor quality yarns and sacrifice careful weaving for speed. She was then left with little choice but to accept these pieces in order to recover her investment and meet her deadline with urban buyers. Most weavers do not have ready access to good quality yarns because as independent producers, they do not buy in bulk. While some artisans are able to negotiate individual arrangements with Manila or Baguio City factory workers, usually through kinship connections, others' choices in yarns are often restricted to the materials they can find in stock overruns and in discounted yarn bins.

Drawing on her weaving experience, Cecille now designs her own line of products, instructing artisans how to reproduce her specific patterns and colors. She has negotiated a bulk-buying agreement with a small Baguio supplier and distributes her self-selected yarns to weavers; and in a piecework arrangement she deducts the cost of the yarn from the value of the weavings producers deliver. Although Cecille pays artisans only for their labor, she has earned a reputation for paying the market price for woven yardage and, in most instances, for paying promptly upon delivery. In addition, she often includes an in-kind bonus such as vegetables from her household garden. Some weavers explain that since they often lack the capital necessary to buy their own yarn, Cecille's arrangement facilitates an optional avenue for them to earn cash especially when childcare demands preclude extra-household work. On the other hand, Cecille also makes a profit on the yarn as she buys it wholesale, but advances it to the weavers at the retail price.

Still, it does not take long before unique designs are copied. In the spring and summer of 2000, Cecille was accumulating runners woven in a unique black-and-white optical design that she had developed with one of her weavers. She planned to take this line of products to a Manila exporter in the busy December season when they would command a higher price. On a selling trip in October, however, she noticed that one craft store was already selling bags manufactured in this fabric. Neighboring Banaue weavers had already duplicated the design and had taken the sewn products to Baguio City and to Manila stores. For Cecille, this meant releasing her line of products sooner than she had wanted and receiving a price lower than she had anticipated. In such instances, the balance of power shifts to artisans who are able to usurp designs, materials, and marketing opportunities and, in so doing, constrain traders' capital accumulation.

Cecille's survival tactics illustrate that earning a living is not only a matter of redistributing goods after adding a markup, but involves more proactive strategies. On the one hand, she tries to maximize the return on each transaction by buying as cheaply as possible, within community expectations, and selling for as much as the market will bear. This style of trading involves patience on the part of traders and nurturing skills with both producers and buyers, qualities of high cultural value within the Philippines (Karim 1995:19). Success depends on careful balancing of one's shrewd business prowess with fulfilling cultural community expectations. Like other petty capitalists manufacturing weavings, Cecille must also nurture ties with her urban buyers who market crafts both nationally and globally. To increase sales she gives, as a gift, samples of her new products in which her buyers have expressed interest. If these samples sell well, she increases the likelihood of receiving new orders. Similarly, if buyers do not bargain to reduce the amount of their payments, Cecille offers a gesture of good faith by rounding off the total due to make a small deduction.

In an innovative initiative to expand the reach of her sales, Cecille has entered into limited arrangements with neighbors and relatives allocating to them the responsibility for operating a separate section of her business. Based on the cultivation of trust, Cecille consigns her woven products to these emergent traders who, in turn, sell the weavings at the numerous regional public sporting events and village fiestas. Cecille receives her usual price while the latter sellers add a small markup for their profit. Cecille, explains, however, that this is a high-risk option for her and hesitates to commit to any immediate expansion until she identifies additional women on whom she can depend.[8]

Within such a variable craft market, Cecille hesitates to reinvest her profits solely back into her business. Instead, she uses some of her accumulated capital to purchase local signs of status and prestige such as rice land and lowland pigs. Such business investments, common throughout the Philippines, provide Cecille with both in-kind income (rice and meat) and social capital through sharecropping and joint-venture agreements that can facilitate community and family members' access to land and income (Milgram 1999; Rutten 1993).[9] Independent female petty capitalists like Cecille increasingly participate in such informal activities as their inability to predict economic outcomes encourages reliance on informal associations that can provide access to local knowledge, opportunities, and support (see also Alexander and Alexander 2001). Even petty capitalists such as Cecille with small livelihood operations want their businesses to be successful, no matter how petty they may be (Cook and Binford 1990:21; Gates, this volume).

### Poitia Handicraft Cooperative

In the mid-1990s, in response to the limited applicability of the Department of Trade and Industry's high-end trade fairs, a number of female artisans in different Banaue villages organized themselves into self-managed weaving cooperatives. Here I consider one collective organization, the Poitia Handicraft Cooperative, which has forged links with Manila-based alternative trade organizations engaged in fair trade practices.

In 1995, with support from the NEED initiative, a local nongovernmental organization provided initial loan funds to the Poitia cooperative, as they did to other similar associations, to construct a basic frame building and to purchase the equipment (looms) and yarn supplies needed to establish a weaving business. Like other new cooperative enterprises, the Poitia cooperative suffered initial growing pains. Loan repayments were due before weavers could establish a regular production schedule. With the strong leadership of a few board directors, however, members are now repaying their loan, albeit in smaller than expected amounts and in 1999 the collective was able to raise the 2,500-peso fee ($60) to formally register themselves as a cooperative.

Jean Calingun, a backstrap weaver in her early forties with four children, joined the cooperative in late 1995 to learn how to weave on an "upright" or *tilar* loom and to access the cooperative's broader marketing networks. As a novice weaver on the *tilar* loom, Jean worked slowly at first. In addition to weaving at the center, she continued to weave at home on her backstrap loom but using the cooperative's yarns and selling her products through the organization's marketing structure. Indeed, a majority of cooperative members engage in a similar pattern of multisited production depending upon the demands of childcare and domestic responsibilities and upon the availability of *tilar* looms in the cooperative's building. Determined to improve her weaving skills and to work for the success of the organization, Jean weaves at the cooperative four days a week, often taking her youngest child with her, and earns the standard per piece rate set by cooperative members. Her experience working part-time in a daycare center and as *barangay* (village) secretary makes her an excellent candidate for the three-member management team to which she was elected in late 1996. Jean works closely with the other managers, Kate Pindug, a mother of five also in her early forties, and Helen Dayong, a mother of two in her late thirties. While Helen is a weaver, Kate is the cooperative's master sewer designing many of the collective's unique products. The three women are responsible to a ten-member board of directors.

Members in the Poitia Handicraft Cooperative produce Ifugao's well-known, handwoven, stripe-patterned cotton yardage from which they manufacture a variety of functional products such as bags, backpacks, garments, and household accessories. On a rotating basis, members are responsible for selling these items to local tourist craft shops in Banaue and to regional and national outlets in Baguio City and Manila, as well as directly to tourists who visit the cooperative. Weavers feel they have more control over their income as they earn an agreed-upon fee per finished item; the fee varies depending upon the type of product not upon the whim of wholesale buyers. The cooperative, however, is still striving to mitigate the effects of the fluctuating seasonal demand for crafts that interrupts the cooperatives' cash flow and thus members' source of work.

In spring 2000, to overcome this seasonal cycle, cooperative members offered the use of its registered status to the *barangay* (village) captain who required such an organization through which to channel provincial grant funds given to support livestock raising. The *barangay* captain had obtained a grant from the government's Department of Agriculture (DOA) to purchase young pigs that would be raised by selected village households. Because the DOA would only distribute the funds through an organization formally registered with the SEC (Securities and Exchange Commission), and since some of the cooperative members would be availing of this livelihood enterprise, Jean with her fellow directors offered their association as the conduit for the funds with the stipulation that each recipient join the cooperative for one year. Their initiative thus strengthened local social bonds while members used the increase in revenue to purchase yarn, in bulk, which they retail to local weavers who are not members of the cooperative.

To achieve more autonomy within the current global market structure, members of the Poitia cooperative have recently established linkages with the Community Crafts Association of the Philippines (CCAP) and with Associated Partners for Fairer Trade, Inc. (APFTI), Philippine nongovernmental organizations based in Manila. Both nongovernmental organizations (NGOs) adhere to a philosophy of fair trade rather than to the neoliberal model of free trade practice (see CCAP 1995, 2002; APFTI 2002, 2003).[10] The main potentials of fair trade lie in opening up international markets to small community producers, educating consumers (particularly those in the "North") to select products produced and marketed along ethical lines, thus breaking existing patterns of resource dependency in which poorer artisans remain vulnerable to flows of aid and to uncertain local market conditions (Lewis 1998:135).

Nationally based alternative trade organizations such as CCAP and APFTI assist producer groups to market their products through international ATOs such as Ten Thousand Villages, Oxfam and Sales Exchange for Regugee Rehabilitation Vocation (SERRV). Adhering to fair trade practice, they purchase goods at locally appropriate prices directly from producers to eliminate the layers of middle people and multiple markups. This enables producers to earn more than a subsistence livelihood and to more accurately anticipate future income. In addition, some ATOs provide services such as credit, skills training, and advise on product development. ATOs do not work to maximize shareholders' profits, but rather to foster more democratic and equitable systems of international exchange, systems that confront the dominant disciplinary authority of the free market (APFTI 2002; CCAP 2002).

Working with fair trade organizations, however, does not insulate suppliers like the Poitia cooperative from the discipline of global markets—delivery deadlines, communication and quality standards, and changing consumer tastes all have to be met. Fair trade organizations employ the same "just-in-time" rationale as commercial companies, importing crafts in accordance with the statutory trading regulations (Grimes 2000:14; Littrell and Dickson 1999:158–163, 2000). Lewis (1998) cautions then, that a key challenge in fair trade practice is to convert producers and their organizations into successful marketing operations with the ability to sell high-quality goods in competitive, complex, and rapidly changing international markets.[11] Thus, petty capitalists like the Poitia managers devote as much time to strengthening members' social relations of production as they do to working with ATOs to develop marketing strategies and educational campaigns aimed at increasing consumer support for fair trade crafts.

While the formal market mode of ordering is present throughout the fair trade network, it is mediated through the mode of connectivity. The Poitia cooperative's new product label, for example, makes such linkages explicit:

> This handwoven product is made by women artisans at the [Poitia Handicraft Cooperative], an independent business started by weavers and sewers in Ifugao Province, Philippines. More of the money you pay for this product goes directly to these small-scale artisans who have few other employment opportunities. This livelihood project encourages the use of local and recycled materials and provides funds to assist in educational needs.

Such labeling establishes a physical connection between those who produce and those who buy crafts as Banaue artisans package their culture into the products they make. These bridges establish the performance of fairness that stands in sharp contrast to the rationale of cost-minimizing and self-interest privileged in free market exchange (see also Whatmore and Thorne 1997:297–299).

In summer 2001, the Poitia cooperative started to use fair trade linkages to market some of their products on the Internet. Both CCAP and APFTI subscribe to services of PEOPLink, a fair trade Internet site that features food and craft products on a rotating basis (see also Littrell and Dickson 1999:171–172, 185–190). In addition, APFTI maintains its own, somewhat smaller website to feature the Philippine producer groups that it specifically supports.[12] Although such linkages certainly offer rural artisans broader marketing possibilities, they come with the challenge of meeting the varied shifts in global market demand.

Such a challenge confronted Poitia weavers in mid-2002 when they received one of their first large Internet-sourced orders. Earlier, when cooperative managers obtained orders they could not commit immediately to agreements with prospective buyers until they had consulted with producers about whether or not, and within what time period, artisans could complete the order. Contacting cooperative members, especially those who often weave at home, can be time-consuming as some members' houses, located near their rice fields, are up to a one-hour walk from one another. Thus when orders are received or when artisans' availability changes due to increased childcare or cultivation tasks, the managers often have to visit houses individually to confirm production and delivery schedules. After missing the delivery deadline for a smaller order in the fall of 2001 and wanting to ensure that they meet the requirements of this new order, the cooperative managers applied for a special project loan from APFTI. In 2001, in an innovative initiative with one of its producer groups in Aklan province, APFTI offered loans to cooperative members to purchase cell phones. To facilitate the Poitia cooperative's new order, APFTI made a similar suggestion. The construction of a cell phone site in Banaue in 2002 opened up communication possibilities previously unfeasible with limited land line availability. Currently with their cell phones, once orders are received, the managers can quickly contact some of the members thus facilitating a timely response to buyers. The cooperative managers can also keep in closer contact with producers not working at the organization's building in case unexpected problems arise. The managers confirm that although it might be easier to centralize production by equipping a larger cooperative building, Jean explains, "We are committed to community development and to giving women options in their work conditions; thus we sponsor cell phones instead."

Cooperative managers Jean, Kate, and Helen acknowledge that at this point in the association's development, they are most often the voice of the organization and, indeed, garner the additional benefit of earning an honorarium for their work, 250 pesos ($6 in accordance with government guidelines) per day for two days work per week. Their educational achievements (two have some college education and one finished high school) plus their ownership (or long-term tenancy) of rice land have equipped them with the literary skills and social positions necessary to administer the cooperative. The demands of childcare and domestic tasks periodically preclude some female members from participating in the association's operation beyond their work in production. To facilitate the sharing of knowledge, skills, and power across a broader membership base, the managers, in conjunction with members' requests, are working with APTFI to develop leadership and skills training seminars for interested members. The current situation of the Poitia Handicraft Cooperative does not mean that instances of exploitation will not surface in the future given the differential in members' class-based positions. Clearly, the cooperative leaders enjoy the status and power implicit in their managerial roles. Given the youth of the program and the continuing challenge of fluctuating markets, however, to ensure sustainability, these women currently focus on strengthening the organization's administrative structure and its connections to global markets, even as they simultaneously garner an edge during their three-year term in office.

## Conclusion

In her discussion of globalization, Anna Tsing (2000:330) argues that although the international flow of goods, information, and technology is valorized, the manner in which the channel is carved is not. In Ifugao, the diverse channels that female petty capitalists pursue, independently and in craft cooperatives, demonstrate Tsing's position. As most craft enterprises remain family proprietorships in which petty capitalists work in production and distribution, continue to occupy pivotal positions between local producers and international buyers, and activate fair trade linkages, the bifurcation between domestic and economy or between formal and informal dissolves. As "small-scale" operators, they engage "in a complex of activities that are both embedded within and at the same time transforming practices of global capitalism" (Freeman 2001:1008).

Petty capitalists such as Cecille Kimmay and members of the Poitia cooperative address the risks in crafts by diversifying activities, mobilizing resources, and consolidating networks across multiple spheres. They employ better-qualified laborers, negotiate varied sites of supervision, enter into subcontracting or consignment relations, and develop more favorable and broader market opportunities (e.g., fair trade networks). The variable market for crafts, however, means that petty capitalists quickly reach the economic limits on the expansion of their businesses, not due solely to the lack of financing, but rather due to the limitations of local-to-regional sales. Cecille, for example, bought rice land and rented it out in a sharecropping arrangement, a traditional avenue of gaining cultural prestige, rather than reinvesting accumulated capital into her business, an initiative she feels can be more risky. Such initiatives increase petty capitalists' incomes, less by reinvesting in physical expansion than by solidifying the number and the quality of subsidiary relationships. They increase their turnover of products by extending their relationships both downward toward production (employing more artisans on contract when needed), and upward toward marketing (employing traders who take goods on consignment when demand is high). At the same time, if individual enterprises like Cecille's are to grow beyond a certain size, they must be accompanied by access to technology that enables larger production when needed, such as the upright floor looms used by the Poitia cooperative. Lacking this, artisans will work longer and longer hours to meet the larger product orders they have worked so hard to obtain.

It is certainly the case that women who have a higher education, own land, or have a long-term land tenancy are better positioned to accumulate capital and potentially exploit those they employ. Based on such class-based distinctions those women successful in business will often employ other women to perform domestic responsibilities not assumed by their male family members. However, because craft commodities are unique, handcrafted goods requiring intensive and skilled labor, petty capitalists often recruit artisans on the basis of local renown, their reliability and connection to community networks, and must maintain good social relations for business success. This personalized situation affords bargaining power to the artisans regardless of traders' class. Although artisans' earnings are low, the personal relation offers them an opportunity to bargain for favorable working conditions that act as compensation for wages (e.g., interest-free loans and in-kind gifts). Other artisans are better able to gradually start trading for themselves, especially when they have little access to capital, as Cecille's consignment initiatives illustrate. Although petty capitalists derive most benefit from the craft industry, the fluidity of Ifugao's socioeconomic climate means that "today's [petty] capitalist may be yesterday's" producer, "just as tomorrow's" producer may be "today's [petty] capitalist" (Cook and Binford 1990:31). Female petty capitalists thus use capital in creative ways to mitigate the practical difficulties in effectively appropriating the labor of others.

In initiatives similar to those of independent businesswomen, the Poitia Handicraft Cooperative has also hybridized their operation. Members established horizontal activities such as retailing yarns or offering the organization's status as a conduit for community activities. The options in fair trade practice that the Poitia cooperative is currently pursuing dispel the common expectation that the artisan trades and the livelihood opportunities they offer will be pushed out by global capital, displaced by machine-made commodities, and subordinated to capitalist production. As Priscilla Connolly (1985:85–86) suggests, women's power to operationalize such options constitutes a social movement mobilized on the basis of economic activities that have been labeled "informal" (see also Grimes, forthcoming). Organizations, such as neighborhood groups, she continues, "consciously defend not only their housing, but also their territorially prescribed petty trade and production interests: not only where and how they live but also the integration of their habitat to where and how they work" (Connolly 1985:85–86). Understanding fair trade networks as a social movement enables another channel through which women can realize the potential of their cross-sector activities.

Female petty capitalists' initiatives in craftwork push analyses beyond simple dichotomies and beyond unidirectional shifts from one steady state to another (Winslow 1996:726; Colloredo-Mansfeld 2002:115–116). In the Philippine Cordillera women operationalize different spaces that mobilize forms of ordering, particular rationalities, technologies, and routinized socioeconomic practices that resist and indeed compromise the singular neoliberal model of the global capitalist enterprise. By considering the multiple channels and the varied reach of the local-to-global networks within which these women work, we can engage in a critical study of social change. We can begin to understand how female petty capitalists reconfigure gendered patterns of interaction as "performative orderings (always in the making)" rather than as "systemic entities (always already constructed)" (Whatmore and Thorne 1997:289).

## Notes

Field research for this chapter was conducted over several periods in the northern Philippines between 1995 and 2003. Financial support for this research was provided by the Canada/ASEAN Centre, the Academic Support Program, the Social Sciences and Humanities Research Council of Canada, Doctoral Fellowship, a Postdoctoral Fellowship, (1997-1999) and a Standard Research Grant. In the Philippines, I am affiliated with the Cordillera Studies Center (CSC), University of the Philippines Baguio, Baguio City. I thank my colleagues at the CSC for their generous support of my research. I also wish to thank the volume editors Alan and Josephine Smart and the anonymous reviewers for their thoughtful comments. To the residents of Banaue, Ifugao, I owe a debt of gratitude.

1. Whatmore and Thorne, in turn, ground their research in actor-network theory as argued by Law (1994) and Latour (1993).

2. Rovine (2001) similarly argues that global markets have meant international fame and profitable opportunities to some makers of "mud-cloth" textiles in Mali.

3. This chapter builds upon and expands previously published material (Milgram 2000, 2001). For a further discussion of Ifugao's wood-carving trade, in particular, see Milgram (2001).

4. For similar terms of loan repayment documented in other Southeast Asian enterprises see, for example, Brenner (1998), Onchan (1992), and Alexander and Alexander (2001).

5. Structural adjustment policies designed to "modernize" economies typically include monetary devaluations, privatization of industry, deregulation of markets and prices, and a policy of austerity such as massive cutbacks in government social spending (Balisacan 1995; Broad 1988).

6. In 2001 the exchange rate was $1 = 42–44 Philippine pesos. The following average monthly incomes in 2001 contextualize these fees. A government employee (including teachers) earns approximately 3,500 pesos per month, a tourist service industry worker earns 2,500 pesos, most artisans earn 1,000-1,500 pesos, and vegetable venders earn 2,000-3,000 pesos per month.

7. Personal names of individuals as well as specific village names are all pseudonyms.

8. In Banaue's craft industry, as noted, most petty capitalists maintain their roles as producers and work not carried out by owners is paid on a fee-for-service basis whether working full- or part-time. This lack of delegated tasks is related to the problems of supervising staff especially in circumstances where prices are seldom fixed. A distinctive feature of Banaue's craft businesses is that even in situations where some form of collective household enterprise might appear economically efficient, throughout the Philippines, petty capitalists usually ensure that individual contributions, including those of family members, are calculated and paid for separately. Each individual retains considerable control over her own finance and labor. This inability to use the nuclear family as a cost-free business resource is one constraint on the growth of Ifugao enterprises (see also Alexander and Alexander 2001).

9. Throughout the Philippines, people often enter into agreements in which they share the purchase, raising, and selling of the faster-growing lowland pigs and then divide the profits from the sales.

10. With roots in nongovernmental organizations dedicated to reducing poverty in Southern countries, the fair trade "movement" has grown in North American, Europe, and Asia over the past twenty-five years. For a full discussion of fair trade organizations see Grimes (2000, forthcoming); Littrell and Dickson (1999), and Lewis (1998).

11. Lewis suggests that NGOs promoting fair trade ventures face a distinctive set of problems, many of which are caused by the location of such organizational activities in the "ambigous zone that exists between the for-profit and NGO sector," (1998:147). This has led to problems of confused expectations, management tensions, and lack of sustainability. He suggests that keys to strengthening such partnerships will involve greater transparency, market diversification, long-range planning, and the building of a set of more realistic expectations (1998:144-146).

12. Effective May 2001, the Craft Center in Washington, DC, launched the Artisan Enterprise Network, another site mandated to showcase fair trade products worldwide. Both CCAP and APFTI, as members of the Craft Center, are currently negotiating avenues through which to involve their producer groups in the numerous Craft Center initiatives.

# 12

## The Moral Significance
## of Petty Capitalism

### *Michael Blim*

Though our moral memories of the last thirty years will no doubt be crowded with thoughts of wars, little and large, endless and sporadic, we might also note two other striking passages that significantly altered human trajectories. First, the combination of poverty and disease, specifically that of AIDS, has triggered a dramatic fallback in human life expectancy for a vast proportion of the region of Africa in a path of destruction that may soon include Asia. This would be the first such fallback since Western-born diseases wiped out indigenous populations throughout the New World in the sixteenth century. Second, after sundry economic crises pushed capitalism into serious difficulties during the seventies throughout Western societies, a great tide of industrial development throughout Asia has swept up hundreds of millions of workers into a new industrial proletariat, whose labors are remaking the workshops of the world.

Wars, and the specter of a world in violence without end, cloud our view of both our immediate past as well as our future. Failed economies, failed states, overweening imperial ambitions, nationalist demagogueries—each can be found as a casus belli. The phenomena of economic stagnation and demographic fallback in Africa and the pell-mell economic development of Asia, on the other hand, find some roots in the abrupt and jagged flows of world capitalist development. Investment and economic activity, so often

directed by the restless international consensus of "business confi-
dence," abandoned other speculative domains such as Africa in
pursuit of increased profits, and fed instead the powerful indigenous capitalist growth machines of Asia. Following on earlier
Japanese success, the "smart money" went to Asia, and in buckets
to support the shift of world production across the international
dateline. After landing on the shores of East Asia's active commercial centers such as Hong Kong and Singapore, industrial capitalism established new beachheads under United States' military
protection in South Korea and Taiwan. From there it spread
throughout the hinterlands of the Pacific Rim, China, and finally
to all of Southeast Asia. Just as one would be unwilling to ascribe
the rise of AIDS to the simple "diffusion" of a disease without a
closer analysis of the social, economic, and political conditions
structuring a particular environment, so too our understanding of
how capitalism has spread requires more complex explanations
than the notion of "contact" with the contagion requires. States via
their ruling elites throughout East and Southeast Asia brought
their markets and institutions into sustained contact with capitalism. The results of this contact in each case vary by the kinds of
social struggle in each of these lands that ensued among groups,
some of whom had much to gain, and some of whom had much to
lose in the opening to the capitalist world economy.

In Asia industrial capitalism is a mix of the very big and the
small, but none have yet called it beautiful. The emplacements of
capital and labor can be truly gargantuan: consider that in
Dongguan, a city in the Guangdong region of southern China, one
factory employs 80,000 workers making upward of a 100 million
running shoes a year. They join over 30 million workers in the
Pearl River Delta who along with hundreds of millions of Chinese
workers throughout the country have made their country the
world's new industrial giant (Roberts and Kynge 2003:13).

The River Rouge-like dimensions of some of China's capitalist
development is a reminder that firms can still build great factories
and manufacturing facilities that would make even Henry Ford
envious, when the circumstances are suitable. Too, these industrial behemoths can still find customers for their long runs of standardized goods, even though they have mastered flexible
manufacturing with its speedy changeovers, just-in-time supply
systems, and reprogrammable machines. While small firms have
prospered via the adoption of the information revolution's technologies as well, neither big nor small firms seem to have gained a
decisive advantage in the new industrial age, now at least a quar-

ter of a century old. Indeed, one senses—in lieu of what are probably unattainable data anyway—that neither big nor little has won the day and that the sizes of industrial locations continue to reflect continuous, if zigzagging attempts to calculate price and profit.

However, firm size, large or small, it seems, may have succumbed to hierarchy. It is useful to keep in mind the rather sobering fact that four-fifths of the world's industrial output is a product, directly or indirectly, of the world's thousand largest companies (*Economist*, January 29, 2000:21). Let us even suppose that 20 percent of the world's industrial output of $10 trillion, or $200 billion, flows through the productive capacities of small- and medium-sized firms (World Bank 2001:297).[1] While certainly not small change, brief contemplation of these facts helps one to keep in perspective the actuality of the kind of world in which petty capitalists live and compete. Large firms continue to dominate world industrial production. In addition, the progressive incorporation of the output of small businesses into the production chains organized by the world's megafirms seems as much a fact as any claims that the information revolution has bequeathed a fetching future for the small and innovative (Harrison 1994).

And the observation that hierarchy—the subordination of production to the organizational needs and desires of large corporations—seems to have won out in many cases damages in an obvious way a purely instrumental argument for the virtues of petty capitalism. If one could see petty capitalism growing, overtaking "big" capitalism in important ways, and becoming something of a normative phenomenon, then "the propaganda of the deed" that would result would take one toward a certain kind of argument for the good. Certainly, it would have to be more than a sanctification of what is. Growing success for small firms would help establish their claim as the wave of the future and solidify a presumption that petty capitalism was somehow better adapted to the evolutionary path of capitalism as an economic system.

After a quarter century of anticipation, this outcome, it appears, is not to be. Though a literature praising their greater agility and general superiority as a business model in a quicker, more complicated world economy burgeoned, big business is still "the big business" of the world economy.

## Virtuous Petty Capitalism?

Perhaps a question is being begged here that should be asked in a straightforward way: Need petty capitalism have "a reason,"

or even more demanding, a "moral reason?" This is an important
question, and one that would seem to require one to provide some
justification for asking it—if nearly a quarter century of investiga-
tions of petty capitalism had not been undercoated with an implicitly moral rhetoric supporting its virtues, especially as against the
alternatives of "big" capitalism. Among the accounts that explored
the role of small business in a world capitalist economy recovering
from a worldwide economic trough in the latter half of the seventies, one detects a persistent theme in which the moral value of
petty capitalism vis-à-vis "big" capitalism was being appraised,
and mostly positively. Networks of small producers became like
bands of brothers linked in a kind of associative creation of goods
and a better society. Sometimes the relatively egalitarian division
of labor and the sophisticated technological linkages firms maintained with their partners through networks encouraged a kind of
technological moral reason: this new system of production and
labor, some argued, released and nurtured a better framework for
human affairs. It was a general good for society, in other words,
that its economy ran more humanely (see Perrow 2002).

Still, there was some looking-backward in this forward-looking
vision. Social scientists and economists, otherwise occupied with
documenting the rise or return, depending upon their point of
view, of petty capitalism, sought historical antecedents and justifications for their more favorable view of the small. The early capitalist period in Europe and in the United Kingdom was
reimagined as the capitalist road not taken (Sabel and Zeitlin
1985, 1997). Intellectual forerunners including the anarcho-syndi-
calist Pierre Joseph Proudhon were invoked as visionaries who
saw how social democracy could be implemented through work and
small firms without resorting to the construction of a costly, and
ultimately politically unsupportable welfare state (Piore and Sabel
1984). Others fastened upon a time in the United States before
Wall Street seized control of the nation's economy from Main
Street, and small business provided a competitive wedge between
people and economic power (Perrow 2002).

Other accounts claimed petty capitalism virtuous because it
affected the other aspects of society so little. I am reminded of an
early volume in the development of the Third Italy intellectual
boom, *Industrialization without Fractures* (Fua and Zacchia
1983),[2] whose title implies how much it was devoted to showing
how petty capitalism could create significant economic progress
without fatally disrupting the structures and tenor of local social

life. Instead of a band of brothers, this account, unaided as it was at the time of its writing by an analysis of gender, praised the efforts of another band—the hardworking, former peasant patriarchal extended household and its ability to work harmoniously, if self-exploitatively, to produce a new economy out of an old society.

These accounts are illustrative of the fact that I think it is fair to suggest that the "moral question" reflecting on the ultimate value of petty capitalism finds its way into many of our economic and social analyses. I do not claim to have ignored moral arguments myself. On several occasions, my work has expressed a certain amount of disappointment in the petty capitalists of the central Italian Marche region whom I studied throughout the eighties over their failures to invest in radically upgrading their production processes so as to assure their own survival and the region's well-being. I was also outspoken in my criticism of their continued resort to illegal and undocumented labor processes, again something I attributed to lack of foresight as well as to outright cupidity (Blim 1990, 1992).

Thus, based as much on my own personal reflections as on the accounts of others, I do not think it too great a leap to venture that social scientists identify with at least some aspects of the lives and works of petty capitalists. They provide some economic alternatives in societies that have become dominated by gigantic corporate power. They provide instances for authorizing efficacious individual agency in tableaux so often otherwise organized by bureaucratic structures. One need not share Russell Jacoby's (1987) worm's-eye view of the diminished capacities of intellectuals in the United States to note the rightness of his observation that the vast majority of American intellectuals (if I may be permitted) and putatively others occupying parallel posts in rich societies, operate from inside the great house rather than from outside. We staff the enormous structures of cosmopolitan higher education, and find ourselves heteronomously "housed" in large organizations in which we are carefully monitored for our quality and output, and otherwise treated as subalterns in what often seems to be a dizzying hierarchy of academic bureaucrats. Given the depths of our own domination, nonetheless marked by our professional strivings for autonomy and by the perfection of craft in teaching as well as in thought, our appreciation of petty capitalists may derive as much from our own confinement as from their relative freedom to take on the world economically on at least a few of the terms they choose.

Of course, the politics of petty capitalists may dismay, even alienate those who study them. Once again, I am reminded of my own experience of knowing a highly benevolent as well as paternalistic factory owner who has remained a committed Fascist, Mussolini and all. By my informant's lights, there was little Il Duce hadn't anticipated as answers to contemporary social and political problems. One thinks a bit more carefully about my informant's outbursts now that a reformed fascist party cogoverns Italy in a center-right coalition. Yet, it strikes me that even the most ideologically insulated among us, faced periodically with the seemingly inexplicable demands of a tax return or a research funding proposal, would at least nod knowingly to a petty capitalist's plea to be released from the manifold reporting requirements touched off by the ordinary workday.

Let it also be said that the combination of risk, determination, and hard work—such as they are in evidence—often creates admiration in many, and not simply those of an intellectual cast of mind. In the United States, autonomy, independence, doing something one's self, and for one's self remains a mythical component of everyday life, even if the reality of doing for one's self has grown steadily out of reach, given the capacities of most of the nation's people (Wiebe 1995).

In all, though, the admiration such as it is of academic intellectuals for petty capitalists reminds one of the attraction that the late social critic Christopher Lasch felt for the petty bourgeois sensibilities of the lower middle class. Lasch (1991) was charmed by the fact that the lower-middle class was attached to family and neighborhood and respected workmanship and hard work. He appreciated that its members valued loyalty, thrift, and self-denial, and acknowledged the fundamental limits governing human potential. One imagines that these stolid, responsible folk represented for Lasch the last virtuous group in a society he viewed as overrun with elites no longer interested in the plight of the masses, and of masses drugged by fetishized consumption into a narcissistic sense of self-regard—and inner emptiness (see Lasch 1979, 1995).

But does this account of virtue, however scaled back, suffice? Shall we measure value solely via a reflection of our own heteronomy or via a properly misguided populist celebration of the self-assertion and self-actualization of the petty capitalist?

## Applying Equality

Suppose, instead, that we examine petty capitalism with the value of equality, specifically economic equality, in mind. To that end, we might ask: To what degree do petty capitalist enterprises generally contribute to greater economic equality?

This is not the place to present a full-fledged defense of why we should place economic equality above other possible values that could be applied to the predicaments of petty capitalism.[3] It is important, however, to clarify briefly what we might mean by taking economic equality into consideration. We actually can retrieve little help from the Marxist tradition, for as G. A. Cohen (2000:103) points out, there wasn't much thought given to the concept of equality, since it was assumed to be an historically inevitable outcome of proletarian revolutions. In contrast, modern liberals have thought a great deal about the meanings and implications of equality; the accounts of John Rawls and Ronald Dworkin provide us with some concepts and language useful to the task. Equality for Rawls is a situation where all have similar rights and duties, and income and wealth are evenly shared. The distribution of basic goods can be unequal, Rawls (1971) writes, so long as any existing inequalities benefit society as a whole, and surplus in compensation for disadvantage is transferred to improve the condition of those in greater need. Dworkin, in contrast with the position of Rawls, argues that the kinds of resources that societies must provide to ensure equality are constantly changing. He believes that it is the duty of politics in states to manifest "equal concern" for all citizens by continuously advancing equality (2000, 2002).[4]

On the face of it, petty capitalism would seem to be an unlikely and unlucky candidate for creditable valuation with respect to equality. It would seem, almost by definition, to be an inequality-maker: by becoming a petty capitalist, one places one's self in a better position when contrasted with dependent workers and unemployed people in a given society. Of course, this need not always be the case, as workers protected by good union contracts and unemployed persons by a generous welfare state can often obtain enviable positions of relatively greater security, if not wealth, than can the petty capitalist. Even in societies without strong unions and welfare states of note, the petty capitalist, if imagined as the street-corner entrepreneur in the informal economy of a poor country, may find that she has only the freedom to starve, as the late Michael Harrington would have put it, and few if any comforts, let alone privileges attached to her class. In all, then, we can't assume, a priori, that petty capitalists are automatically excluded from any project to increase equality.

Then there is the hard-nosed constraint of context that any
valuation must face: More or less equal compared with what?
Starting with our own characterization of the international industrial economy as dominated by a thousand of the world's largest
firms, can we imagine their sector of the economy as highly redistributive? Their profits flow into a tiny portion of the world's
households in the form of dividends. Given the pressures of profitability, it seems highly unlikely that as labor-users, the world's
largest corporations are great engines of equalization. To the
extent that they provide wages in areas where there are none, one
might argue, via a theory of proletarianization, that some, however slight, incremental gains could be predicated on multinational expansion. Some studies over the past several decades, for
instance, have suggested that women in poor countries, given their
prospects in patriarchal households or facing gender discrimination on a society-wide basis, have improved their economic and
social status through employment in the factories and offices of
multinational corporations, or those producing for them (see Lim
1983; A. Ong 1987; C. K. Lee 1998; Freeman 2000).

And to return to our starting-point with the petty capitalists, it
seems unlikely that their presence would send a nation's Gini
index, (a common measure of inequality) a conventional indicator
of national economic inequality, skyrocketing. If anything, small-
firm preponderance, one hazards a guess, would be likely to lower
the rate of total economic inequality in given societies, all things
being equal.

However, it is one thing to acknowledge hypothetically the
modest effects that petty capitalism might have on the distribution
of income.[5] It is another to undertake state and international projects to promote petty capitalism on the theory that increasing
their presence will increase economic equality. For instance, even
if extremely unfashionable to contemplate today, it may make
more sense to return to the formulas of enlightened corporatism,
whereby the state and large corporations increased the social
wage, and unions agreed to provide labor peace and to tolerate
technological innovation in the workplace. Even more unpopular
for these times still might involve states nationalizing major
industries once more. In addition to gaining more political control
over their economic destinies, states could advance directly the
living standards of the firms' workers, and by example positively
influence outcomes for workers at large. These strategies may not
stand the test of neoliberalist politics, but each had modest posi-

tive equality effects in the United States, Eastern, and Western Europe during the so-called Golden Age of post-World War II economic expansion.

If we focus on the "petty" of petty capitalism, there are solutions other than interventions to support entrepreneurial, for-profit capitalism that would warrant close attention. Collective entities like cooperatives, though they account for very small proportions of business activity everywhere they are found, typically emphasize redistribution and equity among their members. The so-called third or nonprofit sector run by nongovernmental organizations, charitable foundations, and the like, provide public goods and perform services on an economically and socially significant scale in many parts of the world (Bruyn 2000).[6] Some have argued that this form of enterprise could be extended downward to include small-service providers and others dealing directly with clients. With the protection and assistance of the state, nonprofit providers could develop useful niches in the human services economy, while the state and clients would receive valuable services at the lower costs that the providers could charge (Block 1996; Revelli 1997). The cooperative and nonprofit options could undoubtedly profit from greater scrutiny as well as from social experiment (Milgram, this volume).

## Petty Capitalism's Virtues and Gender Inequality

Suppose, however, that we set aside the evaluation of the equality effects of these alternatives for the moment, and turn instead to a consideration of the value in these terms of widespread initiatives undertaken currently around the world in support of for-profit entrepreneurship via microlending. While I cannot provide an exhaustive reporting of its history and use, it is certainly fair to say that the promotion of small businesses and its finance have been constant features of international economic development programs for the better part of half a century. Important international development advocacy documents such as the Pearson Commission in 1969 and the Brandt Commission in 1980 both included the need to encourage small businesses, and suggested the extension of small credits to small businesses, particularly to those engaged in agricultural production for markets.[7]

Microlending per se has strong roots in women's self-help and development-minded communities around the world, but it began to find external support in the eighties from states and nongovernmental organizations as policy makers sought ways of supporting economic change initiated by local people themselves. The result is that microlending support became a key policy strategy for addressing the manifest economic disadvantages of women in poor countries. Because it has become such a key economic intervention, it is important that we examine critically its equality effects. It would also provide an excellent instance for attempting to evaluate a social policy by a yardstick other than by the instrumental one of market efficiency. If we followed the latter, for instance, we would be concerned with whether microlending overcame an obvious market failure in poor countries, where banks fail to provide small business people with liquidity. In contrast, let us ask whether microlending to small business enterprises of women reduces or eliminates economic inequality among women and/or vis-à-vis men.

"With Little Loans, Mexican Women Overcome," the headline of the *New York Times* story reads. Tim Weiner, a highly experienced liberal reporter, has his lead:

> Guadalupe Castille Urena was widowed at 31, left alone with five children when her husband died trying to get to the United States from their hut here in the foothills of Mexico's southern Sierras. She was among the poorest of the poor—scraping by, like half the people in Mexico, and half the world's six billion people, on $2 a day or less, barely surviving. Then an organization called Finca came to the village. It asked the women there—and only the women—whether they would be interested in borrowing a little money, at the stiff interest rate of 6% a month, to start their own businesses. Change came. With a loan of about $250, Ms. Urena, now 35, started making hundreds of clay pots this winter. With Finca's help, they were sold in bulk to a wholesaler, who sells them in the city. She pocketed $15 to $20 a week in profit. That sum, the first real money she had ever earned, was enough to help feed her children and pay their school expenses. "It's exhausting," she said, "kneading the mud, stoking the kiln. But it's something. An opportunity." (March 19, 2003:A8)

Microlending, Weiner argues, "is producing wealth in some of the world's poorest countries."

In addition to providing poor women with small-business loans, Weiner notes that the nongovernmental organizations involved in lending have also begun providing other financial services, effectively becoming the banks of the poor. "The fact is that poor people can save money," one World Bank expert who had been involved in microcredit start-ups tells Weiner, who also observes that this fact was "something of a revelation to economists."

The high interest rates of microlenders do catch Weiner's eye. The article ends with the story of another client, Escolatica Medina, who had borrowed the equivalent of $500 from the Finca microlenders. The sales of the clay pots she produced with the loan amounted to $800. The $300 "profit" calculated as the difference between the loan and the sales—and not counting her labor as a cost of production—was split between her and the microlender. She received $190 and Finca received $110, the latter a consequence of what Weiner describes as an interest rate "about five times higher than any United States credit card company could legally charge."

As a result of her loan-assisted business, Escolatica and her children could probably not be said to be living richly. "A little money for when my children need something—enough for food, for school, for their health" is how she puts it. Conveniently for Weiner's conclusion, though, she says just the right thing. Presumably as a result of her small business success through microlending, she says that now, "I feel equal to anyone."

Though perhaps with less skill, this story has been told time and again in development policy and political circles. Microlending, and through it the fostering of microenterprises works for women otherwise weighed down by childcare and household labor, and beaten down by males in patriarchal societies. The microlending movement, dating roughly to the establishment of Bangladesh's Grameen Bank in 1974, has moved quickly to become one of the premier development interventions designed to wrest disadvantage from the shoulders of women around the world. The World Bank estimates that 7,000 microlending institutions have made loans to 25 million people, 75 percent of them women, in over 40 countries (World Bank 2002a:9). In Bangladesh alone, owing to the success of Grameen Bank, 7 million people, largely women, have received small loans. Grameen has branched out as a bank and as a nongovernmental organization into a variety of income-generating businesses including dairies, fisheries, textiles, and telecommunications. In the case of the last, it can

now boast to be the largest mobile phone company in Asia, using
its links with local lending circles to distribute handheld telephone
service operated by women microentrepreneurs throughout poor
rural villages in Bangladesh (Lawson-Tancred 2002:6).[8] Other
credit banks engaged in microlending have reported similar successes in Latin America, and of late in the United States.[9]

It is a concept with many advocates, for it fits nicely in the
niche that neoliberalism has carved for itself as the friendly alternative that can find favor with the centrists of the former Clinton
administration and Washington's center-right new masters. World
Bank James Wolfensohn, a structural straddler between the two
camps, puts the case in an ideologically adept way: "It is about
scaling up—moving from individual projects to programs, building
on and then replicating, for example, micro-credit for women or
community-driven development where the poor are at the center of
the solution, not the end of a handout (World Bank 2002b:4)."

Women becoming The Solution, rather than the problem: this
is an attractive slogan in these times when redistribution is seen
as charity rather than right. If women can do something for themselves, a greater moral dignity is attached to them and some
change in their character is inferred. They are, in a word, *empowered.* That is, women exercise more everyday autonomy over their
bodies, their labor, their associations, and their time, and they
have greater access to, and control over, material resources in
their environments.

Microlending has achieved mixed results, as measured in
terms of the goal of empowerment. Putting money in women's
hands through loans in Bangladesh, for instance, is highly associated with improving children's nutritional status, an outcome not
typically found when money is given to men (World Bank
2001:119). As one Salvadorian woman told a microlending
researcher, microloans beat depending upon the local loan shark:
instead of "feeding the fat man," the loan shark, she could feed her
children (Cosgrove 1999:46-47).[10] However, there is contradictory
evidence as to whether microlending helps women overcome the
practical conditions of patriarchy at home. In one Bangladesh
study, women microloaners as compared with nonloaners did
increase their say in household decision making (Amin, Becker,
and Bayes 1998). Another study, once more from Bangladesh, suggests the opposite, except that it notes that women do have access
to more financial resources and do acquire more control over fertility decisions in family planning (Osmani 1998).

Moreover, microlending may also have unintended downside effects on participating women. It appears that men advantage themselves from programs otherwise directed toward improving the lot of women relative to their men. While evidence from Bolivia suggests that women were able to put the loan money to good use and to maintain control over their businesses (Buechler et al. 1998), a detailed Bangladeshi study of households to whom loans in the name of the senior woman were made revealed that in about half of the cases, men—not women—controlled the loan monies (Goetz and Sen Gupta 1995; Rahman 1999). It also is reported that women experience enormous peer pressure from their co-loan recipients, other women organized into lending circles by credit banks, to pay off their loans. More vulnerability, rather than the expected empowerment, can be the result (Fernando 1997; Rahman 1999).

But what of the equality effects? That is, do microlending programs create greater economic equality? In actuality, this is presently impossible because microlending is but an economic drop in the bucket, even in nations where it is highly diffused. The Grameen Bank, to recall, is not only a pioneering microlender, but can boast of loan operations in 40,000 of Bangladesh's 68,000 villages. Yet, its turnover, the amount of money it contributes on an annual basis to the country's gross domestic product, varies between 1 and 1.5% a year.[11] Perhaps the dilemma of BancoSol, a successful Bolivian microlender, illustrates the point best: despite providing 40% of all bank loans in Bolivia, BancoSol holds only 2% of the country's banking assets.[12]

However, based upon the evidence of how microlending has been working in local situations, we can get some measure of its impact on reducing economic inequality. We can begin to get some idea of whether it is an intervention to be promoted in achieving greater economic equality, or whether the present and future assets devoted to it might be better placed elsewhere. To develop our assessment, we must take and adapt the findings of studies for which the question of equality was not directly evaluated. First, we can review studies analyzing the degree to which microlending has reduced poverty among its client populations, a focus of much current research. They can be helpful at least indirectly because a society that reduces poverty in most cases is likely making progress in reducing overall economic inequality.

Several international aid agencies, having analyzed the results of a wide range of empirical studies have concluded that microlending is not directly effective in reducing poverty. Noting that while some research has highlighted the microlending's potential for significant poverty reduction, while others have found minimal impact on poverty reduction, the International Fund for Agricultural Development argues:

> It is now increasingly recognized that microfinance alone is not a magic bullet for poverty reduction, but only one of the many factors that may contribute to it. In fact, in an effort to dispel the impression that microfinance is a cure for poverty, it is argued that "the claims that microfinance assists 'the poorest' and 'the poorest of the poor' are unfounded within national contexts, microfinance institutions virtually never work with the poorest...and many microfinance institutions have high proportions of clients who are non-poor, using national poverty lines." (2001:209)

The World Bank in similar fashion concludes that microlending is "no panacea for poverty," noting too that studies of microfinance programs suggest participants living at or above the national poverty line derive significantly greater benefits than do those below the poverty line (World Bank 2001:75).

Based upon these findings, a second observation would seem warranted. Are these programs *increasing* rather than decreasing economic inequality? The question needs to be qualified in two ways. On the one hand, has microlending, a program historically targeted at women, reduced their inequality compared to men? Discussion of the data related to research on women's empowerment suggests that women do get access to money to which they would otherwise not have access, but the research also notes that women in some contexts lose control over the loan money to male residents of their households. Aside from the softer measures of "empowerment," there is not much evidence available to confirm or deny that women's equality vis-à-vis men in their immediate surroundings or in areas with lively microlending programs has increased (Newaz 2000).[13] If a positive equality effect vis-à-vis men were significant, it would likely be noted widely. Perhaps all we can infer is that in the matter of men versus women, microlending neither increases nor decreases equality.

On the other hand, analysis does suggest that microlending increases economic inequality among women as a whole in contexts where it is prevalent. We have just noted that reviews by large international development agencies such as the World Bank and the International Fund for Agricultural Development found that more advantaged participants, again overwhelmingly women, do better in microlending programs, and that poor women are underserved relative to those who are better off. Several ethnographic studies show that microlending can actually deepen class differences among women by providing limited social mobility for a better-off minority that is able to capture microloans as a new local resource. A field study of the activities of three microlending nongovernmental organizations in Bangladesh shows that women of the local elite monopolized receipt of microloans. They did so in part because of their superior social connections, and in part because nongovernmental organizations (NGOs), both desiring elite participation and needing lending successes for their own institutional reasons, favored them. Microenterprises funded by microlending, the author argues, reinforce existing inequality (Fernando 1997).

Lesley Gill's ethnographic inquiry outside LaPaz, Bolivia (2000) reveals much the same thing, except that the pattern she believes she has discovered is far more insidious. Gill notes too that NGOs create clientelist ties with economically advantaged women who become organizational "successes." But she also posits that the growing involvement of a microlender like BancoSol that has become for-profit businesses signals that microlending is being transformed into another circuit for the capitalist exploitation of the poor through the extension of small loans at rates little lower than offered by the local loan shark. Like the U.S. banking giant Citicorp that has dipped down through acquisitions of "consumer finance" corporations, a.k.a. usurious lenders to lend to "substandard," a.k.a. poor clients at high rates, Gill sees an agency like BancoSol leading the way in the transformation of grassroots microlending into a profitable, private banking business.

## Conclusion

Whether microlending will take the route spotted by Gill in the case of BancoSol, or if it will remain largely the province of nongovernmental organizations interested in self-sufficiency rather than, strictly speaking, a profit, one cannot at this point say.

If one, however, were interested in increasing equality, specifically in this case economic equality—and one would be expectant about increasing social equality as well if one succeeded—then microlending would not be a wise intervention. It appears to have no measurable effect in narrowing the economic inequalities between men and women. It would also seem less than efficacious in reducing the social inequalities that arise between men and women in households, as suggested by the empowerment studies that attempt to capture precisely the closing of social status differentials at home.

Supporting microlending for women may be virtuous when seen in the light of other values. Surely it supports the development of petty capitalism, and may ease the impact of market failures to provide credit at reasonable prices for women in small enterprises. To the degree that petty bourgeois values such as thrift and hard work are associated with small business, microlending may strengthen these kinds of value orientations among women entrepreneurs. Many ascribe additional value to people "making something of themselves," and "pulling themselves up by their bootstraps," no less than the persons trying to do it for themselves.

Those valuing equality, particularly economic equality in this case, however, will probably not find in microlending a highly congenial solution. It remains to be seen whether the same can be said for petty capitalism more generally. With respect to the condition of women and the poor, for instance, there is some evidence suggesting that public works programs, education, and job-training programs provide more concrete support for people's earnings, and thus eat away at income inequality more directly (Dollar and Collier 2002).

Other segments or institutions within capitalist economies may produce more economic equality than petty capitalism. Cooperatives, because they typically seek to distribute wages and redistribute profits on an egalitarian basis, hold out more prospects for positive equality effects. Insofar as fair trading scheme help producers retain more of the surplus they generate, they also may have positive local equality effects. Even large-scale corporate capitalism, when tamed by unions or harnessed by the combination of state and unions in corporatism, might perform the function well.

The point, it seems to me, is to measure our economic results differently and act accordingly.

# Notes

1. This rough estimate is based upon the World Bank's report that the world gross domestic product (GDP) in 1999 was $30 trillion (2001:table 12).

2. The title of the book in question, *Industrializzazione senza fratture*, triggered more than a few grins, as the title was consistently if somewhat teasingly mispronounced as *Industrializzazione senza fatture*, or as "industrialization without invoices or receipts" in recognition of one of the more notorious traits of Third Italian development: its flagrant tax evasion and use of *lavoro nero*, "illegal and undocumented labor," to speed its accumulative success.

3. See Blim (forthcoming) for a statement of the argument for equality.

4. Dworkin (2002:1, 86-109). Dworkin and Rawls also disagree over the extent to which disadvantaged persons should be guaranteed equality of resources. While Dworkin offers full support for the notion, Rawls's position is more qualified, a position closer to equality of opportunity, and having to do with the kinds of resources and the nature of handicaps that disadvantaged people suffer.

5. The Gini index only calculates disparities in income, not the distribution of wealth in a given society.

6. Severyn Bruyn (2000:40-41) suggests that sometimes success can alter cooperative equality efforts. He notes that although the well-known Basque region cooperatives of Mondragon in 1993 had 26,000 people and 150 businesses and $3 billion turnover, its co-op character was shifting, as it moves production overseas and hires temporary nonowner workers at home.

7. The Commission on International Development, was known as the Pearson Commission and the Independent Commission on International Development Issues, the latter that was published was known as the Brandt Commission.

8. See also Women's World Banking website, www.swwb.org. Women's World Banking accounts for roughly half of the microcredit loans being to women through its forty agents throughout the world.

9. Americans for Community Co-operation in Other Countries (ACCION) International, a network of credit banks operating in 13 Latin American countries, as well as in Africa and the United States served 2.7 million clients between 1999 and 2002, and disbursed $4.6 billion in loans with a loan loss rate of 3 percent. See www.accion.org, <April 7, 2003>.

10. Reduced dependence on local loan sharks is also reported in Buechler et al. (1998:102).

11. See the fact page of the Grameen Bank at www.grameen-info.org/bank, <April 4, 2003>.

12. www.accion.org, <April 7, 2003>.

13. Newaz (2000) reports that no women in her sample of twenty microlenders were able to purchase land with their increased earnings. In this context, property ownership would probably figure as a significant measure of economic equality.

# Bibliography

Abu-Lughod, J. L. 1989. *Before European hegemony: The world system A.D. 1250–1350.* Oxford: Oxford University Press.

Aguilar, F. V., and V. A. Miralao. 1985. Rattan furniture manufacturing in metro Cebu: A case study of an export industry. *Handicraft Project Paper Series,* No. 6. Manila: Ramon Magsaysay Award Foundation.

Ainsworth, M. D. S. 1967. *Infancy in Uganda: Infant care and the growth of love.* Baltimore: John Hopkins.

Alexander, J. 1986. Information and price setting in a rural Javanese market. *Bulletin of Indonesian Economic Studies* 22:88–112.

Alexander, J., and P. Alexander. 2001. Markets as gendered domains: The Javanese Pasar. In *Women traders in cross-cultural perspective: Mediating identities, marketing wares,* ed. L. J. Seligmann. Stanford: Stanford University Press, 47–69.

Alonso, J. A. 1984. The domestic clothing workers in the Mexican metropolis. In *Women and men and the international division of labor,* eds. J. Nash and M. P. Fernandez Kelly. Albany: State University of New York Press.

———. 2000. *Redes de subcontratacion y globalization periferica en Mexico.* Paper presented at the annual meeting of the Southwest Council of Latin American Studies. Puebla, Mexico.

Amendola, M., and J-L. Gaffard. 1988. *The innovative choice.* New York: Basil Blackwell.

Amin, A. 1989. Flexible specialisation and small firms in Italy: Myths and realities. *Antipode* 21:13–34.

———. 1999. An institutionalist perspective on regional economic development. *International Journal of Urban and Regional Research* 23(2): 365–378.

271

——. 1999. The Emilian model: Institutional challenges. *European Planning Studies* 7(4): 389–405.

Amin, A., and K. Robins. 1990. The re-emergence of regional economies? The mythical geography of flexible specialisation. *Environment and Planning D: Society and Space* 8: 7–34.

Amin, A., and N. Thrift. 1992. Neo-Marshallian nodes in global networks. *International Journal of Urban and Regional Research* 16(4): 571–587.

Amin, R., S. Becker, and A. Bayes. 1998. "NGO-promoted microcredit programs and women's empowerment in rural Bangladesh: Quantitative and qualitative evidence," *Journal of Developing Areas* 32(2), Winter, 221–236.

Amin, S. 1972. *Modes of production, social formations, interconnections of the various levels of a formation, classes and social groups, nations and ethnic groups: Introduction to the concepts.* Dakar: United Nations African Institute for Economic Development and Planning.

——. 1973. *Le developpement inegale.* Paris: Les Editions de Minuit.

Amsden, A. 1989. *Asia's next giant: South Korea and late industrialization.* New York: Oxford University Press.

APFTI (Associated Partners for Fairer Trade, Inc.). 2002. *Annual report: Strengthening market links for the global Filipino.* Manila: APFTI.

——. 2003. APFTI E-Bulletin 13 (March 24, 2003).

Appadurai, A. 2000. Grassroots globalization and the research imagination. *Public Culture* 12(1): 1–19.

Babb, F. E. 1989. *Between field & cooking pot: The political economy of marketwomen in Peru.* Austin: University of Texas Press.

——. 1981. Labor market, class structure and regional formations in Italy. *International Journal of Urban and Regional Research* 5(1): 40–44.

Bagnasco, A. 1977. *Tre Italie: La problematica territoriale dello sviluppo italiano.* Bologna: Il Mulino.

Balisacan, A. 1995. Anatomy of poverty during adjustment: The case of the Philippines. *Economic Development and Cultural Change* 44(1): 33–62.

Bateman, M. 1999. Small enterprise policy in transition economies: Progress with the wrong model? *Zagreb International Review of Economics and Business* 2(1): 1–36.

Bateson, P., and P. Martin. 2000. *Design for life: How behavior and personality develop*. New York: Simon and Schuster.

Becattini, G. 1992. The Marshallian district as a socio-econ notion. In *Industrial districts and inter-firm cooperation in Italy*, eds. F. Pyke, G. Becattini, and W. Sengenberger. Geneva: International Institute for Labor Studies.

Begg, R., J. Pickles, and P. Roukova. 2000. A new participant in the global apparel industry: The case of southern Bulgaria. *Problemi na Geographi* 3(4): 121–152.

Begg, R., J. Pickles, and A. Smith. 2003. Cutting it: European integration, trade regimes and the reconfiguration of East-Central European apparel production. *Environment and Planning A*, forthcoming.

Beneria, L., and M. Roldan. 1987. *The crossroads of class and gender: Industrial homework, subcontracting, and household dynamics in Mexico City*. Chicago: University of Chicago Press.

Bennett, J. M. 1996. *Ale, beer, and brewsters in England: Women's work in a changing world, 1300–1600*. Oxford: Oxford University Press.

Bernstein, H. 1986. Capitalism and petty commodity production. *Social Analysis* 20: 11–28.

———. 2000. 'The peasantry' in global capitalism: Who, where and why? In *Working classes, global realities (Socialist Register 2001)*, eds. L. Panitch and C. Leys. London: Merlin Press.

Best, M. 1990. *The new competition*. London: Polity.

Bianchi, G. 1992. Combining networks to promote integrated regional development. In *Problems of economic, transition: Regional development in Central and Eastern Europe*, ed. T. Vasko. Aldershot England: Avebury, 89–105.

Blim, M. 1990. *Made in Italy: Small-scale industrialization and its consequences*. New York: Praeger.

———. 1992. Small-scale industrialization in a rapidly changing world market. In *Anthropology and the global factory: Studies of the new industrialization in the late twentieth century*, eds. F. Rothstein and M. Blim. New York: Bergin and Garvey.

———. 2000. Capitalism in late modernity. *Annual Review of Anthropology* 29: 25–38.

———. 2001. Italian women after development: Employment, entrepreneurship, and domestic work in the Third Italy. *History of the Family* 6: 257–270.

———. Forthcoming *Equality*, Lanham, MD: Rowman and Littlefield.

Block, F. 1996. *The vampire state and other myths and fallacies about the U.S. economy.* New York: New Press.

Bonacich, E., and R. Appelbaum. 2000. *Behind the label: Inequality in the Los Angeles apparel industry.* Berkeley: University of California Press.

Bowlby, J. 1969. *Attachment.* London: Tavistock Institute of Human Relations.

———. 1988. *A secure base: Parent-child attachment and healthy human development.* London: Routledge.

Bowles, S., and H. Gintis. 1990. Contested exchange: New micro-foundations for the political economy of capitalism. *Politics and Society* 18: 165–222.

Boyer, R. 1990. *The regulation school: A critical introduction.* New York: Columbia University Press.

Brenner, S. A. 1998. *The domestication of desire: Women, wealth and modernity in Java.* Princeton: Princeton University Press.

Brhel, J. 1994. *Malé a stredné podnikanie.* Bratislava: FITR.

Broad, R. 1988. *Unequal alliance: The World Bank, the International Monetary Fund and the Philippines.* Berkeley: University of California Press.

Brown, J. K. 1997. Agitators and peace-makers: Cross-cultural perspectives on older women and the abuse of young wives. In *A cross-cultural exploration of wife abuse,* ed. A. Sev'er. Lewiston, NY: The Edwin Mellen Press, 79–99.

Browne, K. E. 1996. The informal economy in Martinique: Insights from the field, implications for development policy. *Human Organization* 55(2): 225–234.

Brusco, S. 1982. The Emilian model: Productive decentralisation and social integration. *Cambridge Journal of Economics* 6: 167–184.

Bruyn, S. 2000. *A civil economy: Transforming the market in the 21st century.* Ann Arbor: University of Michigan Press.

Buechler, H., and J.-M. Buechler. 1992a. *Manufacturing against the odds: Small scale producers in an Andean city.* Boulder: Westview Press.

———. 1992b. Spanish Galician industrialization and the Europe of 1992: A contextual analysis. In *Anthropology and the global factory,* eds. F. Rothstein and M. Blim. New York: Bergin and Garvey, 102–118.

―――. 1999. The bakers of Bernburg and the logics of socialism and capitalism. *American Ethnologist* 26(4): 799–821.

―――. 2000. Farmers, conflict, and identity in Eastern Germany. *Identities: Global Studies in Culture and Power* 7(1): 39–83.

―――. 2002. *Contesting agriculture: Cooperativism and privatization in the new Eastern Germany.* Albany: State University of New York Press.

Buechler, H., J-M Buechler, S. Buechler, and S. Buechler. 1998. "Financing small-scale enterprises in Bolivia, in *The third wave of modernization in Latin America: Cultural perspectives on neoliberalism,* ed. Lynne Phillips. Wilmington, DE: Scholarly Resources Books.

Carlsson, B. 1996. Small business, flexible technology and industrial dynamics. In *Small business in the modern economy,* eds. Z. Acs, B. Carlsson, and R. Thurik. Oxford: Blackwell.

Carrier, J. 1997. Introduction. In *Meanings of the market: The free market in Western culture,* ed. J. Carrier. Oxford: Berg, 1–68.

Cassidy, J., and P. R. Shaver, eds. 1999. *Handbook of attachment.* New York: Guilford Press.

Castells, M. 1996. *The rise of network society.* Oxford: Blackwell.

Castells, M., and Y. Aoyama. 1994. Paths toward the informational society: Employment structure in G–7 countries, 1920–90. *International Labor Review* 133(1): 5–33.

CCAP. 1995. CCAP initiates social development link-ups. *Fair Trader* (January). Manila: Community Crafts Association of the Philippines, 1.

―――. 2002. *Fair Trader: Annual Report.* Manila: Community Crafts Association of the Philippines,.

Census and Statistics Department. 1999. *Statistical digest of the services sector.* Hong Kong: Census and Statistics Department.

Chang, P., C. Shih, and C. Hsu. 1993. Taiwan's approach to technological change: The case of integrated circuit design. *Technology Analysis and Strategic Management* 5(2): 173–177.

Chang, P., C. Shih, and C. Hsu. 1994. The formation process of Taiwan's IC industry—method of technology transfer. *Technovation* 14(3): 161–171.

Chant, S. 1996. Women's roles in recession and economic restructuring in Mexico and the Philippines. *Geoforum* 27(3): 297–327.

Charap, J. 1993. *Entrepreneurship and SMEs in the EBRD's countries of operations.* London: European Bank for Reconstruction and Development.

Chen, H. 1999. Man, machine and the gods: Skill, hegemony and culture in the making of Taiwanese machinists. PhD diss., Rensselaer Polytechnic Institute, Troy, New York.

Chin, C. B. N. 1998. *In service and servitude: Foreign domestic workers and the Malaysian "modernity" project.* New York: Columbia University Press.

Chiu, C. C. H. 1998. *Small family business in Hong Kong: Accumulation and accommodation.* Hong Kong: Chinese University Press.

Christerson, B., and C. Lever-Tracy. 1997. The third China? Emerging industrial districts in rural China. *International Journal of Urban and Regional Research* 21: 569–588.

Christian, W. 1996. *Visionaries: The Spanish Republic and the reign of Christ.* Berkeley: University of California Press.

Clark, G. 1994. *Onions are my husband: Survival and accumulation by West African market women.* Chicago: University of Chicago Press.

Clark, G., and T. Manuh. 1991. Women traders in Ghana and the structural adjustment programme. In *Structural adjustment and African women farmers*, ed. C. Gladwin. Gainesville: University of Florida Press.

Clifford, J. 1997. *Routes: Travel and translation in the late twentieth century.* Cambridge: Harvard University Press.

Cohen, G.A. 2000. *If you're egalitarian, how come you're so rich?* Cambridge: Harvard University Press.

Cole, R. E. 1971. *Japanese blue collar: The changing tradition.* Berkeley: University of California Press.

Collins, J. L. 1991. Housework and craftwork within capitalism: Marxist analyses of unwaged labor. In *Marxist approaches in economic anthropology*, eds. Alice Littlefield and Hill Gates. Lanham, MD.: University Press of America, 91–99.

Colloredo-Mansfeld, R. 2002. An ethnography of neoliberalism: Understanding competition in artisan economies. *Current Anthropology* 43(1): 113–137.

Commission on International Development.1969. *Partners in Development: Report of the Commission on International Development.* New York: Praeger.

Connolly, P. 1985. The politics of the informal sector: A critique. In *Beyond employment, household, gender and subsistence,* eds. N. Redclift and E. Mingione. Oxford: Basil Blackwell, 55–91.

Constable, J. H. 1982. *Lucha de clases: La industria textil en Tlaxcala*. Mexico City: Ediciones El Caballito.

Cook, S. 1986. The 'managerial' vs. the 'labor' function, capital accumulation and the dynamics of simple commodity production in rural Oaxaca, Mexico. In *Entrepreneurship and social change: Monographs in economic anthropology*, No. 2, eds. Sidney M. Greenfield and Arnold Strickon. New York: University Press of America.

———. 1993. Craft commodity production, market diversity, and different rewards in Mexican capitalism today. In *Crafts in the world market: The impact of global exchange on Middle American artisans*, ed. J. Nash. New York: State University of New York Press, 59–84.

Cook, S., and L. Binford. 1990. *Obliging need: Rural petty industry in Mexican capitalism*. Austin: University of Texas Press.

Cooke, P. 2002. *Knowledge economies: Clusters, learning and cooperative advantage*. London: Routledge.

Cooke, P., and K. Morgan. 1993. The network paradigm: New departures in corporate and regional development. *Environment and Planning D: Society and Space* 11: 543–564.

———. 1998. *The associational economy: Firms, regions, and innovation*. Oxford: Oxford University Press.

Cosgrove, S.1999. "Guadalupe's Story: The Complexities of Microcredit," *Grassroots Development: Journal of the Inter-American Foundation* 22(1), 46–47.

Crang, P., and R. Martin. 1991. Mrs. Thatcher's vision of the 'New Britain' and the other side of the 'Cambridge phenomenon'. *Environment and Planning D: Society and Space* 9: 91–116.

Crouch, H. 1996. *Government and society in Malaysia*. Ithaca: Cornell University Press.

Damasio, A. 1999. *The feeling of what happens: Body and emotion in the making of consciousness*. New York: Harcourt.

Davis, W. G. 1973. *Social relations in a Philippine market: Self-interest and subjectivity*. Berkeley and Los Angeles: University of California Press.

De Soto, H. 1989. *The other path: The informal revolution*. New York: Harper.

———. 2000. *The mystery of capital: Why capitalism triumphs in the West and fails everywhere else*. New York: Basic.

Dedrick, J., and K. Kraemer. 1998. *Asia's computer challenge.* New York: Oxford University Press.

Denwood, P. 1974. *The Tibetan carpet.* Warminster, U.K.: Aris and Philips.

Deyo, F. C., ed. 1989. *Beneath the miracle: Labor subordination in the new Asian industrialism.* Berkeley: University of California Press.

Dicken, P. 1998. *Global shift,* 3rd ed. New York: Guilford Press.

Dollar, D., and P. Collier. 2002. *Globalization, Growth, and Poverty,* Washington, DC: World Bank, www.//Econ.worldbank.org/prr/subpage.php?sp=2477, <accessed June 27, 2002.>

Dorall, R. 1989. Foreign workers in Malaysia: Issues and implications of recent illegal economic migrants from the Malay world. In *The trade in domestic helpers: Causes, mechanisms and consequences.* Kuala Lumpur, Malaysia: Asian and Pacific Development Centre.

DTI (Department of Trade and Industry). 1992. *Presidential Council for countryside development. Summary report.* Lagawe, Ifugao, Philippines: Department of Trade and Industry, Provincial Government of Ifugao.

Dunford, M., A. Fernandes, B. Musyck, B. Sadowski, M. R. Cho, and S. Tsenkova. 1993. The organisation of production and territory—small firm systems—an intensive ERASMUS course held in Lombardy, July 4–16 1992. *International Journal of Urban and Regional Research* 17: 132–36.

Dunford, M., R. Hudson, and A. Smith. 2001. *Restructuring of the European clothing industry.* Economic and Social Research Council (ESRC) research project interim report.

Durrenberger, E. P., ed. 1984. *Chayanov, peasants, and economic anthropology.* New York: Academic.

Dworkin, R. 2000. *Sovereign Virtue: The theory and practice of equality.* Cambridge: Harvard University Press

Eberts, D., and G. Norcliffe. 1998. New forms of artisanal production in Toronto's computer animation industry. *Geographische Zeitschrift* 2: 120–133.

*Economist.* 2000. "The World's View of Multinationals," January 29 21.

Ehlers, T. B. 1990. *Silent looms: Women and production in a Guatemalan town.* Boulder: Westview.

Elson, D., and R. Pearson. 1981. Nimble fingers make cheap workers: An analysis of women's employment in Third World export manufacturing. *Feminist Review* 8: 87–107.

Elvin, M. 1973. *The pattern of the Chinese past.* Stanford: Stanford: University Press.

Engelen, T., and A. P. Wolf, eds. In press. *Marriage and the family in Eurasia.* Stanford: Stanford University Press.

Erickson, M. 1989. Incest avoidance and familial bonding. *Journal of Anthropological Research* 45(3): 280–295.

———. 1993. Rethinking Oedipus: An evolutionary perspective on incest avoidance. *American Journal of Psychiatry* 150(3): 413–430.

Ernst, D. 1998. What permits David to defeat Goliath? Inter-organizational knowledge creation in the Taiwanese computer industry. *DRUID Working Paper,* No. 98: 3.

Errington, S. 1990. Recasting sex, gender, and power: A theoretical overview. In *Power and difference: Gender in Island Southeast Asia,* eds. J. Monnig, and S. Errington. Stanford: Stanford University Press, 1–59.

ERSO. 1995. *Yearbook of semiconductor industry* (in Chinese).

Escobar Latapi, A., and M. de la o. Martinez Castellanos. 1991. Small-scale industry and international migration in Guadalajara, Mexico. In *Migration, remittances and small business development,* eds. S. Diaz-Briquests, and S. Weintraub. Boulder: Westview.

European Bank for Reconstruction and Development (EBRD). 1995. *Transition Report 1995.* London: Her Magesty's Stationery Office (HMSO).

Faaland, J., J. Parkinson, and R. B. Saniman. 1990. *Growth and ethnic inequality: Malaysia's new economic policy.* New York: St. Martins Press, in association with Chr. Michelson Institute, Bergen, Norway.

Faist, T. 2000. Transnationalization in international migration: Implications for the study of citizenship and culture. *Ethnic and Racial Studies* 23: 189–222.

Far Eastern Economic Review. 1998. Migration: Deport and deter: Indonesian illegal workers get a harsh send-off from Malaysia. *Far Eastern Economic Review*: 16–17, 20.

Featherstone, M. 1990. *Global culture: Nationalism, globalisation, and modernity.* London: Sage.

Feith, H. 1982. Repressive-developmentalist regimes in Asia. *Alternatives* 7: 491–506.

Fernandez-Kelly, M. P. 1983. *For we are sold: I and my people: Women and industry in Mexico's frontiers.* Albany: State University of New York Press.

Fernandez-Kelly, M. P., and S. Sassen. 1991. *A collaborative study of Hispanic women in garment and electronics industries.* Final report presented to the Ford, Revson, and Tinker Foundations.

Fernando, J. 1997. "Nongovernmental organizations, microcredit, and empowerment of women," *Annals of the American Academy of Political and Social Science* 554, November: 150–177.

Fóti, K. 1993. Lessons for industrial restructuring: Experiences of some Hungarian enterprises. *Institute of Development Studies Discussion Paper*, No. 322. Sussex, England: IDS.

Foucault, M. 1991. Governmentality. In *The Foucault effect: Studies in governmentality*, eds. G. Burchell, C. Gordon, and P. Miller. Chicago: University of Chicago Press.

Frank, A. G. 1998. *ReORIENT: Global economy in the Asian age.* Berkeley: University of California Press.

Frank, T. F. 2000. *One market under God: Extreme capitalism, market populism, and the end of democracy.* New York: Random House.

Freedman, M. 1950. Colonial law and Chinese society. *Journal of the Royal Anthropological Institute* 80: 97–126.

Freeman, C. 2000. *High tech and high heels in the global economy: Women, work, and pink-collar identities in the Caribbean.* Durham, N.C.: Duke University Press.

———. 2001. Is local: Global as feminine: Masculine? Rethinking the gender of globalization. *Signs: Journal of Women in Culture and Society* 26(4): 1007–37.

Fricke, T. 1986. *Himalayan households: Tamang demography and domestic process.* Ann Arbor, MI: University Microfilms International Research Press.

Friedmann, H. 1978. World market, state, and family farm: Social base of household production in the era of wage labor. *Comparative Studies in Society and History* 20(4): 545–586.

Frigolé Reixach, J. N.d. *La evolución de la relación de aparcería en un pueblo murciano desde la postguerra a los años setenta.* Manuscript. University of Barcelona.

———. 1991. 'Ser cacique' y 'ser hombre' o la negación de las relaciones de patronazgo en un pueblo de la Vega Alta del Segura. In *Antropología de los pueblos de España*, eds. J. Prat, U. Martinez, J. Contreras, and I. Moreno. Madrid: Taurus.

―――. 1997. *Un hombre: Género, clase y cultura en el relato de un trabajador.* Barcelona: Muchnik Editores.

Fua, G., and C. Zacchia, eds. 1983. *Industrializzazione senza fratture.* Bologna: Il Mulino.

Garofoli, G. 1991. The Italian model of spatial development in the 1970s and 1980s. In *Industrial change and regional development: The transformation of new industrial spaces,* eds. G. Benko, and M. Dunford. London: Belhaven, 85-101.

Gates, H. 1979. Dependency and the part-time proletariat. *Modern China* 5(3): 381-407.

―――. 1996. *China's motor: A thousand years of petty capitalism.* Ithaca: Cornell University Press.

―――. 2001. Footloose in Fujian: Economic correlates of footbinding. *Comparative Studies in Society and History* 43(1): 130–148.

―――. In press. Girls' work in China and Northwestern Europe. In *Marriage and the family in Eurasia,* eds. T. Engelen, and A. P. Wolf. Stanford: Stanford University Press.

―――. This volume. *Petty production: The enduring alternative.*

Geras, N. 1983. *Marx and human nature: Refutation of a legend.* London: Verso.

Gereffi, G. 1994. The organization of buyer-driven global commodity chains: How U.S. retailers shape overseas production networks. In *Commodity chains and global capitalism,* eds. G. Gereffi and M. Korzeniewicz. Westport, CT: Praeger.

―――. 1999. International trade and industrial upgrading in the apparel commodity chain. *Journal of International Economics* 48(1): 37–70.

Gereffi, G., and L. Hempel. 1996. Latin America in the global economy: Running faster to stay in place. North American Congress on the Americas *(NACLA): Report on the Americas* 24(4): 18–27.

Gereffi, G., and M. Korzeniewicz. 1994. *Commodity chains and global capitalism.* New York: Praeger.

Gereffi, G., D. Spener, and J. Bair, eds. 2002. *Free trade and uneven development: The North American apparel industry after NAFTA.* Philadelphia: Temple University Press.

Gibson-Graham, J. K. 1996. *The end of capitalism (as we knew it).* Oxford, England: Blackwell Publishers.

Gill, L. 2000. *Teetering on the Rim.* New York: Columbia University Press.

Glick Schiller, N., L. Basch, and C. Szanton Blanc. 1992. Trans-nationalism: A new analytical framework for understanding migration. In *Towards a transnational perspective on migration*, eds. N. Glick Schiller, L. Basch, and C. Szanton Blanc. New York: New York Academy of Sciences, 1–24.

Goetz, A., and R. Sen Gupta. 1995. "Who takes the credit? Gender, power, and control over loan use in rural credit programs in Bangladesh," *World Development* 24(1), 45–63.

Goodman, A. H., and T. L. Leatherman, eds. 1998. *Building a new biocultural synthesis*. Ann Arbor: University of Michigan Press.

Goody, J. 1996. *The East in the West*. Cambridge: Cambridge University Press.

Gordon, C. 1991. Governmental rationality: An introduction. In *The Foucault effect: Studies in governmentality,* eds. G. Burchell, C. Gordon, and P. Miller. Chicago: University of Chicago Press.

Gough, I. 1972. Productive and unproductive labor in Marx. *New Left Review* 76: 47–72.

Government of Malaysia. 1979. *Mid-term review of the third Malaysia Plan 1976–1980*. Kuala Lumpur, Malaysia: Government Publications Department.

Gowan, P. 1995. Neo-liberal theory and practice for Eastern Europe. *New Left Review* 213: 3–60.

Grabher, G. 1993. The weakness of strong ties: The lock-in of regional development in the Ruhr area. In *The embedded firm: On the socioeconomics of industrial networks,* ed. G. Grabher. London: Routledge.

Granovetter, M. 1985. Economic action and social structure: The problem of embeddedness. *American Journal of Sociology* 91(3): 481–510.

Green, C. 1998. The Asian connection: The US-Caribbean apparel circuit and a new model of industrial relations. *Latin American Research Review* 33(3): 7–47.

Green, N. 1997. *Ready-to-wear and ready-to-work*. Durham, N.C.: Duke University Press.

Greenfield, S. M., and A. Strickon. 1986. Introduction. In *Entrepreneurship and social change: Monographs in economic anthropology*, No. 2, eds. S. M. Greenfield and A. Strickon. New York: University Press of America.

Greenhalgh, S. 1986. Is inequality demographically induced? The family cycle and the distribution of income on Taiwan. *American Anthropologist* 87(3): 571–594.

———. 1994. De-orientalizing the Chinese family firm. *American Ethnologist* 21(4): 748–775.

Grimes, K. M. 2000. Democratizing international production and trade: North American alternative trading organizations. In *Artisans and cooperatives: Developing alternative trade for the global economy*, eds. K. M. Grimes and B. L. Milgram. Tuscon: University of Arizona Press, 9–25.

———. Forthcoming. Changing the rules of trade in global partnerships: The fair trade movement. In *Social movements: A Reader*, ed. J. Nash. Oxford: Basil Blackwood.

Gulliver, P. H., and M. Silverman. 1995. *Merchants and shopkeepers. A historical anthropology of an Irish market town, 1200–1991*. Toronto: University of Toronto Press.

Hafter, D. M., ed. 1995. European women and preindustrial craft. Bloomington: Indiana University Press.

Hajnal, J. 1965. European marriage patterns in perspective. In *Population in history*, eds. D.V. Glass and D. E. V. Eversley. London: Edward Arnold, 101–143.

———. 1982. Two kinds of preindustrial household formation system. *Population and Development Review* 3: 449–494.

Haldon, J. 1993. *The state and the tributary mode of production*. London: Verso.

Halperin, R. 1996. Rethinking the informal economy: Implications for regional analysis. *Research in Economic Anthropology* 17: 43–79.

Halperin, R. H., and S. Sturdevant. 1990. A cross-cultural treatment of the informal economy. In *Perspectives on the informal economy*, ed. E. M. Smith. New York: Lanham, 321–342.

Hamilton, G. 1996. The organization of business in Taiwan. *American Journal of Sociology* 96(4): 999–1006.

Hamilton, G., and C-S. Kao. 1990. The institutional foundations of Chinese business: The family firm in Taiwan. *Comparative Social Research* 12: 135–151.

Hardt, M., and A. Negri. 2000. *Empire*. Cambridge: Harvard University Press.

Hardy, J., and A. Smith. 2004. Governing regions, governing transformations: Firms, institutions and regional change in post-Soviet Central and Eastern Europe. In *Placing Institutions*, eds. A. Wood and D. Valler. Ashgate: Aldershot, forthcoming.

Harper, T. N. 1999. *The end of empire and the making of Malaya*. Cambridge: Cambridge University Press.

Harrell, S. 1998. *Human families*. Boulder: Westview Press.

Harrison, B. 1994. *Lean and mean: The changing landscape of corporate power in the age of flexibility*. New York: Basic.

Harrison, B., and R. Kuttner. 1997. *Lean and mean: Why large corporations will continue to dominate the global economy*. New York: Guilford Publications.

Hart, K. 1973. Informal income opportunities and urban employment in Ghana. *Journal of Modern African Studies* 11: 61–89.

———. 1992. Market and state after the Cold War: The informal economy reconsidered. In *Contesting markets: Analyses of ideology, discourse, and practice*, ed. R. Dilley. Edinburgh, Scotland: Edinburgh University Press, 214–230.

Harvey, D. 1989. *The condition of postmodernity*. Oxford: Basil Blackwell.

Hendrickx, F. 1997. *In order not to fall into poverty: Production and reproduction in the transition from proto-industry to factory industry in Borne and Wierden (the Netherlands), 1800–1900*. Nijmegen, Netherlands: International Institunt voo-Socicle Geschiedenis (IISG) Studies and Essays, International Institute of Social History.

Herrigel, G. 1996. Crisis in German decentralised production: Unexpected rigidity and the challenge of an alternative form of flexible organization in Baden Württemburg. *European Urban and Regional Studies* 3(1): 33–52.

Heyman, J. M., ed. 1999. *States and illegal practices*. Oxford, England: Berg.

Heyman, J. M. and A. Smart. States and illegal practices. An overview. In J. M. Heyman, ed. *States and Illegal Practices*. Oxford, England: Berg.

Hilowitz, J. 1997. Social labelling to combat child labor: Some considerations. *International Labor Review* 136(2): 215–232.

Hirschman, A. O. 1970. *Exit, voice, and loyalty: Responses to decline in firms, organizations, and states*. Cambridge: Harvard University Press.

HMG (His Majesty's Government of Nepal). 1999. *Report on the Nepal labor force survey 1998/1999*. Kathmandu, Nepal: Central Bureau of Statistics.

Hobsbawm, E. 1977 [1975]. *The age of capital, 1848–1875*. London: Association of Bibliographic Agencies of Britain, Australia, Canada and the United States (ABACUS).

Hong Kong Government. 1986. *Hong Kong annual report 1985*. Hong Kong: Government printer.

Hooker, M. B. 2002. English law and the invention of Chinese personal law in Singapore and Malaysia. In *Law and the Chinese in Southeast Asia*, ed. M. B. Hooker. Singapore: Institute of Southeast Asian Studies.

Horn, N. E. 1994. *Cultivating customers: Market women in Harare, Zimbabwe*. Boulder: Lynne Rienner Publishers.

Hrdy, S. B. 1999. *Mother nature: A history of mothers, infants, and natural selection*. New York: Pantheon Books.

Hsing, Y-T. 1997. Building *guanxi* across the straits: Taiwanese capital and local Chinese bureaucrats. In *Ungrounded empires: The cultural politics of modern Chinese transnationalism*, eds. A. Ong and D. Nonini. London: Routledge.

HSIP. 1998. *1998 Yearly Report of the Hsinch Science-Based Industrial Park (HSIP)*. Hsinchu, Republic of China: Administration of the HSIP.

Hsiung, P-C. 1996. *Living rooms as factories: Class, gender, and the satellite factory system in Taiwan*. Philadelphia: Temple University Press.

Hsu, J. 1997. A late industrial district? Learning networks in the Hsinchu science-based industrial park, Taiwan. PhD diss., University of California at Berkeley.

———. 1999. Floating embeddedness: The labor market and high-technology development in the Hsinchu science-based industrial park. *Taiwan: A Radical Quarterly in Social Science* 35: 75–118 (in Chinese).

Hsu, J., and A. Saxenian. 2000. The limits of *guanxi* capitalism: Transnational collaboration between Taiwan and the US. *Environment and Planning A* 32(11): 1991–2005.

Huang, P. C. C. 1990. *The peasant family and the rural economy in the Yangzi Delta, 1350–1988*. Stanford: Stanford University Press.

Hüber, D. 1995. Institutional support for small business in Poland—lessons for Central and East European countries. *Small Enterprise Development* 6(3): 18–24.

Hudson, R., M. Dunford, D. Hamilton, and R. Kotter. 1997. Developing regional strategies for economic success: Lessons from Europe's economically successful regions? *European Urban and Regional Studies* 4(4): 365–373.

Illo, J. F., and J. Polo. 1990. *Fishers, traders, farmers, wives: The life stories of ten women in a fishing village*. Quezon City: Ateneo de Manila University Press.

Independent Commission on International Development Issues. 1980. *North-South: A Programme for Survival*, Cambridge: Massachusett Institute of Technology Press.

INEGI (Instituto Nacional de Estadistica, Geografia, y Informatica). 1994. XIV Censo Industrial, XI Censo Comercial y XI Censo de Servicios: Tlaxcala, Mexico.

International Fund for Agricultural Development. 2001. *The challenge of ending rural poverty: Rural poverty report 2001*. New York: Oxford University Press.

ITRI. 2000. *Yearbook of the semiconductor industry.* Hsinchu: Industry Study Center, Industrial Technology Research Institute (ITRI) (in Chinese).

Jacoby, R. 1987. *The Last Intellectuals: American Culture in the Age of Academe*, New York: Farrar.

James, A., C. Jenks, and A. Prout. 1998. *Theorizing childhood*. New York: Teacher's College Press.

Jankowiak, W., ed. 1995. *Romantic passion: A universal experience?* New York: Columbia University Press.

Jefremovas, V. 2000. Women are good with money: Cash cropping and gender relations in the Philippines. In *Women farmers and commercial ventures: Increasing food security in developing countries*, ed. A. Spring. Boulder: Lynne Rienner Publishers, 131–150.

Joffe, A. 1990. 'Fordism' and 'Post-Fordism' in Hungary. *South African Sociological Review* 2(2): 67–88.

Ka, C-M. 1993. *Market, social networks, and production organization of small-scale industry in Taiwan: The garment industries in Wufenpu*. Taipei: Institute of Ethnology, Academia Sinica (in Chinese).

Kabeer, N. 1994. *Reversed realities: Gender hierarchies in development thought*. London and New York: Verso.

Kahn, J. S. 1996. Growth, economic transformation, culture and the middle classes in Malaysia. In *The new rich in Asia: Mobile phones, McDonald's and middle-class revolution*, eds. R. Robison and D. S. G. Goodman. London and New York: Routledge, 49–78.

Kao, J. 1993. The worldwide web of Chinese business. *Harvard Business Review*, March-April: 24–36.

Karim, W. J. 1995. Introduction: Genderising Anthropology in Southeast Asia. In *'Male' and 'female' in developing Southeast Asia*, ed. W. J. Karim. Oxford and Washington: Berg Publishers, 11–34.

Kessler, J. 1999. The North American Free Trade Agreement, emerging apparel production networks and industrial upgrading: The southern California/Mexico connection. *Review of International Political Economy* 6(4): 565–608.

Khan, M. H., and K. S. Jomo. 2000. Introduction. In *Rents, rent-seeking and economic development: Theory and evidence in Asia*, eds. M. H. Khan and K. S. Jomo. Cambridge: Cambridge University Press, 1–20.

Kim, S. 1992. Women workers and the labor movement in South Korea. In *Anthropology and the global factory: Studies of the new industrialization in the late twentieth century*, eds. F. Rothstein and M. Blim. New York: Bergin and Garvey.

Konner, M. 2002. *The tangled wing: Biological constraints on the human spirit* 2d ed. New York: Henry Holt and Company.

Kornai, J. 1992. *The socialist system: The political economy of socialism*. Princeton: Princeton University Press.

Krajská sprava Štatistického úradu Slovenskej republiky v Prešove (KS ŠÚSR). 2000. *Štatistický bulletin za 1. Polrok 2000*. Prešove, Slovakia: KS ŠÚSR.

Krugman, P. 1991. *Geography and trade*. Cambridge: Massachusetts Institute of Technology Press.

Kussmaul, A. 1981. *Servants in husbandry in early modern England*. Cambridge: Cambridge University Press.

Kwong, P. 1998. *Forbidden workers: Illegal Chinese immigrants and American Labor*. New York: New Press.

Lasch, C. 1995. *The revolt of the elites and the betrayal of democracy*, New York: Norton.

———. 1991. *The true and only heaven: Progress and its critics*. New York: Norton.

———. 1979. *The culture of narcissism: American life in an age of diminishing expectations*. New York: Norton.

Lash S., and J. Urry. 1987. *The end of organized capitalism*. Madison: University of Wisconsin Press.

Laslett, P. 1977. Characteristics of the Western family considered over time. *Journal of Family History* 2: i–115.

Latour, B. 1993. *We have never been modern*. Brighton, U.K.: Harvester Wheatsheaf.

Law, J. 1994. *Organizing modernity*. Oxford: Basil Blackwell.

Law, J., ed. 1986. *Power, action and belief*. London: Routledge.

Lawson-Tancred, A. 2002. "Micro-Credit System Comes under Fire," *Financial Times*, May 21: 6.

Leach, E. R. 1961. *Pul Eliy: A village in Ceylon*. Cambridge: Cambridge University Press.

———. 1964. *Political systems of Highland Burma*. London: Athlone Press.

LeDoux, J. 2002. *Synaptic self. How our brains become who we are*. New York: Viking Penguin.

Lee, A. 2004. *In the name of harmony and prosperity: Labor and gender politics in Taiwan's economic restructuring*. Albany: State University of New York Press.

Lee, C. K .1998. *Gender and the South China miracle: Two worlds of factory women*, Berkeley: University of California Press.

Lee, J. Z. 2000. *Malthusian mythologies and Chinese realities*. Stanford: Stanford University Press.

Lem, W. 1991. Gender, ideology, and petty commodity production: Social reproduction in Languedoc, France. In *Marxist approaches in economic anthropology,* eds. A. Littlefield and H. Gates. Lanham, MD: University Press of America, 103–118.

———. 1999. *Cultivating dissent: Work, identity and politics in rural Languedoc*. Albany: State University of New York Press.

Lessinger, J. 1992. Nonresident-Indian investment and India's drive for industrial modernization. In *Anthropology and the global factory*, eds. F. Rothstein and M. Blim. New York: Bergin and Garvey, 62–82.

Lever-Tracy, C., D. Ip, and N. Tracy. 1996. *The Chinese diaspora and Mainland China: An emerging economic synergy*. Houndmills, U.K.: Macmillan Press.

Levy, B. 1988. Korean and Taiwanese firms as international competitors: the challenges ahead. *Columbia Journal of World Business* 23, (1b:43–52).

Lewis, D. 1998. Non-governmental organizations, business and the management of ambiguity: Case studies from Nepal and Bangladesh. *Nonprofit Management and Leadership* 9(2): 135–152.

Li, T. M. 1999. Compromising power: Development, culture, and rule in Indonesia. *Cultural Anthropology* 14(3): 295–322.

Lim, L. 1983. Capitalism, imperialism, and patriarchy: The dilemma of Third World women workers in multinational factories. In *Women, men, and the international division of labor*. Eds. June Nash and Maria Patricia Fernandez-Kelly, Albany: State University of New York Press, 70–92.

Lin, T. B., and V. Mok. 1985. Trade, foreign investment and development in Hong Kong. In *Foreign trade and investment*, ed. W. Galenson. Madison: University of Wisconsin Press, 219–256.

Lin, T.B., V. Mok, and Y. P. Ho. 1980. *Manufactured exports and employment in Hong Kong.* Hong Kong: Chinese University Press.

Lin, X. 1987. *Newly rising industries in developing countries—IC industry in Taiwan.* (master's thesis, National Taiwan University, (in Chinese).

Littlefield, A., and L. T. Reynolds. 1990. The putting-out system: Transitional form or recurrent feature of capitalist production? *Social Science Journal* 27(4): 359–372.

Littrell, M. A., and M. A. Dickson. 1999. *Social responsibility in the global market: Fair trade of cultural products.* London: Sage Publications.

Littrell, M.A., and M. A. Dickson 2000. Fair trade products in a competitive global market. *Craft News: Special Issue on Fair Trade* 11(44): 1, 5, 12.

Liu, C. 1993. Government's role in developing a high-tech industry: The case of Taiwan's semiconductor industry. *Technovation* 13(5): 299–309.

Lockwood, V. S. 1993. *Tahitian transformation: Gender and capitalist development in a rural society.* Boulder: Lynne Rienner Publishers.

Loh, F.K.-W. 2002. Developmentalism and the limits of democratic discourse. In *Democracy in Malaysia: Discourses and practices*, eds. F. K-W. Loh and B-T. Khoo. Richmond, U.K.: Curzon Press, 19–50.

Long, N. 1992. From paradigm lost to paradigm regained? The case for an actor-oriented sociology of development. In *Battlefields of knowledge: The interlocking of theory and practice in social research and development*, eds. N. Long and A. Long. London and New York: Routledge, 16–43.

Lorentzen, A. 1995. *Regional development and institutions in Hungary: Past, present and future development.* Paper presented at the Regional Studies Association European conference, Gothenburg, Sweden, May.

Lovering, J. 1999. Theory led by policy: The inadequacies of the 'new regionalism.' *International Journal of Urban and Regional Research* 23: 379–390.

Lundvall, B-A. 1996. The social dimension of the learning economy. Danish Research Unit for Industrial Dynamics *Working Paper* 96–1.

Maccoby, E. 1998. *The two sexes.* Cambridge: Harvard University Press.

MacEwan-Scott, A. 1978. Who are the self-employed? In *Casual work and poverty in Third World cities,* eds. R. Bromley and C. Gerry. Chichester, England: Wiley.

MacLeod, G. 2001. New regionalism reconsidered: Globalization and the remaking of political economic space. *International Journal of Urban and Regional Research* 24(4): 804–829.

Madrick, J. 1999. How new is the new economy? New York Review of Books, September 23: 42–50.

Malinowski, B. 1922. *Argonauts of the Western Pacific.* London: Dutton.

Mann, S. 1997. *Precious records: Women in China's long eighteenth century.* Stanford: Stanford University Press.

Martin, R., and P. Sunley. 2003. Deconstructing clusters: Chaotic concept or policy panacea? *Journal of Economic Geography* 3(1): 5–35.

Martinelli, F., and E. Schoenberger. 1991. Oligopoly is alive and well: Notes for a broader discussion of flexible accumulation. In *Industrial change and regional development: The transformation of new industrial spaces,* eds. G. Benko and M. Dunford. London: Belhaven, 117–133.

Martínez Alier, J. 1968. *La estabilidad del latifundismo.* Ediciones Ruedo Ibérico. Madrid, Spain.

Marx, K. 1963. Theories of Surplus Value. Moscow: Progress Publishers.

Marx, K. 1976 [1867]. *Capital, Volume. I.* Harmondsworth, U.K.: Penguin.

———. 1977. *Capital, Vol. 1.* Introduced by Ernest Mandel, translated by Ben Fowkes. New York: Random House.

———. 1979. *Karl Marx, Frederick Engels. Collected Works [1851–1853],* vol. 11. New York: International Publishers.

Massey, D., and J. Allen. 1995. High-tech places: Poverty in the midst of growth. In *Off the map: The social geography of poverty in the UK,* ed. C. Philo. London: CPAG, 123–132.

Mathew, J., and D-S. Cho. 2000. Child Poverty Action Group (CPAG) *Tiger technology: The creation of a semiconductor industry in East Asia.* Cambridge: Cambridge University Press.

Mathews, J. 1997. A Silicon Valley of the east: Creating Taiwan's semiconductor industry. *California Management Review* 39(4): 26–54.

Mattera, P. 1985. *Off the books: The rise of the underground economy.* London: Pluto Press.

Mayoux, L. 1993. A development success story? Low caste entrepreneurship and inequality: An Indian case study. *Development and Change* 24: 541–568.

McCorriston, J. 1997. The fiber revolution: Textile extensification, alienation, and social stratification in ancient Mesopotamia. *Current Anthropology* 38(4): 517–550.

McGough, J. P. 1984. The domestic mode of production and peasant social organization: The Chinese case. In *Chayanov, peasants, and economic anthropology,* ed. E. P. Durrenberger. New York: Academic: 183–201.

McKenna, J. J. 1996. SIDS in cross-cultural perspective: Is infant-parent co-sleeping protective? *Annual Reviews in Anthropology* 25: 201–216.

McKenna, J. J., S. Mosko, and C. Richard. 1999. Breast-feeding and mother-infant co-sleeping in relation to SIDS prevention. In *Evolutionary Medicine,* eds. W. Trevathan, N. Smith, and J. McKenna. Oxford: Oxford University Press.

Meillasoux, C. 1975. *Maidens, meal and money: Capitalism and the domestic economy.* Cambridge: Cambridge University Press.

Mendels, F. 1981. *Industrialization and population pressure in eighteenth-century Flanders.* New York: Columbia University Press.

Milgram, B. L. 1999. Crafts, cultivation and household economies: Women's work and positions in Ifugao Northern Philippines. *Research in Economic Anthropology* 20: 221–261.

———. 2000. Reorganizing production for global markets: Women and craft cooperatives in Ifugao, Upland Philippines. In *Artisans and cooperatives: Developing alternative trade for the global economy,* eds. K. M. Grimes and B. L. Milgram. Tuscon: University of Arizona Press, 107–128.

———. 2001. Situating handicraft market women in Ifugao, Upland Philippines: A case for multiplicity. In *Women traders in cross-cultural perspective: Mediating identities, marketing wares,* ed. L. J. Seligmann. Stanford: Stanford University Press, 129–160.

Ministry of Construction and Regional Development of the Slovak Republic. 2001. *National Plan of Regional Development of the Slovak Republic*. Bratislava, Slovakia: Ministry of Construction and Regional Development.

Ministry of Economy. 2001. *Rozpracovanie priemyselnej politiky SR vo vybrany'ch odvetviach spracovatel'ského priemyslu do roku 2004*. Bratislava, Slovakia: Ministry of Economy. Available at: http://www.economy.gov.sk/priem/priemysel2. htm. Accessed August 22.

Mintz, S.W. 1998. The localization of anthropological practice: From area studies to transnationalism. *Critique of Anthropology* 18: 117–133.

Miralao, V. A. 1986. *Labor conditions in Philippine craft industries*. Research and Working Papers. Manila: Ramon Magsaysay Award Foundation.

Mitchell, D. 1995. There's no such thing as culture: Towards a reconceptualization of the idea of culture in geography. *Transactions* 20(1): 102–116.

Mitter, S. 1986. Industrial restructuring and manufacturing homework: Immigrant women in the UK clothing industry. *Capital and Class* 27: 37–80.

Mody, A., and D. Wheeler. 1990. *Automation and world competition: New technologies, industrial location and trade* New York: St. Martin's Press.

Morawetz, D. 1981. *Why the emperor's new clothes are not made in Colombia: A case study in Latin American and East Asian manufacturing exports*. New York: Oxford University Press.

Moser, C. O. N. 1978. Informal sector or petty commodity production: Dualism or dependence in urban development? *World Development* 6: 1041–1064.

———. 1994. The informal sector debate, Part 1: 1970–1983. In *Contrapunto: The informal sector debate in Latin America*, ed. C. A. Rakowski. Albany: State University of New York Press, 11–30.

Müller, B. 1993. *Der Mythos vom faulen Ossi: Deutsch-deutsche Vorurteile und die Erfahrungen mit der Marktwitschaft in drei Ostberliner Betrieben*. *PROKLA* 91: 251–268.

Munoz, P., and J. Calderon. 1997. *Se encarecio 8% la canasta basica en el primer trimestre: CT. La Jornada*, April 21: 16.

Munro-Kua, A. 1996. *Authoritarian populism in Malaysia*. New York: St. Martin's Press.

Murray, R. 1992. Flexible specialisation and development strategy: The relevance for Eastern Europe. In *Regional development and contemporary industrial response,* eds. H. Ernste and V. Meier. London: Belhaven, 197–217.

NADSME (National Agency for Development of Small and Medium Enterprises). 1994. *State of small and medium enterprise and its support in Slovak Republic.* Bratislava, Slovakia: NADSME.

———. 1995. *Role of RAICs and BICs in regional development within the Slovak Republic.* Internal document.

———. 1999. *Annual Report.* Bratislava, Slovakia: NADSME.

———. 2000. *State of small and medium enterprises in the Slovak Republic.* Bratislava, Slovakia: NADSME.

Nag, M., B. N. F. White, and R. C. Peet. 1978. An anthropological approach to the study of the economic value of children in Java and Nepal. *Current Anthropology* 19(2): 293–306.

Nagel, T. 2002. *In the stream of consciousness.* New York Review of Books, April 11: 74–76.

Narotzky, S. 1997a. *New directions in economic anthropology.* London: Pluto Press.

———. 1997b. 'Cultura', 'región' y trabajo en la Vega Baja del Segura. *Trabajo: Revista Andaluza de relaciones laborales* 3: 89–107.

———. 2000. The cultural basis of a regional economy: The Vega Baja del Segura in Spain. *Ethnology* 39(1): 1–14.

Narotzky, S., and G. Smith. Forthcoming. *Real life: Conflicting histories in a regional economy.*

Nash, J. 1988. Implications of technological change for household and rural development: Some Latin American cases. In *Lucha: The struggles of Latin American women,* ed. C. Weil. Minneapolis: Prisma Institute, 37–71.

———. 1989. *From tank town to high tech.* Albany: State University of New York Press.

NASPEC (National Society for Protection of Environment and Children). 1994. *Status of child labor in carpet industry.* Kathmandu, Nepal: Institute of Trade and Development (ITAD).

Neumann, L. 1992. Decentralisation and privatisation in Hungary: Opportunities for flexible specialisation? In *Regional development and contemporary industrial response: Extending flexible specialisation,* eds. H. Ernste and V. Meier. London: Belhaven, 233–246.

———. 1993. Decentralization and privatization in Hungary: Towards supplier networks? In *The embedded firm: On the socioeconomics of industrial networks,* ed. G. Grabher. London: Routledge, 179–199.

New Straits Times. 1985. No refuge from Sedition Act. *New Straits Times.* Kuala Lumpur, Malaysia.

Newaz, W. 2000. "Impact of NGO Credit Programs on the Empowerment of Rural Women in Bangladesh: A Case of UTTARAN," Dublin: International Society for Third-Sector Research Conference, July 5–8.

Newberry, D., and P. Kattuman. 1992. Market concentration and competition in Eastern Europe. *World Economy* 15(3): 315–331.

Niehoff, J. 1987. The villager as industrialist: Ideologies of household manufacturing in rural Taiwan. *Modern China* 13(3): 278–309.

Nieuwenhuys, O. 1994. *Children's lifeworlds: Gender, welfare and labor in the developing world.* New York: Routledge.

———. 1996. The paradox of child labor and anthropology. *Annual Review of Anthropology* 25: 237–251.

Nonini, D. M. 1983. The Chinese community of a West Malaysian market town: A study in political economy. PhD Diss., Stanford University.

———. 1997. Shifting identities, positioned imaginaries: Transnational traversals and reversals by Malaysian Chinese. In *Ungrounded empires: The cultural politics of modern Chinese transnationalism*, eds. A. Ong and D. M. Nonini. New York: Routledge, 204–227.

———. 1998. 'Chinese society,' coffeeshop talk, possessing gods: The politics of public space among diasporic Chinese in Malaysia. *Positions: East Asia cultures critiques* 6(2): 439–473.

———. 2003. All are flexible, but some are more flexible than others: Small-scale Chinese businesses in Malaysia. In *Ethnic business: Chinese capitalism in Southeast Asia*, eds. K. S. Jomo and Brian C. Folk. London: Routledge, 71–88.

Nonini, D. M., and A. Ong. 1997. Introduction: Chinese transnationalism as an alternative modernity. In *Ungrounded empires: The cultural politics of modern Chinese transnationalism*, eds. A. Ong and D. M. Nonini. New York: Routledge, 1–33.

O'Neill, T. 1999. The lives of the Tibeto-Nepalese carpet. *Journal of Material Culture* 4(1): 21–38.

———. 2001. *Nepalese entrepreneurial communities and the European hand-knotted carpet market: Plural globalities and multiple localities*. Lanham, MD: University Press of America.

Odaka, Konosuke, Keinosuke, Ono and Fumihiko, Adohi. 1988. *The automobile industry in Japan: A study of ancillary firm development*. Tokyo: Kinokuniya and Oxford University Press.

Odegaard, S. 1985. *Report on survey of various segments of the Oriental carpet market in the U.S.* Document in author's possession.

OECD. 1999. *The Slovak Republic*. Paris: Organization of Economic Cooperation and Development (OECD).

Ofreneo, R. E., and E. P. Habana. 1987. *The employment crisis and the World Bank's Adjustment Program (Philippines)*. Quezon City: University of the Philippines Press.

Ogilvie, S. C. 1993. Proto-industrialization in Europe. *Continuity and Change* 8: 159–179.

Onchan, T. 1992. Informal rural finance in Thailand. In *Informal finance in low income countries*, eds. D. W. Adams and D. A. Fitchett. Boulder: Westview Press, 103–118.

Ong, A. 1987. *Spirits of resistance and capitalist discipline: Factory women in Malaysia*. Albany: State University of New York Press.

———. 1999. *Flexible citizenship: The cultural logics of transnationality*. Durham, NC: Duke University Press.

Ong, H. C. 1985. Fight is fierce in the lorry industry. *Sunday Star*. Penang, Malaysia.

Onta-Bhatta, L. 1997. Political economy, culture and violence: Children's journey to the urban streets. *Studies in Nepali History and Society* 2(2): 207–253.

Osmani, L. K .1998. Impact of credit on the relative well-being of women: Evidence from the Grameen Bank, *Institute for Development Studies (IDS) Bulletin* 29(4), October: 31–38.

Palmeri, C., and J. Aguayo. 1997. Good-bye, Guangdong, Hello Jalisco. *Forbes* 22(3), Feb. 10: 56.

Paniccia, I. 1998. One, a hundred, thousands of industrial districts: Organizational variety in local networks of small and medium-sized enterprises. *Organization Studies* 19(4): 667–699.

Perrow, C. 2002. *Organizing America: Wealth, Power, and the Origins of Corporate Capitalism*. Princeton: Princeton University Press.

Phizacklea, A. 1990. *Unpacking the fashion industry: Gender, racism, and class in production.* London: Routledge.

Pickles, J. 2001. Gulag Europe? Mass unemployment, new firm creation, and tight labor markets in the Bulgarian apparel industry. In *Work, employment and transition: Restructuring livelihoods in post-Communism,* eds. A. Rainnie, A. Smith, and A. Swain. London: Routledge.

Pickles, J., and R. Begg. 2000. Ethnicity, state violence, and neoliberal transitions in post-Communist Bulgaria. *Growth and Change* 31(2): 179–210.

Pickles, J., and A. Smith, eds. 1998. *Theorising transition: The political economy of post-Communist transformations.* London: Routledge.

Pinch, S., and N. Henry. 2001. Neo-Marshallian nodes, institutional thickness, and Britain's 'motor sport valley': thick or thin? *Environment and Planning A* 33: 1169–1183.

Pineda, R. V. 1995. Domestic outwork for export-oriented industries. In *The Filipino woman in focus,* ed. A. T. Torres. Manila: University of the Philippines Press, 153–167.

Piore, M., and C. Sabel. 1984. *The second industrial divide: Possibilities for prosperity.* New York: Basic.

Portes, A. 1994. Paradoxes of the informal economy: The social basis of unregulated entrepreneurship. In *The handbook of economic sociology,* eds. N. J. Smelser and R. Swedburg. Princeton: Princeton University Press.

Portes, A., and S. Sassen-Koob. 1987. Making it underground: Comparative material on the informal sector in Western market economies. *American Journal of Sociology* 93(1): 30–61.

Poulantzas, N. 1975. *Classes in contemporary capitalism.* London: Verso.

Pratt, A. 2001. New media, the new economy and new spaces. *Geoforum* 31: 425–436.

Rahman, A. 1999. Micro-credit initiatives for equitable and sustainable development: Who pays? *World Development* 27(1), January: 67–82.

Rakowski, C. A., ed. 1994. *Contrapunto: The informal sector debate in Latin America.* Albany: State University of New York Press.

Rawls, J. 1971. *A Theory of Justice,* Cambridge: Harvard University Press.

Rebel, H. 1989. Cultural hegemony and class experience: A critical reading of recent ethnological- historical approaches, Part 1. *American Ethnologist* 16(1): 117–136.

———. 1991. Reimagining the Oikos: Austrian Cameralism in its social formation. In *Golden ages, dark ages—Imagining the past in anthropology and history,* eds. J. O'Brien and W. Roseberry. Berkeley: University of California Press, 48–80.

Reid, A. 1988. *Southeast Asia in the age of commerce 1450–1680, Vol. 1: The lands below the winds.* New Haven: Yale University Press.

Revelli, M. 1997. *La Sinistra Sociale: Oltre la civilta del lavoro.* Torino, Italy: Bollati Boringhieri.

Richards, M. 1998. *A time of silence: Civil war and the culture of repression in Franco's Spain, 1938–1945.* Cambridge: Cambridge University Press.

Rivero Rios M. A., and E. Suarez Aguilar. 1994. *Pequena empresa y modernizacion: Analisis de dos dimensiones.* Cuernavaca, Mexico: Universidad Nacional Antínoma de México (UNAM) Centro Regional de Investigaciones Multidisciplinarias.

Roberts, B. 1978. *Cities of peasants: The political economy of urbanization in the Third World.* Beverley Hills: Sage Publications.

———. 1994. Informal economy and family strategies. *International Journal of Urban and Regional Research* 18(1): 6–23.

Roberts, D., and J. K. Kynge. 2003. How cheap labour, foreign investment and rapid industrialisation are creating a new workshop of the world, *Financial Times,* February 4: 13.

Robison, R., and D. S. G. Goodman, eds. 1996. *The new rich in Asia: Mobile phones, McDonalds and middle-class revolution.* New Rich in Asia Series. London: Routledge.

Roseberry, W. 1998. Political economy and social fields in *Building a new biocultural synthesis,* eds. A. H. Goodman and T. L. Leatherman. Ann Arbor: University of Michigan Press, 75–92

Rothstein, F. 1992. Conclusion: New waves and old—industrialization, labor, and the struggle for a new world order. In *Anthropology and the global factory,* eds. F. Rothstein and M. Blim. New York: Bergin and Garvey, 238–246.

———. 1999. Declining odds: Kinship, women's employment and political economy in rural Mexico. *American Anthropologist* 101: 579–593.

Rothstein, F., and M. Blim. (editors) 1992. *Anthropology and the global factory.* New York: Bergin and Garvey.

Rovine, V. 2001. Bogolan. Shaping culture through cloth in contempory Mali. Washington, D.C.: Smithsonian Institution Press.

Rugmark. 2001. *Nepal Rugmark Bulletin 2001.* Kathmandu: Nepal Rugmark Foundation.

Rutten, R. 1993. *Artisans and entrepreneurs in the rural Philippines: Making a living and gaining wealth in two commercialized crafts.* Quezon City, Philippines: New Day Publishers.

Sabel, C. 1989. Flexible specialisation and the re-emergence of regional economies. In *Reversing industrial decline? Industrial structure and policy in Britain and her competitors,* eds. P. Hirst and J. Zeitlin. Oxford: Berg.

Sabel, C., and J. Zeitlin, eds. 1985. Historical Alternatives to Mass Production: Politics, Markets, and Technology in Nineteenth Century Industrialization, *Past and Present,* 108, August: 133–176.

———. 1997. *Worlds of Possibilities: Flexibility and Mass Production in Western Industrialization,* Cambridge: Cambridge University Press.

Sacks [Brodkin], K. 1982. *Sisters and wives: The past and future of sexual equality.* Urbana: University of Illinois Press.

Sahlins, M. 1972. *Stone age economics.* Chicago: Aldine-Atherton.

Said, Y. 1995. *The applicability of the industrial district model to Martin, Slovakia* (master's thesis, Sussex European Institute, University of Sussex).

Sandhu, K. S. 1964. The saga of the squatter in Malaya: A preliminary survey of the causes, characteristics and consequences of the resettlement of rural dwellers during the Emergency between 1948 and 1960. *Journal of Southeast Asian History* 5: 143–177.

Sangren, S. 1985. *History and magical power.* Stanford: Stanford University Press.

Saxenian, A. 1983. The urban contradictions of Silicon Valley: Regional growth and the restructuring of the semiconductor industry. *International Journal of Urban and Regional Research* 7(2): 237–261.

Saxenian, A., and Hsu, J. 2001. The Silicon Valley-Hsinchu connection: Technical communities and industrial upgrading. *Industrial and Corporate Change* 10(4): 893–920.

Sayer, A., and R. Walker. 1992. *The new social economy—reworking the division of labor.* Cambridge: Blackwell.

Sayers, S. 1998. *Marxism and human nature.* London: Routledge.

Schmitz, H., and B. Musyck. 1993. Industrial districts in Europe: Policy lessons for developing countries? *Institute of Development Studies Discussion Paper* 324. Sussex, England: Institute for Development Studies (IDS).

Scott, A. 1988. *New industrial spaces.* London: Pion.

———. 2000. *The cultural economy of cities.* London: Sage.

Scott, A., and M. Storper. 1992. Industrialization and regional development. In *Pathways to industrialization and regional development,* eds. M. Storper and A. Scott. London: Routledge, 3–17.

Seccombe, W. 1993. *Weathering the storm: Working-class families from the industrial revolution to the fertility decline.* London: Verso.

Seligmann, L. J. 2001. Introduction: Mediating identities, marketing wares. In *Women traders in cross-cultural perspective: Mediating identities, marketing wares,* ed. L. J. Seligmann. Stanford: Stanford University Press, 1–24.

Sen, K., and M. Stivens, eds. 1998. *Gender and power in affluent Asia.* New Rich in Asia Series. London: Routledge.

Shieh, G. S. 1992. *'Boss' Island: The subcontracting network and micro-entrepreneurship in Taiwan's development.* New York: Peter Lang Publication.

Sider, G., and G. Smith. 1997. Introduction. In *Between history and histories: The making of silences and commemorations,* eds. G. Sider and G. Smith. Toronto: Toronto University Press.

Simmons, C., and C. Kalantaridis. 1994. Flexible specialisation in the Southern Europe periphery: The growth of garment manufacturing in Poenia County, Greece. *Comparative Studies in Society and History* 36: 200–223.

———. 1996. Entrepreneurial strategies in Southern Europe: Rural workers in the garment industry in Greece. *Journal of Economic Issues* 30: 121–143.

Simon, S. 2003. *Sweet and sour: Life worlds of Taipei women entrepreneurs.* Landham, MD: Roman and Littlefield.

Simoniya, A. N. 1961. *Overseas Chinese in Southeast Asia—A Russian study.* Southeast Asia Program, Dept. of Far Eastern Studies, Data Papers, No. 45. Ithaca: Cornell University.

Singh, A. M., and A. Kelles-Viitanen, eds. 1987. *Invisible hands: Women in home-based production.* London: Sage.

Sit, V. F. S., S. Wong, and T. S. Kiang. 1979. *Small-scale industry in a laissez-faire economy.* Hong Kong: Centre of Asian Studies.

Smart, A. 1995. Local capitalisms: Situated social support for capitalist production in China. Dept. Geog. Occ. Pap. Hong Kong: Chinese University.

———. 1998. Economic transformation in China: Property regimes and social relations. In *Theorising transition: The political economy of post-communist transformations,* eds. J. Pickles and A. Smith. London: Routledge, 428–449.

———. 1999. Getting things done across the Hong Kong border. In *Qiaoxiang ties: Interdisciplinary approaches to "cultural capitalism" in South China,* ed. L. Douw. London: Kegan Paul, 158–186.

———. 2001a. The Hong Kong/Pearl River delta urban region: An emerging transnational mode of regulation or just muddling through? In *The new Chinese city,* ed. J. Logan. Oxford: Blackwell.

———. 2001b. Restructuring in a North American city: Labour markets and political economy in Calgary. In *Plural globalities in multiple localities: New world borders,* eds. M. Rees and J. Smart. Lanham: University Press of America, 167–193.

Smart, A., and J. Smart. 1992. Capitalist production in a socialist society: The transfer of production from Hong Kong to China. In *Anthropology and the Global Factory,* eds. F.A. Rothstein and M. Blim. New York: Bergin and Garvey, 47–61.

———. 1998. Transnational social networks and negotiated identities in interactions between Hong Kong and China. In *Transnationalism from below,* M. P. Smith and L. E. Guarnizo. New Brunswick, N.J.: Transaction Publishers, 103–129.

———. 2000. Failures and strategies of Hong Kong firms in the PRC: An ethnographic perspective. In *The globalization of Chinese business,* eds. H. W. Yeung and K. Olds. New York: Macmillan, 244–271.

Smart, J. 1989. *The political economy of street hawking in Hong Kong*. Hong Kong: Centre of Asian Studies.

————. 1990. Self-employment versus wage employment in Hong Kong: A reconsideration of the urban economy. In *Perspectives on the informal economy*, ed. E. M. Smith. New York: Lanham, 251–279.

Smart, J., and A. Smart. 1991. "Personal relations and divergent economies: A case study of Hong Kong investment in China." *International Journal of Urban and Regional Research* 15 (2): 216–233

————. 1993. Obligation and control: Employment of kin in capitalist labor management in China. Critique of Anthropology 13 (1): 7–31.

Smith, A. 1997. Constructing capitalism? Small and medium enterprises, industrial districts and regional policy in Slovakia. *European Urban and Regional Studies* 4(1): 45–70.

————. 1998. *Reconstructing the regional economy: Industrial transformation and regional development in Slovakia.* Cheltenham, England: Edward Elgar.

————. 2002a. Imagining geographies of the 'new Europe': Geoeconomic power and the new European architecture of integration. *Political Geography,* 21,5: 647–670.

————. 2002b. 'Sweatshop' production and the politics of work in the East European garment industry'. Paper presented at the annual conference of the Royal Geographical Society, Belfast, January.

————. 2003. Power relations, industrial clusters and regional transformations: Pan-European integration and outward processing in the Slovak clothing industry. *Economic Geography* 79: 17–40.

Smith, A., A. Rainnie, M. Dunford, J. Hardy, R. Hudson, and D. Sadler. 2002. Networks of value, commodities and regions: Reworking divisions of labor in macro-regional economies. *Progress in Human Geography*, forthcoming.

Smith, G. 1979. The use of class analysis in social anthropology. In *Challenging anthropology*, eds. G. Smith and D. Turner. Toronto: McGraw-Hill, Ryerson.

————. 1991. The production of culture in local rebellion. In *Golden ages, dark ages: Imagining the past in anthropology and history*, eds. J. O'Brien and W. Roseberry. Berkeley: University of California Press.

————. 1994. Towards an ethnography of idiosyncratic forms of livelihood. *International Journal of Urban and Regional Research* 18: 71–87.

Smith, M. E. 1990. A million here, a million there, and pretty soon you're talking real money. In *Perspectives on the informal economy,* ed. E. M. Smith. New York: Lanham, 1–22.

Smith, M.P. 2001. *Transnational urbanism.* New York: Blackwell.

Sommer, M. H. 2000. *Sex, law, and society in late Imperial China.* Stanford: Stanford University Press.

Spener, D., and R. Capps. 2001. North American free trade and changes in the nativity of the garment industry workforce in the United States. *International Journal of Urban and Regional Research* 25(2): 301–326.

Staber, Udo. 2001. Spatial Proximity and Firm Survival in a Declining Industrial District: The Case of Knitwear Firms in Baden-Württemberg, Regional Studies, 35, pp. 329–341.

Štatistický úrad Slovenskej republiky. 1997. *Statistická ročenka Slovenskej republiky.* Bratislava, Slovakia: ŠÚSR.

Stephen, L. 1991. Culture as a resource: Four cases of self-managed indigenous craft production in Latin America. *Economic Development and Cultural Change* 40(1): 101–130.

Stevens, S., ed. 1995. *Children and the politics of culture.* Princeton: Princeton University Press.

Stinchcombe, A. 1987. Flexible specialization. *Sociological Forum* 1(2): 185–190.

Storper, M. 1995. The resurgence of regional economies, ten years later: The region as a nexus of untraded interdependencies. *European Urban and Regional Studies* 2(3): 191–221.

————. 1997. *The regional world.* New York: Guilford.

Storper, M., and A. Scott. 1993. *The wealth of regions: market forces and policy imperatives in local and global context.* Working Paper, University of California at Los Angeles.

Tadao, Kiyonari. 1983. The unsung mainstays Small businesses. In *Politics and economics in contemporary Japan,* eds. M. Hyoe and J. Hirschmeier. Tokyo: Kodansha, 157–183.

Tan, L. E. 1992. Dongjiaozong and the challenge to cultural hegemony 1951–1987. In *Fragmented vision: Culture and politics in contemporary Malaysia,* eds. J. S. Kahn and F. L. Kok Wah. North Sydney, NSW, Australia, Asian Studies Association of Australia/ Allen & Unwin. 22: 181–201.

Tanter, R. 1982. The militarization of ASEAN: Global context and local dynamics. *Alternatives* 7(4): 507–532.

Taplin, I. 1996. Rethinking flexibility: The case of the apparel industry. *Review of Social Economy* 54: 191–121.

Teichova, A., and P. Cottrell. 1983. Industrial structures in West and East Central Europe during the interwar period. In *International business and Central Europe, 1918–1939*, eds. A. Teichova and P. Cottrell. Leicester, England: Leicester University Press, 31–55.

*The Independent*. 1992. Carpets continued: The human cost. April 15.

Thrift, N. 1999. The globalisation of the system of business knowledge. In *Globalisation and the Asia-Pacific*, eds. K. Olds, P. Dicken, P. Kelly, L. Kong, and H. Young. London: Routledge, 57–71.

Tiano, S. 1994. *Patriarchy on the line: Labor, gender, and ideology in Mexican Maquila industry*. Philadelphia: Temple University Press.

Transparency International. 2002. *Transparency International: The global coalition against corruption*. Available at www.transparency.org.

Tsing, A. 2000. The global situation. *Cultural Anthropology* 15(3): 327–360.

Uberoi, J. P. S. 1962. *Politics of the Kula Ring: An analysis of the findings of Bronislaw Malinowski*. Manchester, England: University of Manchester Press.

United States Department of Commerce, International Trade Commission, Office of Textiles and Apparel. May 30, 1998. *Major Shippers Report: Section One: Textiles and apparel imports by category*. Available: http:otexa.ita.doc.gov/msr/carvo.htm.

USAID (United States Aid to Developing Countries). 1994. The end of the carpet induced boom? *USAID ECON Internal*, June 16.

Vangstrup, U. 1997. *Globalization of industry in Mexico—A commodity chain approach to the analysis of linkage capabilities*. Paper presented at the annual meeting of the Latin American Studies Association, Guadalajara, April 17–19.

Verdery, K. 1993. What was socialism and why did it fall? *Contention* 3: 1–23.

Waldinger, R. 1986. *Through the eye of the needle: Immigrants and enterprise in New York's garment trades*. New York: New York University Press.

Walton, D. 1999. Canadians speed selling to Japan. *Calgary Herald*, August 17: B10.

Weiner, T. 2003. With little loans, Mexican women overcome, *New York Times*, March 19: A8.

Whatmore, S., and L. Thorne. 1997. Nourishing networks: Alternative geographies of food. In *Globalising food: Agrarian questions and global restructuring*, eds. D. Goodman and M. Watts. London and New York: Routledge.

Whitford, J. 2001. The decline of a model? Challenge and response in the Italian industrial districts. *Economy and Society* 30(1): 38–65.

Whitley, R. 1993. *Business system in East Asia: Firms, markets, and societies*. Thousand Oaks, CA: Sage.

Wiebe, R. 1995. *Self-rule: A cultural history of American democracy*. Chicago: University of Chicago Press.

Williams, R. 1961. *Culture and society 1780–1950*. Harmondsworth, U.K.: Penguin.

———. 1977. *Marxism and literature*. Oxford: Blackwell.

Williamson, O. 1985. The economic institutions of Capitalism: Firm, markets, relational contracting. New York: Free Press.

Wilson, F. 1990. *De la casa al taller: Mujeres, trabajo y clase social en la industria textil y del vestido, Santiago Tangamandapio*. Michoacan, Mexico: El Colegio de Michoacan.

Winslow, D. 1996. Pottery, progress, and structural adjustments in a Sri Lankan village. *Economic Development and Cultural Change* 44(4): 701–726.

Wolf, A. P. 1995. *Sexual attraction and childhood association: A Chinese brief for Edward Westermarck*. Stanford: Stanford University Press.

———. 2001. Is there evidence of birth control in late Imperial China? *Population and Development Review* 27(1): 133–154.

Wolf, A. P., and W. B. Durham, eds. In press. *Inbreeding, incest, and the incest taboo: The state of the art at the turn of the century*. Stanford University Press.

Wolf, E. R. 1966. *Peasants*. Englewood Cliffs, N.J.: Prentice-Hall.

———. 1982. *Europe and the people without history*. Berkeley: University of California Press.

Wood, G., and I. Sharif, eds. 1997. *Who needs credit: Poverty and finance in Bangladesh*. London: Zed Books.

World Bank. 2002a. *World Bank Development News*, March 18: 9.
———. 2002b. *World Bank Development News*, April 2: 4.
———. 2001. *World Development Report, 2000/2001: Attacking Poverty*. New York: Oxford University Press.
———. 1994. *Slovakia: Restructuring for recovery*. Washington, DC: International Bank for Reconstruction and Development (IBRD).
Wright, E. O. 1981. Reconsiderations. In *The value controversy*, ed. I. Steedman. London: Verso.
Wrigley, E. A., and R. S. Schofield. 1989. *The population history of England 1541–1871: A reconstruction*. Cambridge: Cambridge University Press.
WTO. 1999. *Annual Report: International Trade Statistics*. Geneva: World Trade Organization (WTO).
Yoruk, D. 2001. *Growth of Central and East European clothing firms in relation to networks and industrial upgrading*. Paper presented at ESRC project workshop on 'The emerging industrial architecture of the wider Europe: The Co-evolution of industrial and political structures.' University of Sussex, June 28.
Ypeij, A. 2000. *Producing against poverty: Female and male micro-entrepreneurs in Lima, Peru*. Amsterdam: University of the Netherlands Press.
Yu, T.F.-L. 1997. *Entrepreneurship and economic development in Hong Kong*. London: Routledge.

# Contributors

**Michael Blim** is Associate Professor of Anthropology in the Ph.D. Program in Anthropology at the Graduate Center of the City University of New York. He is the author of Equality and Economy (forthcoming), *Made in Italy: Small-Scale Industrialization and its Consequences* (1990), and co-editor with Frances Rothstein of *Anthropology and the Global Factory* (1992).

**Hans Buechler** is Professor of Anthropology at Syracuse University. **Judith-Maria Buechler** is Professor of Anthropology at Hobart and William Smith Colleges. They are authors of *Manufacturing Against the Odds*, and *Contesting Agriculture*.

**Hill Gates** was born in Fort William, Ontario and received her degrees in Anthropology from Radcliffe College, Harvard University (BA), University of Hawaii (MA and PhD). She taught for twenty years at Central Michigan University, and retired as Professor Emerita to take up a Lectureship at Stanford University. She is the author of *China's Motor: A Thousand Years of Petty Capitalism* (1996, Cornell UP) and *Looking for Chengdu* (1999, Cornell UP). She presently divides her research time between a Taiwan/Netherlands Demographic Project and a book on women's labor and footbinding to be called *Hand and Foot*.

**Simone Ghezzi** is currently a contract researcher at the Dipartimento di Sociologia e Ricerca Sociale, Università di Milano-Bicocca, Italy. He received a Master of Arts (1996) and a Ph.D. (2002) in Anthropology from the University of Toronto. He was a Donner Post-Doctoral Fellow at the Watson Institute for International Studies, Brown University, Providence, RI (2003). He has carried out extensive fieldwork on informal economy, and on workshops in Lombardy, Northern Italy. He is currently writing a book on entrepreneur-workers and workshops in Lombardy.

**Dr. Jinn-yuh Hsu** is currently an associate professor in Geography at National Taiwan University. He received his Ph.D. degree from the University of California at Berkeley. He is an economic geographer who specializes in high-technology industries and regional development in late-industrializing countries, particularly Taiwan. Dr. Hsu has published a series of papers (in Chinese and English) on the labor market, technology learning, industrial organization and dynamic institutionalism of the Hsinchu Region and its connection with Silicon Valley. Currently he is conducting research on high technology industries in the triangle connection among Silicon Valley, Taiwan and Shanghai.

**B. Lynne Milgram** is Associate Professor in the Faculty of Liberal Studies at the Ontario College of Art and Design, Toronto, Canada, and Adjunct Graduate Faculty (Anthropology), York University, Toronto. Her research on gender and development in the Philippines analyzes the cultural politics of social change with regard to fair trade, women's entrepreneurial work in crafts, and microfinance initiatives. This research has been published in *Atlantis: A Women's Studies Journal* (2002), *Human Organization* (2001), *Research in Economic Anthropology,* (1999) and *Museum Anthropology* (1998). She has also co-edited, with Kimberly M. Grimes, *Artisans and Cooperatives: Developing Alternative Trade for the Global Economy*. Tuscon, AZ: University of Arizona Press. Her current research explores Philippine women's engagement in the global trade of secondhand clothing through trans-Asian commodity networks.

**Susana Narotzky** is Profesora Titular de Antropologia at the Universitat de Barcelona. Among her recent publications are "New Directions in Economic Anthropology" (London, Pluto 1997) and "La Antropologia de los pueblos de España. Historia, cultura y lugar" (Barcelona, Icaria, 2001). With Gavin Smith, Narotzky is completing an historical ethnography on a regional economy in contemporary Spain.

**Donald M. Nonini** is Professor of Anthropology at the University of North Carolina at Chapel Hill. He is the author of *British Colonial Rule and the Resistance of the Malay Peasantry,* 1900–1957 (New Haven: Yale Southeast Asia Studies, 1992), editor with Aihwa Ong of *Ungrounded Empires: The Cultural Politics of Modern Chinese Transnationalism* (New York:

Routledge, 1997), and the author of numerous articles on the cultural politics of Chinese ethnic identity and citizenship in Malaysia. He is currently completing a book entitled *"Getting Through Life": Classed and Gendered and The Cultural Politics of Chinese Identity in Malaysia*. He is also the co-author with Dorothy Holland, Catherine Lutz, et al. of *If This is Democracy: Public Interests and Private Politics in A Neoliberal Age* (under contract, New York University Press), a study of local politics, neoliberal government, and the effects of globalization in the United States. His most recent research deals with issues of nationality and citizenship among Chinese Indonesians who fled Indonesia for Australia in the wake of the ant-Chinese violence of mid-1998.

**Tom O'Neill** received his Ph.D in anthropology from McMaster University in Hamilton, Canada and is Associate Professor in the Department of Child and Youth Studies at Brock University in St. Catharines, Canada. He has written on the dynamics of child labor rhetoric in the Nepalese carpet industry, and is currently investigating the transnational remittance economy in Nepal and its impact on Nepalese youth.

**Frances Abrahamer Rothstein** is Professor of Anthropology at Towson University. Her research in rural Mexico has examined the effects of the Mexican "economic miracle" in the 1960s and early 70s and "the lost decade" in the 1980s. More recently, she has looked at the consequences of trade liberalization. She is the co-editor (with Michael Blim) of *Anthropology and the Global Factory* and has authored numerous articles on gender, development, and globalization.

**Alan Smart** is Professor at the Department of Anthropology, University of Calgary, and has been conducting field research in Hong Kong and China since 1982. In 1986, he completed his Ph.D. in Social Anthropology at the University of Toronto, on the topic of the political economy of squatter clearance in Hong Kong. His research has focused on urban issues, housing, foreign investment, and social change. He is the author of *Making Room: Squatter Clearance in Hong Kong* (Hong Kong: Hong Kong University Press) and articles in journals such as Urban Anthropology, International Journal of Sociology of Law, Cultural Anthropology, Critique of Anthropology, International Journal of Urban and

Regional Research, Society and Space, City & Society, American Anthropologist and a variety of edited volumes.

**Josephine Smart** received her Ph.D. in Anthropology from the University of Toronto in 1987. She is Professor of Anthropology at the University of Calgary. Her research interests are informal economies, international mobility of labor and capital, Asian immigration to Canada, development in post-1978 China, NAFTA and its social and economic impact, and her most recent project is a study of Chinese immigrant cuisine and the politics of identity in Canada. She is the author of *The Political Economy of Street Hawkers in Hong Kong* (1989) and her work has been published in International Journal of Urban and Regional Research, Critique of Anthropology, Anthropology of Work Review, Asian Journal of Public Administration, Canadian Journal of Development, Canadian Journal of Regional Sciences, Urban Anthropology and in numerous edited volumes.

**Adrian Smith** is Professor of Human Geography at Queen Mary, University of London, U.K. He has also worked at the Universities of Sussex, Kentucky and Southampton. His main interests are in economic geographies, the political economy of cities and regions, and post-socialist transformations. His work engages with debates over political-economic transformations, non- essentialist Marxism and development theory to try to understand the contemporary geographies of social power. He is author of Reconstructing the Regional Economy (Edward Elgar, 1998) and co-editor of Theorising Transition (Routledge, 1998) and Work, Employment and Transition (Routledge, 2002), and is former deputy editor of Regional Studies.

**Gavin Smith** continues to ask the questions that motivated his Livelihood and Resistance (1989)—about the relationship between the way people put together 'a living' and their forms of political expression. His recent book of essays *Confronting the Present* (1999) was motivated by a desire to explore the ways in which historical realism might inform a more politically effective radical anthropology project. His current work in Europe seeks to explore the interface between programs of rule and localized sites of emergent or failed collective practice. Susana Narotzky and he have a manuscript in press on a regional economy in contemporary Spain.

# Index